Also by McKay Jenkins

THE LAST RIDGE: THE EPIC STORY OF AMERICA'S
FIRST MOUNTAIN SOLDIERS AND THE
ASSAULT ON HITLER'S EUROPE

THE WHITE DEATH: TRAGEDY AND HEROISM
IN AN AVALANCHE ZONE

THE PETER MATTHIESSEN READER (EDITOR)

THE SOUTH IN BLACK AND WHITE: RACE, SEX,
AND LITERATURE IN THE 1940S

BLOODY FALLS

of the

COPPERMINE

BLOODY FALLS

of the

COPPERMINE

—

MADNESS, MURDER, AND THE COLLISION OF CULTURES IN THE ARCTIC, 1913

McKAY JENKINS

RANDOM HOUSE NEW YORK

Copyright © 2005 by McKay Jenkins

All rights reserved under International and Pan-American Copyright Conventions. Published in the United States by Random House, an imprint of The Random House Publishing Group, a division of Random House, Inc., New York, and simultaneously in Canada by Random House of Canada Limited, Toronto.

RANDOM HOUSE and colophon are registered trademarks of Random House, Inc.

LIBRARY OF CONGRESS CATALOGING-IN-PUBLICATION DATA

Jenkins, McKay
Bloody Falls of the Coppermine: madness, murder, and the collision of cultures in the Arctic, 1913 / McKay Jenkins.
p. cm.
Includes bibliographical references and index.
ISBN 0-375-50721-3
1. Inuit—Northwest Territories—Coppermine River Valley—History. 2. Inuit—Legal status, laws, etc.—Northwest Territories—Coppermine River Valley.
3. Sinnisiak. 4. Uluksuk. 5. Murder—Northwest Territories—Coppermine River Valley—History. 6. Catholic Church—Missions—Northwest Territories—Coppermine River Valley—History. 7. Missionaries—Crimes against—Northwest Territories—Coppermine River Valley. 8. Trials (Murder)—Alberta—Edmonton—History. 9. Coppermine River Valley (N.W.T.)—History. 10. Coppermine River Valley (N.W.T.)—Social conditions. I. Title.
E99.E7J46 2005   364.152'3'0971955—dc22   2004046433

Printed in the United States of America on acid-free paper

Random House website address: www.atrandom.com

2 4 6 8 9 7 5 3 1

FIRST EDITION

Book design by Barbara M. Bachman

For

CHRIS SHELDRICK AND BRIAN JENKINS,
ARCTIC EXPLORERS,

for

DR. DENNY JENKINS, SURGEON,

and for

ANNALISA SWAN,
MY BABY GIRL

Author's Note

A note on the use of the word *Eskimo*. In some contemporary Canadian communities, where the term *Inuit* is preferred, *Eskimo* has become an anachronism, even a pejorative, in part because of a disputed etymology that traces the word to an expression meaning "eaters of raw meat." In other places, *Eskimo* is still widely used. In any case, *Inuit* does not serve as a blanket substitute for *Eskimo*, either historically or geographically. *Inuit*, the plural of the noun *Inuk*, for "human being," refers only to the Inuit-speaking peoples of Arctic Canada and parts of Greenland. In Alaska and Arctic Siberia, where Inuit is not spoken, the comparable terms are *Inupiaq* and *Yup'ik*. Given the historical period in which the story recounted here took place, and the hundreds of original documents and newpaper clippings on which my research was based, it seemed appropriate to use the historical and inclusive term *Eskimo*. When describing my own recent journey to the town of Kugluktuk, I used the term *Inuit*.

PROLOGUE

—

No one would claim to understand every part
of these stories, or to have a ready explanation
for people, events, or processes that are
confusing and strange. These are stories that
defy any complete understanding. To tell and
to listen to them is to experience the delight
and enigma of incomprehension. Mysteries
are repeated, not explained.

—HUGH BRODY, *The Other Side of Eden*

I N THE DARK, NEARLY SUNLESS DAYS OF AN ARCTIC NOVEMBER, two Catholic priests, exhausted, freezing, and nearly mad from starvation, were hauling their gear south, away from the continent's northern edge. Father Jean-Baptiste Rouvière, slight and dark-eyed, and Father Guillaume LeRoux, strong chinned and defiant, were dressed unusually, given the increasingly severe weather. Under their parkas, their long black cassocks, buttoned down the front, seemed insufficient protection against weather that in winter has been described as feeling like "iron on stone." Indeed, the priests seemed to be in retreat from their pioneering mission of spreading religion to a group of people named for the Coppermine River, which bisected the tribe's hunting grounds. The year was 1913, exactly three years after the Copper Eskimos became some of the very last North Americans to encounter Europeans.

Living above the Arctic Circle had taken its toll on the missionaries. A diary, discovered later by police, would reveal their last written thoughts: "We are at the mouth of the Coppermine. Some families have already left. *Disillusioned* with the Eskimos. We are threatened with starvation; also we don't know what to do." The priests were members of the Oblates of Mary Immaculate, a group known for some of the Catholic Church's most remote missionary work. Oblate priests had been offering spiritual solace to the Dog Rib and Hare Skin Indians in Canada's far Northwest for years. Fathers Rouvière and LeRoux, at the ages of thirty and twenty-eight, were pushing this work to the very edge of the continent. They planned to follow the migrating Eskimos to the sea, live with them, care for them. They intended to build a church and get the Eskimos to come. They wanted to conduct baptisms, and marriages, and funerals. The fact that they spoke little of the native language did not deter them. "There will be some tough nuts up there," Father Rouvière had said, "but they are too good-hearted to put up much of a fight against grace."

In fact, Eskimo country did not, on its face, seem to offer promising soil in which to plant the seeds of Christianity. For one thing, the landscape itself offered few parallels to the places where the religion had been born. There were no gardens, no vineyards, no deserts with which to illustrate biblical parables. There were no sheep or shepherds. There was no daily bread. There was no easy way to describe a crucifixion, because there were no trees. There was no notion of "God." Early translators of the Lord's Prayer had settled on "Our boat owner, who is in heaven."[1]

Where Eskimos had encountered Europeans, mostly to the west, near whaling ports in the mouth of the Mackenzie River, they thought the strangers a bit odd. Among other things, white trappers, missionaries, and police officers seemed to insist on traveling without the skills and companionship of women. Europeans arrived with useful tools, it was true, but most were unable to clothe, feed, or protect themselves. Many of them died of starvation or exposure.

The priests were unbowed by the unlikeliness of their mission. They were favored by their bishop, Gabriel Breynat, who oversaw a region stretching between Hudson Bay and the Alaskan border, and from just north of Edmonton in the south to Victoria and Banks Islands at 72 degrees north—all told, about a million and a half square miles. Breynat, a gregarious man with a twinkle in his eye and an enormous, bushy beard, admired Father Rouvière's sensitivity, his gentleness, his ability to accommodate adversity. Father LeRoux was a polished, well-educated man who also seemed rugged, physically capable of living in a place that demanded resiliency. The priests and their brethren had spent years traveling from outpost to outpost, building a network of tiny churches across the Northland. But this fall, for Rouvière and LeRoux, things had gotten dicey. Months of hard living and a diet that consisted almost entirely of scraps of caribou meat had left their bodies malnourished and weak. They had been making little headway with the Eskimos. They were utterly frustrated with the Eskimo language. How could they teach about the mysteries of the Immaculate Conception, of Communion, of the Resurrection, when they were frequently limited to communicating with hand gestures? It was hard even to be sure if the Eskimos knew what the priests were doing there. Their simple wardrobes, which at home projected humility and a willingness to live apart from the world of getting and spending, meant nothing here, except perhaps that white men did not know how to dress against the cold. Worse, as inexperienced hunters, they were able to contribute nothing to the survival of the group with whom they were traveling, especially at a time in the season when food was getting extremely scarce. By this point, in early winter, the caribou had all but vanished, and the ice was not yet firm enough to allow for seal hunting. For the Eskimos, the priests, in a very real sense, were just two more mouths to feed. "There is contempt for the white man that no argument on your part can eradicate, or even lessen very much," another Oblate priest would write. " 'Krabloonak ayortok!' The white man does not know a thing."[2]

Fathers Rouvière and LeRoux spent five days with a group of Eskimos at a camp where the Coppermine River dumps into the Arctic Ocean. The time did not pass easily. After quarreling bitterly over the ownership of a rifle, Father Rouvière harnessed his weak body to a sled, Father LeRoux gathered up a couple of dogs, and the odd little team started hiking south. They never made it home.

Two days after the priests began their journey, a pair of Eskimo hunters named Sinnisiak and Uluksuk found the priests struggling along near a stretch of the Coppermine already heavy with history. In July 1771, just two days before he had become the first white man ever to see the Arctic Ocean, the explorer Samuel Hearne had witnessed a scene of overwhelming violence between Copper Eskimos and Chipewayan Indians at Bloody Falls, a dramatic cataract that for centuries had been a favorite Eskimo fishing spot. Arriving at Bloody Falls fifty years to the day later, the doomed British explorer Sir John Franklin stumbled on "several human skulls which bore marks of violence, and many human bones." Given the rarity of white visitors to the banks of the Coppermine, it seems certain that the two priests would have known about the legend of Bloody Falls. Whether they pondered the story is unknown. What we do know is that the priests also ended up dead. Their livers were removed and eaten. Their bodies were thrown aside, and left to the wolves.

It took months for rumors of the killings to blow far enough south to reach a Catholic mission post. The Royal North West Mounted Police were called in for an investigation that had no precedent. For two years, a handful of young constables used canoes and dogsleds to cross thousands of miles of the continent's least-charted terrain. It was a dangerous assignment, requiring the patrol to overwinter in the Arctic and face the same challenges that routinely caused the far hardier and more experienced Eskimos to starve to death. Some of the most famous Arctic explorers of the twentieth century, including the anthropologists Vilhjalmur Stefansson and Diamond Jenness, overlapped with the search; they mediated encounters between officers and Eskimos, helped them find their suspects, allowed the patrol to transport the prisoners on board their research vessel.

Once Sinnisiak and Uluksuk had been arrested and carted off to Edmonton for trial, they became instant curiosities, attracting crowds wherever they went. Here, for the first time, city dwellers could ogle two men lifted straight out of the Stone Age. Newspapers swooped down on them, snapping photographs and parsing their every movement for evidence of prehistoric behavior. "More primitive than any race of people to be found in darkest Africa, less touched by civilization than any other humans, the Eskimos offer to ethnologists the most fertile subject for study," one white "expert" told the newspapers. "If treated well the white man is as safe with the Eskimo as he is anywhere on earth. But anyone who plays them false must expect to die. Death is the only penalty the Eskimo knows."[3]

For their part, Sinnisiak and Uluksuk had never dreamed that so many people could exist in one place. They were amazed by the city's technology. They saw trams held up by wires, and newspapers they could not read but that carried their photographs. An Eskimo translator, taken to a ballet, was seen by reporters covering his eyes at the sight of the half-naked dancers.

When Sinnisiak and Uluksuk entered the Edmonton courthouse, they became the first Eskimos ever put on trial in a white man's court. The prosecutor in the case lost little time telling the jury that their conviction would send an important message to all native North Americans. "These remote savages, really cannibals, the Eskimo of the Arctic regions, have got to be taught to recognize the authority of the British Crown," the prosecutor told the jury. "The code of the savage, an eye for an eye, a tooth for a tooth, a life for a life must be replaced among them by the code of civilization. . . . The Eskimo must be made to understand that the lives of others are sacred, and that they are not justified in killing on account of any mere trifle that may ruffle or annoy them."[4]

On the witness stand, Sinnisiak and Uluksuk claimed that the priests had threatened their lives. Father LeRoux had bullied them, brandished a loaded rifle, threatened to shoot. "Any man, whether he is white or black, civilized or uncivilized, is justified in killing another in his own self-defense," their attorney argued. "Was it not reasonable, considering the extent of their mind, the little knowledge they had of the white race, the two greatest fears they had—fear of the spirits and fear of the white man, the stranger—were they not justified in believing that their lives were in danger?"[5]

Who was the jury to believe? Even the judge refered to Sinnisiak as a "poor, ignorant, benighted pagan." There were no witnesses, save the two suspects, and their perspective on life and death in the Arctic was utterly outside the jury's ken. Forget about their not speaking a word of English. Until three years before they met the priests, they hadn't even known white men *existed*. Attorneys for both sides would tell the press the trial was "the strangest that has ever taken place on the continent."

A question that hovered in the courtroom, and that would haunt the Far North for decades to come, can be boiled down to this: did the priests themselves, in their ravaged state, in their desperation, become murderous? Were they, stripped of all vestiges of their civilized training, reduced to their own brand of savagery? This question prompted still larger questions. Two men from Europe had commited their lives to missionary work in a landscape that was as alien to them as the surface of the moon. What did they imagine their lives would be like up there, surrounded by a vastness that could have swallowed all of Europe and that contained over its entire expanse fewer people than a small French village? How did they imagine the flow of human wisdom and experience? The story of the priests and the Eskimos, and the police investigation and the trials that followed, became a kind of a crucible in which to ponder the history of the North American frontier.

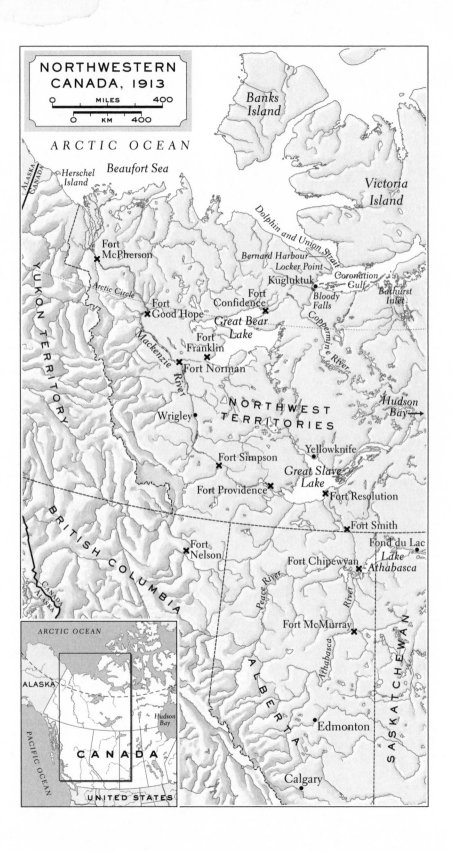

NORTHWESTERN
CANADA, 1913

MILES 400
KM 400

ARCTIC OCEAN

Banks
Island

Beaufort Sea

Herschel
Island

Victoria
Island

Dolphin and Union Strait

Fort
McPherson

Bernard Harbour
Locker Point

Arctic Circle

Kugluktuk

Coronation
Gulf

Bathurst
Inlet

Fort
Good Hope

Fort
Confidence

Bloody
Falls

Fort
Franklin

Great Bear
Lake

Coppermine River

Mackenzie River

Fort Norman

Hudson
Bay

Wrigley

NORTHWEST
TERRITORIES

Yellowknife

Fort Simpson

Great Slave
Lake

Fort Providence

Fort Resolution

Fort Smith

Fort
Nelson

Fond du Lac
Lake

Fort Chipewyan

Athabasca

BRITISH COLUMBIA

Peace River

Athabasca River

Fort McMurray

SASKATCHEWAN

ALBERTA

Athabasca

Edmonton

Calgary

ALASKA
CANADA

YUKON TERRITORY

CANADA
ALASKA

ARCTIC OCEAN

ALASKA

PACIFIC OCEAN

Hudson
Bay

CANADA

UNITED STATES

PART ONE

CHAPTER ONE

—

Very little investigation has been made in Canada
of the native races, and what has been done had
been under the auspices of foreign institutions. The
opportunities for such studies are fast disappearing.
Under advancing settlement and rapid development
of the country the native is disappearing, or coming
under the influence of the white man's civilization.
If the information concerning the native races is
ever to be secured and preserved, action must
be taken very soon, or it will be too late.

—GEOLOGICAL SURVEY OF CANADA, 1908

ONE MORNING IN EARLY JULY 1911, AN ODD LITTLE MAN
walked into a saloon on the shore of the mighty Mackenzie River and
dipped his filthy fingers in a sugar bowl. John Hornby was just twenty-
seven years old, five feet four inches tall, and barely one hundred pounds,
but in the north country he was, among white men at least, a legend.
Once, it was said, he ran next to a horse for fifty miles, trotting sideways,
like a wolf. Another time, on a bet for a bottle of whiskey, he ran one hundred miles in under twenty-four hours. And Hornby was not a drinking
man. His instincts most resembled a trapper's, but he loved animals and
hated traps. He never hunted except for food, and often, like the native

people with whom he traveled, he went without eating for days at a time. He probably knew the Barren Lands, the country in which he lived, more intimately than any other white man in history.

Hornby had fierce blue eyes that seemed to always be focused on something off in the far distance. Exactly why Hornby decided to explore Canada's north country has been lost to history. He may have ventured north with vague notions of finding gold, but the Klondike rush had long since dried up. He may have been lured by rumors of vast giveaways of land, which the government had promised in an effort to populate the north. More likely he went north to go north, to see what he could see.

John Hornby did not like darkening the doorways of Fort Norman, the dreary oupost that comprised little more than a Hudson's Bay Company store, the Anglican Mission of the Holy Trinity, and the Catholic Mission of Saint-Thérèse. Even among the usual rough men who passed through such places, Hornby stood out for his disinterest in the trimmings of civilized society. He didn't need the company of white men, and he usually did as much as he could to avoid them. He was happiest living among the Barren Land Indians, chopping wood, carrying water, stalking caribou. But the previous summer, Hornby had had a stirring experience. Scouting territory north of Great Bear Lake, he had come upon a group of people he believed to be the last in North America to have remained outside the reach of white explorers. They were not Indians; they were Eskimos who had followed the caribou inland from Coronation Gulf, some 150 miles to the northeast. Hornby had been so excited by his discovery that he had written a letter to the only other permanent European resident of the Barren Lands: the priest in charge of the Mission of Saint-Thérèse. "We have met a party of Eskimos who come every year," Hornby's letter said. "The Eskimos come at the end of August and leave when the first snow falls. They seem very intelligent." The letter then sounded a somber note. "The Eskimos and Indians are frightened of each other and it would be dangerous for Indians to try and meet Eskimos without having a white man with them, because the Eskimos have a bad opinion of the Indians. If you intend on sending someone to meet the Eskimos, we shall be pleased to give you all the help we can."[1]

Word of Hornby's letter moved through Canada's northwest Catholic missions and quickly landed in the hands of Gabriel Breynat, a man so exhuberant about wilderness missionary work that he had been made bishop for all of northwestern Canada by the age of thirty-two. Breynat had made his reputation ministering to Dog Rib, Hare Skin, and Slave Lake Indians, but for nearly a decade he had been praying for the chance to extend his missionary work to the continent's northernmost people. "No one knows how many they are, or what they are like," he had written the Oblate chapter general seven years before, "but we would like to send a few specimens to Paradise."

Breynat had also begun to worry that the Catholic Church might be beaten to the region by the Church of England. Just as French and British trappers had battled for territory all over the Canadian west, so did their churches compete, often using the language and strategies of warfare, for their nationals and the natives with whom they traded. They established outposts. They recruited hardy missionaries and sent them out as scouts. In the Canadian hinterlands, Europe's age-old religious struggle found a new battleground. "We have against us here, a silent, vexatious and persistent opposition on the part of a handful of Protestants, freemasons and materialists, old-fashioned adherents of Darwinian theories who think they are in the vanguard of progress," a Catholic missionary would write some years later. "Souls cost dear, and they have to be gained one by one."[2]

The subtleties of the conflict between Catholics and Protestants, of course, were often lost on the Eskimos. They had a hard enough time understanding that these strange men in black robes were holy men and not just another batch of traders.

To say the least, bringing religion to Eskimos would require talents that were not part of the typical seminarian's training. The territory between the church's northern outposts and the central Arctic coast were virtually unmapped. Even the survival techniques that missionaries had learned through their work with Indians would be of limited value. There would be no building a log church on the Arctic coast, which sat at least a hundred miles above the tree line. And what would these people think of European religion, when many of them had never even met a European?

Nonetheless, when Bishop Breynat read John Hornby's letter, he could sense the veil lifting over the northland. Hornby's letter "had every appearance of an invitation from heaven," Breynat wrote. And he had just the man for the job.[3]

Father Jean-Baptiste Rouvière was a small-boned, dark-haired man with melancholic eyes set deeply behind prominent cheekbones. He had a sensitive mouth and an expression that seemed not dour but resigned, as if he had come to terms with the difficult but rewarding life of remote missionary work. Rouvière had been born on November 11, 1881, in Mende, France, to Jean Rouvière and Marie-Anne Cladel. After his traditional studies, he entered the novitiate of Notre-Dame de l'Osier on September 23, 1901, took vows at Liège on August 15, 1903, and was ordained as a priest three years later. In 1907 he transferred to the Northwest Territories, spending his first four years at Fort Providence on Great Slave Lake, then moving to Fort Good Hope, about one hundred river miles north of Fort Norman.

To Breynat, Rouvière seemed to have a number of qualities that would serve him well in the Far North. He was patient. Deliberate. Slow to anger. He had a certain seriousness of purpose that Breynat considered appropriate to a country that for many months of the year was cloaked in darkness. On the other hand, Rouvière was, as Breynat had been upon his own arrival from France, utterly inexperienced. Natives acknowledged that learning the skills needed to survive in their country took a lifetime. Rouvière had arrived in northern Canada as an adult, with few skills and no experience living outside a temperate European climate. The warmest clothing he had was made of wool. He planned to live through winters that would kill a sheep in a day. And though he had been ministering to Indians living near Fort Good Hope, Rouvière had spent little time away from the relative security of a mission in the middle of the Mackenzie River's busy trading route. Compared to where he would end up, the posts along the Mackenzie were practically crowded.

Yet like all Europeans who came to the Arctic, Rouvière seemed both enamored of and intimidated by the breadth of the land. Vast open spaces of any kind—save the odd belt of mountains running through Switzerland or between Spain and France—had been in exceedingly short supply in Europe for centuries. Dropped into a world where forests blanketed many thousands of square miles—where trees might cover a landmass as large as France—colonists were shaken to their bones. A young priest, in other words, could be forgiven his early trepidation.

Bishop Breynat showed his young priest the letter he had received from John Hornby, and asked Rouvière if he would be willing to take the church's work into the Barren Lands, and from there to the Arctic coast. Though Rouvière would be on his own, at least initially, Breynat promised to try to find him a companion. "I will do everything I can to send someone to keep you company next year," he said. In the meantime, Rouvière could at least count on help from Hornby. To Breynat's delight, Rouvière agreed to the challenge with happiness in his eyes, a smile on his lips, and a quote from Isaiah: *Ecce ego, mitte me.* Here I am, send me forth.

AS A YOUNG missionary trying to navigate the people and places of Canada's vast wilderness, Father Rouvière knew he was standing on the shoulders of some of the church's most adventurous men. The Oblates of Mary Immaculate had been founded in Provence in 1816 by Eugène de Mazenod, who would later become bishop of Marseilles. They first came to Montreal from France in 1842, and within three years had already placed a missionary at Fort Chipewyan on Lake Athabasca, five hundred miles to the north of Edmonton. In 1853, a priest named Father Henri Grollier became the first priest to visit the Eskimos, and seven years later he even managed to perform four baptisms at Fort McPherson. But compared to Rouvière's overland assignment, this had been relatively easy, requiring only a trip to the mouth of the Mackenzie River. Grollier was to die in his prime near the Arctic Circle, after founding the mission of Our Lady of Hope. "I die happy," he said on his deathbed. "I have seen the cross planted at the extremities of the earth."[4]

In 1865, a priest named Father Petitot made it to the Arctic coast with a Hudson's Bay Company man and met several Eskimo families. Just three years later, Petitot began suffering from a "painful disease"—doubtless a kind of darkness-induced psychosis—that manifested as an obsessive terror of being killed by Eskimos. Overtaken by a fit, Petitot abandoned his canoe and his gear and fled south. He was not the first European to become traumatized by the sheer emotional difficulty of living through months of total darkness. Nor would he be the last.[5]

AS IT DID in other remote corners of the globe, Arctic missionary work presented the Catholic Church with both real opportunity and real expense, and calls went out from early on to support this difficult work. "The great Catholic Church cannot be too generously supported, and great rewards hereafter must be in store for all those who ungrudgingly by acts of self-sacrifice aid on Christ's work on earth," a Catholic newspaper reported. "Without a thought for personal comfort, these Oblate Fathers harness their dogs and render all that great comfort which they alone can give, giving all the last sacraments so that a happy death shall be theirs. Yes, it is a touching sight, all too frequent, as epidemics are not rare in the Far North. Indians are a delicate race, and their human frames will not stand much in the way of the various fever outbreaks." The article did not mention that whites were the likely source of the epidemics. Native people were only "delicate" in the face of European viruses to which they had never needed to be immune.[6]

Indeed, during the winter of 1899, Breynat and the Indians suffered a terrifying epidemic of influenza. Breynat could do nothing. People began dying in large numbers, often before he could arrive to offer last rites. How the virus first infected the community is unclear, but foreign illnesses routinely followed European settlers into native regions, often with disastrous results. With their immune systems unaccustomed to the microbes, people died in swaths.

With so little firewood, and no way to dig graves in the frozen ground, bodies began to pile up. Those who did not succumb found themselves with still less food, and fewer people to find it. Those who had taken to Breynat's religion seemed resigned to their fate. "Father," an elderly Indian said to Breynat. "I have never suffered so much before. The Almighty is punishing us. But it will only be for a day. Look at us: don't we scold our children? Give them a clout sometimes, a bit of a spanking? But it's for their good. Well, our Father in Heaven does the same with us. We have displeased Him. That's why He corrects us. But it won't be forever. It's for our great good."[7]

BY THE TIME Father Rouvière set off for Eskimo country, the Catholic Church had already converted most of the Indians living around Great Bear Lake. The Anglican Church, by comparison, had only a half dozen churches north of Edmonton, and seemed to be struggling to keep up. Finding someone up to the task of proselytizing among the Eskimos had become one of Bishop Breynat's most passionate ideas. Had he had fewer responsibilities, Breynat might have done the work himself. By the time he approached Father Rouvière, Breynat must have seen something of himself in the young priest. He could only hope that Rouvière would be as enthusiastic about his work as Breynat had remained about his own. No one in the Catholic Church knew more about the challenges of ministering to people in the Far North than Breynat, who over the next fifty years would become known as "the Flying Bishop" for winging around the Arctic in a single-engine plane.[8]

For Breynat, as for all missionaries in remote areas, there had been significant challenges along the way. Up in the Barren Lands, Indians would arrive at the settlements shortly before Christmas, and would stay for only a week or two. Though most had long since been converted to Catholicism and many attended church, they came primarily to trade furs for tea and tobacco, cartridges and shot, axes, knives, and needles. Breynat was fascinated by his new charges and the ingeunuity with which they navigated their lives. Their summer clothes were made of caribou hide, its hair scraped off with a piece of bone. Brains were rubbed on the hide to make it supple, and it was smoked for rain resistance. Their winter clothes were similar but were worn with the animal's hair left in place. Young animals, including those that had been stillborn, provided a luxurious material for hoods. Skin clothing, Breynat would find, could keep a human body warm in weather reaching forty below zero, yet was never too heavy to wear traveling on foot. Tents were also made of caribou skins and were left empty, except for a few packages of meat. Family members squatted on their heels around a stove in the center of the tent and lay down at night side by side, fully dressed and wrapped in a blanket or caribou-skin gown. Breynat called his charges "the Caribou-Eaters." The Indians referred to Breynat equally simply: *"Yalt'yi gozh aze sin"*: There's a new little praying man.

For their part, priests who had grown up on the agricultural bounty of France had to get used to a diet that consisted, at its most diverse, of caribou and fish and the occasional potato. Priests learned to clean trout and slice chips off caribou-grease candles to light a campfire. They learned to toss a little altar wine in the skillet for flavor. There were no vegetables, of course. And there wouldn't be; none grew in the north country. Yet compared to the people to whom they ministered, Breynat and Rouvière had it easy. As long as they stayed near their mission base, there was little chance that they would starve to death or die of exposure. It was only out in the field that things got dangerous.[9]

On his way home one day from the hunting grounds, Breynat found himself in snow up to his knees. His legs were spent, his food nearly gone, the sun almost set. His dogs, starving and exhausted, were barely moving. A common enough situation for a native, but Breynat was at a loss. He didn't know how to build a snowhouse or a bough shelter. He had no sleeping bag. He had no family around him to lay a fire or hunt a caribou.

Should he push on to the mission or turn around and return, humbled, to the camp he had just left? Breynat decided to follow an Indian hunter who was tracking a gut-shot caribou.

Suddenly, to his right, Breynat heard the blows of an axe. Breynat's dogs shuffled forward. There, up ahead, was the hunter, deftly butchering the caribou. Exhilarated, Breynat gathered up some spruce branches and laid a fire. Warmed by the flames and waiting for the meat to roast, Breynat and his provider treated themselves by sucking the frozen marrow from one of the caribou's foot bones. They threw some meat and entrails to the starving dogs and settled in for a feast.[10]

With his newfound admiration for native hunting skills, Breynat decided soon afterward to try his own hand at bringing down a caribou. Armed with an old carbine, he managed to shoot an animal, but his prey did not die. It lay where it fell, quivering. Rather than expend another precious cartridge, he smashed the butt of his rifle into the caribou's skull, killing it instantly. But now he had no knife or axe to dress the kill. Instead, he undid the girdle on his black cassock, tied it around the caribou's neck, and dragged it to the top of a nearby woodpile.

Word quickly spread among the Indians. They were horrified at the blundering indignity of the kill. Breynat had disregarded rituals of respect for prey animals that hunters had long held dear; his actions might, at the spirit level, cause the caribou to let the people starve. "It was a major scandal among the whole population," Breynat wrote. "The spirit of the caribou thus struck would go and tell all the rest of its race. These would never come back. Very shortly there would be a complete famine. An utter disaster!"

After working so hard to earn the trust of his congregants, Breynat now had to figure out how to repair a gaff of shocking proportions. He decided to try to convince the Indians that "there was nothing in it, that their belief was mere superstition. The good God, I told them, had created the caribou to serve as their food, and it was of little or no importance with what instruments they were killed." Breynat's choice—to argue against traditional beliefs rather than confess to his own ignorance—did not go over well. The tribe's chief arrived and reproached the priest for his foolishness. In a fury, he blamed Breynat for exposing his people to the risk of starvation.

Breynat responded by saying that he would write to his bishop and ask his opinion about whether Breynat should leave his post. The chief did not understand, but he grudgingly let Breynat go off to conduct a service. It was Christmas Eve. With hundreds of dogs tied up outside the church, baying at the moon, Breynat somehow got his "Caribou-Eaters" to chant the liturgy in Latin and sing "Il est ne le Divin Enfant" in their native tongue.

Three months later, a letter arrived from Monsignor Grouard. Breynat addressed his people. "The Big Praying-Man wishes me to inform you that he had not the time, still less the inclination, to address you a pastoral letter in order to explain that God created the caribou to provide you with the food you need, and that you can kill them any way you like, with the snare, with a gun, or if necessary by hitting them with a stick!"

Breynat then read an excerpt from the letter. "Tell your Caribou-Eaters to understand what you have told them, and what I now repeat myself, that I can do nothing about it. Let them ask the Author of all good to give them such understanding. . . . I bless them, just the same, with all my heart."[11]

IF ANYTHING, the cultural divide separating Europeans and Eskimos would be far wider than it had been between Europeans and Indians. Just a few years before Hornby delivered his fateful letter, the explorer Vilhjalmur Stefansson had learned that extreme isolation had made the native people highly suspicious of people they did not know. The introduction of Christianity, and especially Christian prohibitions of certain behaviors, would make a complicated fit for the Eskimos, Stefansson predicted. On its face, some of the Church's rituals might wear well. Since as far as he could tell the Eskimo religion consisted primarily of prohibitions and taboos, the many prohibitions of Christianity were easy for them to understand, Stefansson wrote. Eskimos, he observed, believed that sickness, famine, and death were caused by the breaking of a marrowbone with the wrong kind of hammer, or the sewing of deerskin clothing before enough days had elapsed from the killing of the last whale or walrus. To avoid breaking these taboos meant prosperity and good health. Adding notions of sin and salvation seemed perfectly logical.[12]

But even early on, Stefansson wondered about the impact of Christian doctrine on the practical realities of Arctic life. For one thing, Stefansson had talents most missionaries did not. An excellent linguist, he would eventually become fluent in several Eskimo dialects. More important, he had an unusual willingness to learn from native intelligence rather than ignore it. He often relied on a small handful of Eskimo guides and interpreters, notably a young man named Ilavinik, who had become one the region's most reliable translators. Over the next few years, Ilavinik would use his language skills in an increasingly complex series of negotiations, from translating for wandering anthropologists to interpreting details of a grisly double murder in an Edmonton courtroom. In 1911, of course, all that seemed impossibly far away.

Now that they had been admonished against breaking the Sabbath, the Mackenzie Eskimos refused to "work" on Sundays, a decision that yielded some strange results. Around Christmastime in 1908, an Eskimo couple came into Stefansson's encampment at Cape Smythe hoping to sell skins. They had traveled some two hundred miles, they said, and had left another couple, including the man's sister, behind. There had not been enough food to feed both the people and the dogs, they said; they had left the man's sister and her husband forty miles to the east. Their dogs were already dead of starvation.

As soon as the Eskimos living near the cape heard this story, they organized a party to go out and rescue the man and his wife before they starved to death. But just as the rescue party was about to depart, someone pointed out that since it was Sunday, no journeys could begin. It was not until after midnight that the group finally set out. A fair day had turned foul, with snow blowing into great drifts that covered any sign of the sled trail. The search party had no luck.

Later that morning, the man of the abandoned couple turned up, barely alive, at a cabin three miles north of the Cape Smythe encampment. A second search party went out immediately and found his wife, a half day's journey away, sitting beside a dead fire, her hands and feet completely frozen. Curious as to why the stronger man had decided to abandon his sister and her husband, and why they had waited so long to rescue them, Stefansson asked the man from the stronger couple his thoughts on the matter. The man had been a Christian for about ten years, knew more prayers than any other Eskimo, and was very careful not to break any Christian commandments. For many years he had done no work on Sunday; for many years he had never eaten a meal without saying grace; and he had in every other way lived according to the Christian law as he understood it. "I asked him whether he had never heard that such things as leaving his sister to starve to death were also against the law of the Lord," Stefansson wrote. "He replied that he had never heard anything about that. His Christianity, he told me with evident regret, might not be the best and most up-to-date, for he had never had the chance to get any firsthand from a missionary. He had learned his Christianity entirely from the converted Eskimos of the Kuvuk River who, he said, might not be well informed about all the prohibitions necessary for salvation."[13]

CHAPTER TWO

—

"Of what are you thinking?" Peary asked one
of his Eskimo guides. "I do not have to think,"
was the answer; "I have plenty of meat."

—WILL DURANT, *Our Oriental Heritage*

I
F JOHN HORNBY'S LETTER DESCRIBING HIS MEETING WITH
the Eskimos ignited Bishop Breynat's imagination, Hornby's offer to lead
young Father Rouvière to the Arctic coast was almost too good to believe.
Only a very few white explorers had ever attempted an overland route from
the south, and during those few crossings the Barren Lands had seen some
of the Arctic's most spectacular tragedies. In 1771, Samuel Hearne had
heard rumors of vast Arctic copper deposits from local Indians. When he
arrived at the mouth of the Coppermine River, he became the first white
man to see the Arctic Ocean. The promised mountains of metal, however,
turned out to fit in his palm. But it was something he saw before reaching
the coast that left him permanently shaken. Traveling north along the Cop-

permine, Hearne watched his Chipewayan guides carry out a horrifying "Eskimo hunt," in which they crept upon two dozen Eskimos sleeping in tents above a waterfall twelve miles from its mouth and slaughtered them. Hearne described the scene as "shocking beyond description."

> The poor, unhappy victims were surprised in the midst of their sleep, and had neither time nor power to make any resistance; men, women and children, in all upward of twenty, ran out of their tents stark naked, and endeavored to make their escape, but the Indians having possession of all the land-side, to no place could they fly for shelter. One alternative only remained, that of jumping into the river; but as none of them attempted it, they all fell a sacrifice to the Indian barbarity! The shrieks and groans of the poor expiring wretches were truly dreadful; and my horror was much at seeing a young girl, seemingly about eighteen years of age, killed so near me that when the first spear was stuck into her side she fell down at my feet, and twisted around my legs, so that it was with difficulty that I could disengage myself from her dying grasps. As two Indian men pursued this unfortunate victim, I solicited very hard for her life; but the murderers made no reply till they had struck both their spears through her body, and transfixed her to the ground. Then they looked me sternly in the face, and began to ridicule me, by asking if I wanted an Esquimaux wife; and paid not the smallest regard to the shrieks and agony of the poor wretch, who was twining round their spears like an eel.[1]

From that point forward, the scene of the massacre was known as Bloody Falls. Eskimos had been terrified of strangers ever since, and ventured into Indian hunting grounds only as a last resort. The few white expeditions that moved through Bloody Falls over the next 150 years saw mostly the backs of Eskimos running away from them. In his *Narrative of a Journey to the Shores of the Polar Sea*, John Franklin included a pen-and-ink sketch of Bloody Falls with a pile of human skulls in the foreground.

Not long after this, Franklin would come to his own catastrophic end in the Barren Lands.[2]

Just when Father Rouvière first learned of the legend of Bloody Falls is hard to ascertain. But surely the stories about Samuel Hearne and John Franklin were among the first things he heard in the spring of 1911, when he arrived at Fort Norman to meet John Hornby and begin planning his trip north. And surely he learned of another, far more recent story that must have frightened him to his core. At virtually the same moment that Rouvière reached Fort Norman, a trio of Canadian explorers arrived on the *Mackenzie River* steamer, bound, like Samuel Hearne 150 years before them, to investigate rumors of Barren Land copper. The team, consisting of George Douglas, his brother Lionel, and a geologist named August Sandburg, had outfitted in Edmonton, then hopped steamers along the string of trading posts between Lake Athabasca and Fort Norman, on the Mackenzie River. Though they had never been to the Barren Lands, let alone the Arctic coast, the members of the Douglas team were remarkably confident in their ability to navigate the worst the region could offer. They were competent, experienced woodsmen and sailors. They were physically strong, and—far more important—they had unshakably sound judgment. Over time, this probity would set them apart from the scores of explorers for whom the Arctic had become a graveyard. Yet just days before unloading at Fort Norman and meeting Father Rouvière, the Douglases stumbled across a scene of terrifying violence that to all four newcomers must have seemed a dark archetype of life and death in the Barren Lands.

On their way north on the Mackenzie, the Douglases had been asked to help the Royal North West Mounted Police investigate a report of a murder-suicide that had taken place in a trappers' remote winter base camp. They had obliged. Near a pretty spot with views of both the Salt River and the mighty Mackenzie, they found a log cabin, about twelve feet by fourteen feet. The scene inside was terrible. The stench was overwhelming, "worse than any other form of decomposing animal matter, and blended with it was the peculiarly acrid smell of old smoke from spruce fires," George Douglas reported. The two dead men were still in their bunks, one with his head "a shapeless mass, blown out of all resemblance to anything human by a soft point bullet from a high powered rifle." Beside the bunks, on a small table, lay a filthy notebook and a bottle of carbolic acid, but beyond that, Douglas could not stand in the cabin long enough to take notes. "One could remain in that loathsome atmosphere only a few minutes at a time," he wrote. "The bodies were in a state of decomposition so advanced that it was necessary to break the bunks down and carry them out as they lay."

Once they got the bodies out of the house, Douglas snapped a photograph of the men, laid head-to-head on the ground. He and the police buried them in a single grave, dug as deeply as they could manage in the frozen turf. They then returned to the cabin and tried to make sense of what had happened. In the notebook, they discovered a series of comments, written on different pages and at different times. Apparently the man who'd written the notes had shot his companion and then killed himself by drinking the carbolic acid.

"Cruel treatment drove me to kill Peat," one note said. "Everything is wrong he never paid one sent ship everything out pay George Walker $10. . . . I have been sick a long time I am not Crasy, but sutnly goded to death he thot i had more money than i had and has been trying to find it. I tried to get him to go after medison but Cod not he wanted me to die first so good by."

A final note concluded, "I have just killed the man that was killing me so good by and may god bless you all I am ofle weak bin down since the last of March so thare hant no but Death for me."[3]

What lasting impression the murder-suicide had on the Douglas team can only be imagined, since George Douglas wrote no further about it. To what degree they described it to Father Rouvière also can't be known. But bearing witness to such a horrifying crime, carried out by one man against the companion who was apparently asleep in his bed, could hardly have failed to have unsettled these men as they set out on their own journey north. What had happened in the minds of those trappers, shuttered in against the pressing darkness? What minor disputes, what petty irritations had led to anger so unyielding that death seemed the only escape? Perhaps the alternative—suffering in silence until spring, then hiking the hundred miles back to the nearest trading post, and from there home—seemed impossibly trying. Eskimos, who had faced such conditions since time immemorial, had a term for this malady: *perlerorneq*, an extreme winter depression that brought on symptoms of psychosis. Barry Lopez has described it as "to look ahead to all that must be accomplished and to retreat to the present feeling defeated, weary before starting, a core of anger, a miserable sadness." Under its spell, "the victim tears fitfully at his clothing. A woman begins aimlessly slashing at things in the iglu with her knife. A person runs half naked into the bitter freezing night, screaming out at the village, eating the shit of dogs. Eventually the person is calmed by others in the family, with great compassion, and helped to sleep. *Perlerorneq*. Winter."[4]

No matter how much time the trappers had spent in the region—a year? two?—they were apparently ill equipped to deal with such darkness. For Rouvière, other questions must surely have arisen. Who could say what torments were possible in the middle of this northern country? Compared to where he was heading—the mouth of the Coppermine River, on the coast of the Arctic Ocean and fully five hundred miles north—the scene of the murder was relatively southern and far more accessible. As one of the continent's primary trading routes, the Mackenzie River corridor was dotted with at least a half dozen busy settlements. Where Rouvière, Hornby, and, coincidentally, the Douglas team were going—overland to the deep interior and the farthest reaches of the unexplored Northwest Territories— there was nothing. The Barren Lands. And with plans to spend the winter in the crushing cold and unyielding darkness, in a place where the sun went down at the end of November and didn't come up again until the end of January, each step the team took felt like a step deeper into a Dantean wilderness. Where they were going, twenty-four hours of winter darkness would give cabin fever an entirely new dimension. Even the outside would seem claustrophobic, close, inescapable. Fifty years earlier, Father Petitot, one of the few missionaries to make it to the coast, had apparently lost his mind.

In the early twentieth century, you could count the number of Arctic expeditions on a couple of hands. Yet the reports that had trickled back to the living rooms in Toronto, New York, London, and Paris revealed the place to be as intriguing, in its way, as Africa. This was a place where shamans could turn themselves into wolves. Where polar bears could be seen swimming five miles out in the open ocean. Where women nursed their babies, outside, in howling blizzards. Where in a good season a caribou hunter "might wade in the blood-stained water spearing the bemused animals by the hundred, until strength failed, in a liturgy of destruction that celebrates the bounty and the terror of the land." The land was full of musk ox, and wolves, and wolverines. It was one of the few places in the world that accommodated both grizzly bears and polar bears. The rivers were stuffed with char, the lakes with trout. Formed by the retreat of the Wisconsin ice sheet ten thousand years ago, it was the youngest ecosystem on earth.[5]

For white explorers, traveling to the Arctic was like traveling back in time. The people who lived there were as strange as Pygmies. Esquimaux! The very name seemed to be derived from *Eskiquimantsic*, an Algonquian-Abenaki word meaning "an eater of raw flesh." To the turn-of-the-century urban imagination, one caught up in the anxieties of industry, crime, and warfare, the simple people of the Arctic seemed to offer a culture untainted by the poisons of greed, decadence, and imperial aggression. If the Eskimos had never learned how to farm, let alone compose symphonies or build suspension bridges, they were also not cursed by modern problems. They possessed virtually no material goods, and seemed to desire none. Several white explorers noticed that most Eskimos seemed unable to count beyond two or three. Why was that? And how would they figure in a culture where quantifying possessions—money, furs, souls—was practically a religion in itself? Eskimos had so little variety in the way of food (nothing grew there!) that they seemed almost ascetic. Pure. In fact, Eskimos did not seem like contemporary humans at all. They were more like a culture frozen in time. For people of European descent, visiting an Eskimo community in 1911 was time travel: studying Eskimos, they thought, was studying the very roots of man.[6]

The reality, of course, was that Eskimos were not ancestors of Europeans; they were their contemporaries. Though Western explorers could be forgiven their leaps of imagination, the fact was that they and the Eskimos had been "evolving" for exactly the same amount of time. And despite the rhetoric that Europeans used to describe these primitive "nomads," the Eskimos had been in the same place for at least five thousand years. It was the Europeans who had been wandering. Eskimos didn't search for safe passage to Florida, or make pilgrimages to Rome. They didn't send mining expeditions to California, or look to Africa for slave labor. They stayed home. The fact that they functioned so well, with so few material goods, also made the heroic rhetoric of European Arctic exploration narratives somewhat suspect. Ships from Victorian England would disgorge hundreds of men with tons and tons of equipment to spend a few months or years in a place Eskimos lived domestically with virtually nothing. Europeans imposed themselves on the land; the Eskimos simply adapted to it. Missionaries and explorers often showed up ragged, hungry, and sick. They discovered locals who were healthy and hardy. If the explorers made it home to their drawing rooms—an end that was never guaranteed—they would tell grand tales of having conquered another corner of the globe. Eskimo hunters returned to their tents or their snowhouses, went to sleep, and got up and did it again.[7]

To the traveler from the south, exploration was held closely akin to a spiritual quest. You leave the comfort of a known society and enter an entirely new dimension. Along the journey, you are exposed to dangers both foreseen and unforeseen. You accept as givens the powerful and dangerous challenges of isolation from kin, exposure to new territory and harsh weather, and uncertainty about food and water supplies. Very little can be taken for granted. Heat and shelter and food and drink are not easily gotten. Securing even the most basic components to sustain life requires local experience and native skill, and travelers from the south, by definition, lacked both. Rather than eating vitamin-rich caribou and seal, British explorers ate preserved food and relied on vitamin C supplements that became worthless after a few months in the cold. They treated lethargy as a morale problem; it was often an early sign of scurvy. They treated hunting as a sport rather than a necessity. Knowing how to hunt for fun in a community that would feed you if you came back empty-handed was very different from knowing how to hunt to prevent the starvation of your family. Knowing how to pitch a tent in a temperate climate was very different from knowing how to build a snowhouse to fend off weeks of weather at thirty degrees below zero. Knowing how to lay a fire in a hearth had little value in a place where there was no wood.[8]

Traveling to an extremely remote land, you also expose yourself to strange people, who may or not welcome you. They may or may not offer assistance. They may or may not treat you as a friend. Given the extreme remoteness of the region, and the traveler's relative experience and self-sufficiency, relationships with native people become critical to the traveler's survival. The more skilled, savvy, and diplomatic the traveler, the greater the chance for success. The more rigid, the more arrogant, the more inflexible, the greater the chance for disaster. In 1820, Sir John Franklin and his men, moving through the Barren Lands, had such trouble finding food that they ate their own shoes. Two men starved to death. When a guide brought in some meat, Franklin's men exulted and feasted hungrily. When they discovered that the meat had come from a missing member of their own party, they shot the guide. Two decades later, Franklin tried exploring the Arctic again. This time he brought curtain rods, silver cutlery, and silk shoes. He and more than a hundred of his men died of starvation and lead poisoning from their canned food. They almost certainly cannibalized some of their companions. Just a few months after Father Rouvière arrived at Fort Norman, at the other end of the world, Roald Amundsen, adopting Eskimo survival techniques, particularly the use of sled dogs, reached the South Pole. Robert Falcon Scott had insisted on sticking with British know-how, particularly the use of horses, and perished.

—

THAT FATHER ROUVIÈRE trusted his life to John Hornby, a man he had never met, in a region whose hostility he could not possibly conceive was a testament to the depth of his faith. But if Hornby's wilderness expertise and knowledge of the Barren Lands was infinitely superior to Rouvière's, he was not, in fact, an ideal guide. He was independent to a fault, often picking up and wandering off on his own without concern for his travel companions. Far more worrisome, for a man as inexperienced as Rouvière, was Hornby's apparent refusal to plan more than a day or two ahead. Hornby thought highly enough of his own hunting skills that he rarely stored enough food to get him through the Arctic's inevitable seasons of famine. Another white explorer warned Hornby that the practice would one day lead him to "die like a rat." For now, though, Hornby was the best guide Father Rouvière had.[9]

Just what Hornby's motives had been for contacting the Catholic mission in the first place are hard to fathom. He was not, by a long stretch, a churchgoer, and he seemed deeply ambivalent about the impact a mission in the Barren Lands might have on the native people there. To some degree, he felt proprietary over the country itself. To someone with Hornby's personality, another influx of white people could only make the land seem cramped. But perhaps Hornby believed that the tide of history had already begun to flow, and that it would be better to know the white people setting up shop in the north than not. Perhaps he would get some fur-trading business in the bargain. In any case, he agreed to accompany Rouvière from Fort Norman to the northern shore of Great Bear Lake. They would try to coordinate their departure with the Douglas team, but nothing, at this stage of their respective journeys, was simple. Indeed, as confident as George Douglas felt in his own group's wilderness skills, the fact remained that none of them had been remotely this far north. Their intent from the beginning had been to travel quickly and to rely on the help of no one. They viewed with trepidation the prospect of shouldering the burdens of other travelers. Crossing the Barren Lands and getting to the Arctic coast would be difficult enough without worrying about the mental and physical competence of strangers.

Crossing Great Bear Lake would be one of the most difficult legs of the entire expedition. After leaving the relative comforts of Fort Norman, the men would haul their boats and gear one hundred river miles to a southwestern lobe of the lake. They would use canoes and York boats, fifty-foot-long open vessels with just over three feet of freeboard and a twelve-foot beam that could be rigged with a canvas tarpaulin sail. With a combination of rowing and sailing, they would cross the enormous breadth of the lake itself. Their destination, diagonally across, was the old Fort Confidence site, where a Hudson's Bay Company man had already built a cabin; at a second site, six miles up the Dease River, there was another small camp. The shortest route, straight across the lake, would be risky in the extreme. Great Bear Lake is the ninth-largest freshwater lake in the world, fully 250 miles from the southwestern shore to the northeastern shore. Sailing an open, fully loaded boat across such an expanse of water, in a region that could instantly whip up a ferocious windstorm or a blizzard, would have been foolish. Waves on a body of water that big could reach twenty-two feet, easily five times the height needed to swamp a York boat.

For the first time since they'd left Edmonton, twelve hundred miles to the south, even the supremely self-confident Douglases realized they would need some help getting to the region's fabled mineral deposits. Gathering their gear together at Fort Norman, they approached a group of Bear Lake Indians and said they would trade them their York boat in exchange for help dragging it up Bear River to the lake. The Douglases would not need the York for the river trip to the Arctic coast, and figured they would be able to make their return trip in canoes. The Indians hesitated. They were amazed at some of the gear the Douglases planned to carry, particularly the old floorboards and two small windows they hoped would make a winter cabin more cozy. The offer of the York boat was more troubling. Since it could not be divided, the boat would inevitably end up in the hands of one man, and was therefore likely to cause more

strife than it was worth. The Indians also took offense at the canvas
Duxbak pants the Douglases had on. Apparently, the pants closely resembled the uniforms worn by officers of the Royal North West Mounted Police. They represented something that clearly made the Indians nervous.

Since only one of the Indians spoke English—a man with the unlikely
name of Lixie Trindle—coming to terms was not easy. Finally, after nego-
tiating a more attractive fee that did not include the York boat, six Indians
from around Fort Norman agreed to haul three and a half tons of gear in
the York boat, packed with two canoes on top, up the Bear River. They
would haul the boat "like mules," and when they reached Great Bear
Lake, they would return, floating downriver in their own birchbark
canoe.[10]

Before he left, George Douglas reminded Father Rouvière of his plans
to push as far into Eskimo country as possible before the precious summer
weather changed. If Rouvière wanted to come along, he had to cross Great
Bear Lake as quickly as possible. If too many days passed, there simply
would not be enough time to make it north and back again before winter.
The Douglases would travel fast. They needed to make a reconnaissance
run this summer before embarking on a fuller expedition to the Arctic
coast the following spring. If Rouvière wished to join the party, he was welcome. If he was late coming to meet them, they would leave without him.

Though Rouvière had no reason to expect help from the Douglas
team—they had never promised to take him north—their obvious competence would solve some significant problems for the young priest. Making
a round-trip journey with the Douglases from Great Bear Lake to the Coppermine River, the main trunkline to the coast, would make a lot more
sense than trekking all the way to the coast and spending the winter there
with John Hornby. Rouvière had never spent a warm summer day in the
Arctic, let alone an entire winter. He had few supplies of any kind, and virtually no cold-weather gear. He had no hunting skills. He had never met
an Eskimo. And he barely even knew the mercurial Hornby. What would
it be like living with him in a snowhouse for five months of utter darkness?

But by July 8, when the Douglases and their hired hands left Fort Norman, Rouvière and Hornby were still not ready. Hornby didn't even have a boat. He had planned to borrow one from a retired Hudson's Bay man who had not yet arrived at Fort Norman. With Hornby insisting on waiting, Rouvière made the bold decision to leave without him. He joined some Bear Lake Indians who were planning their own trip across the lake. What Rouvière would do once he got to the far shore of Great Bear Lake, he had no idea. "After that, I don't know how I shall make out," he wrote Bishop Breynat. "Nothing has been decided about where to winter. [Hornby's] idea is to get as close as possible to the Eskimo, perhaps going right to the sea-coast to winter. His scheme seems all right to me; but if we adopt this plan, our winter supplies are no use; almost impossible to take them so far without enormous expense."

If he ever did manage to locate the Eskimos, Father Rouvière also wondered how he would find his way back south. Presumably any Indian guides he could persuade to bring him north would be loath to spend much time in Eskimo country, and Eskimos would be unlikely to travel deep into Indian country. Perhaps Rouvière could find a place to build a cabin in between the two peoples and meet an Eskimo family willing to spend the winter with him. "This way we could learn their language fairly quickly—an indispensable step towards the ministering among them," he wrote. Rouvière ended his letter, as he often would, with a tone that reflected his own humility in the face of trials so far from home. "So far the good God has kept me well and I ask him every day to preserve me to the end, until I can fulfill the difficult mission which has been entrusted to me. I rely also upon your good prayers."[11]

When Rouvière and his Indian guides finally got under way, he quickly realized that even making it to Great Bear Lake would be a trial. For all their seaworthiness on open water, York boats were exasperating to haul against the current on a swift river. Five of the boat's eighteen inches of draft were keel, which helped the boat track in open water but seemed like a plow blade in the river shallows. Although Rouvière and his guides occasionally found a lip of beach that allowed some decent footing, more often than not they were forced to drag the boat through thigh-deep, icy water, navigating all the while an Arctic Scylla and Charybdis—whirlpools on one side of them and sheer ice walls on the other.[12]

THE DOUGLASES made it from Fort Norman to the southwest shore of Great Bear Lake on July 14, and were around the lake on the northeastern shore ten days later. They picked a site for their cabin on the banks of the Dease River, six miles up from the lake, and laid out the windows and floorboards they had hauled five hundred miles from Fort Simpson. They immediately set out their gear for the reconnaissance trip to the Coppermine River, and waited impatiently for Rouvière to arrive. When five days went by with no sign of the priest, George Douglas and the geologist, August Sandburg, set off without him, leaving Lionel Douglas behind to build the team's winter cabin. As always, they executed their plans like clockwork.[13]

The same could not be said for the men lagging to their rear. By the end of July, when Rouvière finally showed up, Hornby was still nowhere to be seen. What was taking him so long was hard to fathom. Perhaps he'd been hampered by equipment troubles or a shortage of food, both of which were constant worries in the Barren Lands. Perhaps Hornby had gotten sidetracked, as he often did. With the summer season quickly slipping away, Rouvière grew anxious to move north. But with his Indian guides unwilling to venture farther into Eskimo country, Hornby lagging behind, and not even an abstract idea about how to get to the Coppermine River, Rouvière was stuck. There were no credible maps, and even if there had been, Rouvière lacked the experience to use them. He had no choice but to hang around Great Bear Lake, day after day, watching the sun slip incrementally lower in the sky. Finally, two critical weeks later, Hornby dragged his canoe ashore. It was August 10. A trip to the coast and back was now out of the question. Winter would be setting in soon.[14]

CHAPTER THREE

———

Unuak naguyuk
Talvani nunami
Uilagahuk nutaganikpaktuk
Angutinuak ataniuyuk
Negiyutikagvingmi-ituk
Anilihaktuk Jesus

—FIRST VERSE OF "SILENT NIGHT, HOLY NIGHT"
IN INUINAQTUN

BEFORE LEAVING GREAT BEAR LAKE, GEORGE DOUGLAS AND August Sandburg packed fifty days' worth of food into a canoe they had dubbed the *Polaris*. If they were unwilling to wait for Rouvière and Hornby, perhaps their string of caches and campsites would serve as useful signposts if Rouvière and Hornby did try to make a run at least partway into Eskimo country before winter arrived.

For both teams, the journey between Great Bear Lake and the Coppermine River would be challenging in ways their trip so far had not. No map had ever been made of this section of Canada. All the men had to go on was an imprecise sketch from the Canadian Geological Survey, and a series of descriptions they'd picked up from reading a narrative written by the explorer David Hanbury. And it had been nearly a decade since Hanbury had passed through this country, going in the opposite direction, from the Arctic Ocean via the Coppermine, Kendall, and Dease Rivers to Great Bear Lake. For much of his trip, Hanbury had had a comparatively easy time of it, for one simple reason: after leaving the Coppermine River, he was traveling downstream, following rivers that led one into the next. For the Douglases and Rouvière, trying to follow small tributary creeks upstream would be far more challenging, since each one could lead to a solitary water source—and a dead end. Since every river has myriad branches leading into it, explorers moving upstream have exactly as many ways of getting lost as there are creeks. Minus one.

The early stages of the trip north would be relatively easy. In its lower reaches the Dease River was a shallow stream typically 130 yards wide, though some sections narrowed to rapids just ten or fifteen yards across. Canoes could be paddled up the wider sections of the river, but in the rapids one man always had to exit the boat and pull the other man through. In camp at the end of the day, they could hunt wild geese and pick blueberries they found growing on the riverbanks.[1]

Farther north, the country became increasingly bleak. The landscape looked pulverized. Blackflies were a torment. The region that lay between the Dease and the Coppermine Rivers, at the north end of the Barren Lands, was a plateau known as the Dismal Lakes. The largest lake was ringed by lowlands, which were, in turn, shut in by high, bare, rocky hills; those to the north still had huge, probably permanent drifts of snow. The hills on the southern side were built of sharp broken rocks "unmitigated by any softening influence of plant life," Douglas wrote. Along the shore were scattered the bones of caribou "like driftwood along the beach."

Navigating this region—getting their canoes safely from one river to the other—would require several miles of overland carrying. As difficult as paddling a canoe upriver can be, there is nothing quite as counterintuitive as carrying a canoe for miles across dry land. This is something like a cowboy carrying his horse, or a cyclist shouldering his bike; it is a physical incongruity, in which the weaker, less efficient half of an otherwise graceful pair is forced to do the dirty work. Shouldering a canoe, perhaps with a bag or two of gear occupying hands that would otherwise be engaged in swatting clouds of blackflies, offers challenges to a paddler's patience that are far less happily engaged than, say, a good set of rapids. It is impossible, for one thing, to see anything other than your own legs and, perhaps, if you are carrying the stern of the boat, the feet of your bowman. Conversation is labored, since every word is strained by the weight of the canoe and hollowed out as it bounces off the inverted hull. The man in front has little more peripheral vision than the man in back; since his face is stuck in the bow, he can see sideways but not much in front. If the portage requires moving through woods, low-lying branches can cause no end of aggravation for both parties. There are no moments of exhilaration when trudging in this fashion across tundra with a hundred pounds of gear on your back. There is only exhaustion, and maybe a blister or two. Unless you are in Eskimo country. Then there are some surprises.

Atop the Dismal Lakes plateau, George Douglas had just risen from a rest and was beginning to make his way back to camp when, raising his binoculars, he spotted a man walking along the top of a hill about a mile away. The figure disappeared as soon as Douglas brought him into view, but Douglas was certain that the man was an Eskimo. Scanning the hilltop, Douglas thought he could also see some sort of a camp, and he and Sandburg, beside themselves with excitement, decided to cautiously investigate. They walked quietly toward the hill, afraid of frightening the man, and got quite close to him before he noticed their approach.

"Whether it was merely the unexpectedness of it, or whether he had never seen any white man before I do not know, certainly he was very much frightened," Douglas wrote. "We threw up our arms calling out 'Teyma Teyma' about the only Eskimo word I knew." In return, the man, trembling with fright, kept repeating something over and over in a low moaning tone. Though Douglas would not have known it, the eerie chant was almost certainly the same sound Vilhjalmur Stefansson and his companions had described just a year before. According to Eskimo legend, a man in the presence of malevolent spirits could be struck permanently dumb if he failed to make a sound with every breath. On and on the surprised man would moan, until his visitors either disappeared or somehow convinced them that they were, in fact, human beings.

The man was sturdily built, about five feet four inches high, and dressed in caribou skins and sealskin boots. Douglas noted his clothes were "quite as clean as our own, and a pleasant contrast to the dirty, sulky Indians we were used to." The man's hair hung straight and black, with the bangs cropped close to the skin. His face seemed open and intelligent, with rosy cheeks and, once he got over his fear, an engaging smile. He carried some spears, and on the ground next to him were a bow, a sealskin case full of arrows, and an animal skin drying on a rack of crossed sticks. Douglas and Sandburg did their best to communicate with him, using what little native language they knew. When they asked if the lake they could see in the near distance was Teshierpi Lake, the man nodded his head and repeated, "Teshi-arping, Teshi-arping." Douglas reached into his pocket and produced a small piece of chocolate and watched as the Eskimo put it dubiously into his mouth. Instantly, the man's face broke into a wide grin, and all three men shared a moment of delight.

With the chocolate working its magic, and seeing an opportunity to lighten their load, Douglas did his best through a variety of hand gestures to ask the man if he would follow them back to their camp and help them portage their gear. At first the man seemed willing, and followed the pair south for a stretch. But after a while he began to lag farther and farther behind, and finally he bolted back to the top of the hill, where Douglas and Sandburg watched him gather up his few belongings and disappear toward the lake. Douglas was perplexed. Had their pace been too quick? Did he have obligations elsewhere that were being compromised by his distraction? Or did he simply not trust them? They would never find out.[2]

Following the creeks flowing down the northeastern slope of the Dismal Lakes plateau, Douglas and Sandburg quickly found the Kendall River, then, at last, the broad Coppermine. Getting from here to the rumored copper deposits near the Arctic Ocean the following spring would be a matter of ruddering the *Polaris* to the coast. Douglas and Sandburg spent a couple of days scouting out the river and its surrounding hills, looking for spots to which they might return. Satisfied that they could make the spring trip without too much difficulty, they declared their reconnaissance mission a success, and began the trip home.

On their way south, Douglas and Sandburg were treated to glorious displays of northern lights, extending across the sky "in the form of a spiral like a loosely twisted rope," Douglas wrote. "There was no color, it looked more like a slightly luminous cloud. A rapid movement was running through it from end to end, and I thought at first it was some kind of a cloud, some violent atmospheric disturbance, and for a few moments I was quite alarmed until I realised what it really was."

They were also struck by a more terrestrial surprise. At a campsite near the junction of Sandy Creek and the Dease River, where they had also stopped on their way north, they saw a number of footprints that had not been there before. Trees had been chopped down, but in a very strange manner—they seemed to have been bludgeoned with blunt tools rather than chopped or sawed, and they lay across the river, as if to form some sort of barricade. Douglas decided the work must have been done by Eskimos rather than Indians, who, as full-time forest dwellers, had more efficient tools. The barricade, he supposed, must have been some sort of deer-hunting blind, but who could say for sure? Douglas also noticed that a canvas bag he had strung between two trees on the way north was now tied up differently. When he opened the bag, he was astonished to find a small sealskin coat and a beautifully made pair of sealskin slippers. In addition, the cache had been restocked with a bunch of arrows fitted with spruce shafts and copper-tipped bone heads, along with some walrus-tusk ivory trinkets. It would be a year before Douglas figured out that one of these last items could be used to shove a sinew-rope through the noses of marmots, to form a kind of carrying stringer; the other, a small handle with a loop of sinew attached, was useful for carrying the stomachs of caribou.

Apparently, a group of Eskimos had found Douglas's cache, rifled it, picked out what they needed, and left what they considered fair compensation. When Douglas cataloged everything that had been taken, he came up with exactly one object: an empty lard pail. The things left by the Eskimos seemed "liberal payment," he wrote, an impressive act of civility from one group of travelers to another.

BY THIS TIME, back at Great Bear Lake, Father Rouvière and John Hornby were just beginning their own reconnaissance trip north. Though he had little chance of making it all the way to the coast and back before winter, Rouvière hoped at least to push into the southern reaches of Eskimo territory. Perhaps he would even get lucky and run into a few people before they disappeared to their frozen winter hunting grounds. Like Douglas and Sandburg, they struggled mightily against the currents of the Dease River as they made their way toward the Dismal Lakes plateau. Locked in by a thick fog that severely limited their line of sight down the river corridor, they found themselves crisscrossing the steppes near the lakes for several days. And Despite Hornby's experience in the region, their early going was never assured; indeed, it was only when they came to a campsite left by Douglas and Sandburg that they were certain they were on the right path. "What a river!" Rouvière wrote to Father Ducot, the priest in charge of the mission at Fort Norman. "The current is very strong and there are places where there isn't enough water for the canoe—and it goes on like that for a distance of fifteen miles. There are at least thirty or forty rapids to go up and each turning of the river is a rapid. We have to take the canoe one at each end and lift it in order to get it forward at all."[3]

Finally, in mid-August, their luck changed. Following an impulse, Rouvière, still wearing his black cassock and carrying his Oblate's cross, decided to try going northwest. Hornby refused to follow. Rouvière went off on his own. Forty-five minutes later, he saw three shapes in a fold in a nearby hill. In the evening light, he was uncertain whether they were caribou or men. Quickening his pace, he trotted along for another ten minutes. Suddenly, on the side of a knoll, he spied a small crowd of people. As soon as they saw him, they moved in his direction; a man in front, his head bent to the side, raised his arms in greeting. Then, several times, he bowed his whole body to the ground. Rouvière stood in silence, stunned. But his mind raced. "Thanks, O mother Mary," he said to himself. "One of the first points of my mission is about to be fulfilled. Be pleased to bless this first encounter." He raised his arm. The entire group of Eskimos picked up their pace.

When he got close enough to see Rouvière's face, the man in front turned to his companions and shouted a single word: *Krabluna!* Rouvière knew the word. Depending on the translation, it could be interpreted differently. "Long Eyebrow" was one translation. "Stranger" was another. With a great show of affection, the man took the priest by the arm and presented him to the rest. The young priest shook hands with everyone. Rouvière's cross captured their attention immediately. What could they have thought it was? An arrowhead? A spearpoint? Flashing his fingers, Rouvière tried to explain. "As they gazed at it I did my best by signs to make them understand that He who was on the cross had sacrificed His life for us."

He then hung some crucifixes around their necks, and accompanied them to their camp. He was famished, after a long day's walk, and accepted their invitation gladly. "Refuse? Not likely, because I had been walking since eight in the morning, it was nine in the evening, and myself nearly starved," he wrote. One cannot help but wonder what he would have done for food had he not met the Eskimos. Here he was, far from camp, with no provisions in his pack. Hornby was nowhere in sight.

In any case, once in camp, Rouvière was immediately crowded and peppered with questions. Not able to communicate, he tried again to tell them of his reason for being so far north, "that I had come on their account, and to stay among them." A group agreed to go back with him to fetch his gear, but Rouvière managed to convince them that one volunteer would be enough.

"These Eskimos are really hospitable people," Rouvière wrote to Bishop Breynat. "The first impression they made on me was very favourable, and I think, if one can meet them often, it should be possible to do a great deal of good." Unfortunately, Rouvière found communicating with the Eskimos frustrating. "We can't understand each other," he wrote, "but their language seems quite easy and very little different from the language of the Mackenzie Eskimo, if I can judge from the few words I've been able to pick out."

Even after the first meeting, Rouvière was aware of the pressure the encroachment of whites was having on the Eskimo community. Already a number of them had been trading with whalers. One had exchanged eight white foxes for a rifle. Clearly, learning their language would become critical to a satisfactory ministry. Whether Rouvière could learn it fast enough to make himself an effective missionary or whether he would need some help from an interpreter remained to be seen.

Perhaps, Rouvière thought, Bishop Breynat would make good on his promise to send along another priest, one with training in the Eskimo language. With its proximity to Eskimo hunting grounds, the Dismal Lakes region would make a far better place to set up a missionary base than the more southerly Great Bear Lake, even if it meant living apart from people like the Douglases and John Hornby. The only thing for Rouvière to do now was to head back to Great Bear Lake, gather up his communion vessels, and return to the Dismal Lakes. Once back north, he would build a winter camp and try to convince an Eskimo family to spend the long, dark season with him. He had an idea of a place to build a cabin: on the shores of a small body of water that would one day be named Lake Rouvière. The natives knew the lake as Imaerinik, "The Place Where People Died."[4]

CHAPTER FOUR

—

Therefore it is that our fathers have inherited
from their fathers all the old rules of life which are
based on the experience and wisdom of generations.
We do not know how, we cannot say why, but we keep
those rules in order that we may live untroubled.
And so ignorant are we in spite of our shamans, that
we fear everything unfamiliar. We fear what we see
about us, and we fear all the invisible things that
are likewise about us, all that we have heard
of in our forefathers' stories and myths.

—AUA, A SHAMAN OF THE IGLULIK INUIT

I F A POOR UNDERSTANDING OF THE ESKIMO LANGUAGE WAS THE most obviously frustrating part of his assignment, at least as significant an obstacle for Father Rouvière would be overcoming a complex system of beliefs his new charges had been passing down since thousands of years before Christ was born. Rouvière could be forgiven for starting at a point of genuine ignorance. Even Vilhjalmur Stefansson, who had spent years talking over such things with Eskimos all along the Arctic coast, admitted to large cognitive gaps in his understanding of Eskimo traditions. "Direct questions seldom bring them out, because one does not know what to ask," Stefansson wrote. "Besides, Eskimos have a very definite idea as to what a white man believes in and approves of, and what he disbelieves in and ridicules, and shape their replies accordingly." What such a demeanor meant for the likelihood of genuine Christian conversion was open to speculation. If Eskimos told white men what they wanted to hear, how could a missionary ever be sure they had truly accepted the faith? And what, exactly, could a missionary say to a group of people to convince them to abandon a system of belief that flowed in their lives like river water?[1]

Traveling near the Horton River, Stefansson had once become friendly with an Eskimo family that included a twenty-five-year-old woman named Palaiyak and her eight-year-old daughter, Noashak, whom Palaiyak insisted on calling "Mother." When another family came to visit, the matriarch of that family also called the child "Mother."

"Why do you two grown women call this child your mother?" Stefansson asked.

"Simply because she is our mother," they said.

Intrigued, Stefansson came to learn that when a Mackenzie River Eskimo died, the body was taken to a nearby hill and covered with a pile of drift logs. The body's soul, however, remained in the house where the person died for four days (if it was a man) or five days (if it was a woman). At the end of this period, a ceremony was held in which the spirit was convinced to join the body on the hill, where it remained until the next child in the community was born.

When a new child was born, it arrived with its own soul, but since it was inexperienced and feeble, it required an older soul to do its thinking and help care for it. The child's mother then summoned the spirit from the grave to become the guardian of the child's spirit. When the departed spirit heard the call, it entered the child's body. From then on the older spirit assisted the child in every way, helping to teach it to walk, to grow strong, to talk. When the child spoke, it spoke with the accumulated wisdom of the ancestor, "plus the higher wisdom which only comes after death." The child, then, was the wisest person in the family, even the community, and its opinions were listened to accordingly. "What it says and does may seem foolish to you, but that is mere seeming; in reality the child is wise beyond your comprehension." If a parent denied a child's request, preferring, in effect, his own wisdom to the wisdom of the spirit, the spirit might grow angry and abandon the child. The child might become stupid, or physically deformed, or even die. To offend a child deliberately would be to actively solicit the child's misfortune, and the parent's act would be construed that way by the community. It was for this reason that Stefansson's translator, Ilavinik, even at the end of an arduous day of traveling, would always put his daughter on his shoulders rather than force her to walk on her own.[2]

That Stefansson spoke the Eskimos' language gave him an almost miraculous advantage over other Europeans who would follow him into the central Arctic. The people he encountered spoke a dialect similar to the one he had mastered years before in the Mackenzie delta, immediately giving him an almost magical credibility. "It cannot have happened often in the history of the world," he wrote, "that the first white man to visit a primitive people was one who spoke their language."

If Stefansson's tongue stunned the Eskimos, he felt sure his next trick—one that white explorers had used to great effect all over the world—would fill them with awe. He brought out his rifle, lifted it to his shoulder, and in a flash shattered a target two hundred yards away.

He didn't get the reaction he expected. The Eskimos were only mildly impressed. They knew a shaman, they said, who could do the same thing with a "magic arrow." Stefansson showed them binoculars, which could make distant things look close. The Eskimos were interested, but then asked him to use the glasses to look into the future. Tell us which way the caribou would be moving, they said. Our shamans can do this.

Stefansson told them of a surgeon he knew who could put someone to sleep and remove a kidney, though he had to admit he had never actually seen this procedure done. An Eskimo told Stefansson of a man he knew who had had back pain. A shaman had put the man to sleep, removed the entire diseased spinal column, and replaced it with a new one—all without leaving a scratch. The man confessed he hadn't actually seen the procedure happen. Stefansson had to admit that this was beyond the skills of his own people. The wonders of Western science "pale beside the marvels which the Eskimos supposed to be happening all round them every day," he wrote.

Though Stefansson's hosts admitted that they had never met white men before, they had apparently heard stories about them. White men, they said, were the farthest of all people to the east. White men were reported to have various physical deformities; some were said to have just one eye in the middle of the forehead, but the veracity of this rumor could not be proven. White men were considered to be of a strange disposition, one moment giving valuable things to Eskimos for no pay and the next demanding exorbitant prices for useless articles or mere curiosities. White men would not eat good, ordinary food but subsisted on things "a normal person could not think of forcing himself to swallow except in case of starvation. And this in spite of the fact that the white men could have better things to eat if they wanted to, for seals, whales, fish and even caribou abound in their country."[3]

AS DEEP AS Stefansson's curiosity ran, it wouldn't be until about the time of Father Rouvière's murder that another white man would begin an intensive study of the spiritual life of the Copper Eskimos. Like Stefansson, Diamond Jenness, a New Zealand member of the 1913 Canadian Arctic Expedition, would report on a remarkable palette of beliefs and practices that vividly reflected the lives he observed over five years of study in the Arctic.

While Christian doctrine considers man to be at the pinnacle of God's creation, the Eskimos had a far more subtle understanding of the relationships between man, animals, weather, and landscape. For the Eskimos, understanding the mysteries of these relationships was not a passive meditation, not a means of musing on the hand of God. In the most concrete, physical sense, the health and survival of an individual, a family, and an entire community depended upon a person's understanding of the threads connecting the seen and the unseen, the human and the nonhuman, the physical and the mystical. With such small margins for existence, ignorance meant death for a man and his family. It wasn't just courage that an Eskimo needed; it was experience and wisdom. "A people that lives by the chase and glories in hand-to-hand combat with such adversaries as the polar and brown bear can hardly be lacking in physical courage," Jenness wrote. "But the Copper Eskimo is the reverse of foolhardy; courage with him is nearly always subordinated to prudence." Even their language reflects this uncertainty. When Eskimos leave one another, they don't say, "When we see each other again." They say, "If we see one each other again."[4]

Indeed, "Eskimos do not maintain this intimacy with nature without paying a certain price," Barry Lopez writes in his masterpiece *Arctic Dreams*. "When I have thought about the ways in which they differ from people in my own culture, I have realized that they are more afraid than we are. On a day-to-day basis, they have more fear. Not of being dumped into cold water from an umiak, not a debilitating fear. They are afraid because they accept fully what is violent and tragic in nature. It is a fear tied to their knowledge that sudden, cataclysmic events are as much a part of life, of really living, as are the moments when one pauses to look at something beautiful. A Central Eskimo shaman named Aua, queried by Knud Rasmussen about Eskimo beliefs, answered, 'We do not believe. We fear.' "[5]

Although Eskimos held a universal belief in an existence after death, their notion of what this existence might look like was vague, or so it seemed to Jenness. Some Eskimos asked Jenness if he had seen their dead living in other parts of the Arctic; one woman thought her dead husband was living on the moon. Whenever he asked a direct question about the fate of an individual after death, Jenness often got an honest answer: "I don't know."

When a man died, his tools were broken and laid beside him, since he would need them in a future life. One day Jenness discovered a very old campsite, where an old woman's implements still lay beside the place where she had died. Jenness wanted to burn two of the woman's tent sticks for fuel, but was told that the woman still needed them to keep warm. Occasionally, when Jenness pressed, he might hear that perhaps a dead man was "still alive in some other place, but we have no knowledge."

It is possible that this vagueness was deliberate, that the people Jenness interviewed preferred not to offer him access to what they knew. It is also possible that something precise was lost in the translation of such difficult ideas. How easy is it to articulate such abstractions in one's own mind? But it is also possible that the answer "I don't know" mirrored the Eskimos' emphasis on knowledge based on experience. Who could say, from their own experience, where dead men went? Who had seen such a thing? It is also possible that the answer reflected a humility in the face of the mystery that was such a full part of their lives. With so much in the world that existed beyond the grasp of the human mind, what better answer was there than "I don't know"?

Of course, like people everywhere and during all times, Eskimos had come up with stories for their mysteries. The universe as Eskimos conceived it comprised a flat, unbroken expanse of land and sea, covered over during the greater part of the year with snow and ice that stretched farther than any man knew. At each of its corners stood a pillar of wood holding up the sky. Above that was another land, abounding in caribou and other animals. Wandering across this upper expanse were semihuman, semispiritual beings: the female sun, the male moon, and the stars, which had once been human. The three stars of Orion's belt were known as the Sealers or the Early Risers. Other constellations were named for other animals. The polar bear. The caribou.

The earth itself was full of magic, and populated by strange and often ominous spirits that could be conjured only with the help of a shaman or the telling of an ancient tale. There were dwarfs and giants, creatures who lived underground, people with mouths in their chests. Indians, for their part, were thought most likely to be human, but beyond them were white men, a people whose customs and manners were utterly strange.

Jenness heard very few stories about benevolent guardian spirits. Indeed, it seemed that the Eskimo spirit world was mostly populated by shades that were malignant, or neutral at best. These spirits remained unseen until they decided to haunt or even kill a hapless person; the shade of a man who died in one place might cause the death of another man a thousand miles away.

The religious doctrines of the Copper Eskimos brought them little or no comfort. "Life would be hard enough if they had none but natural forces to contend with, forces that they could see and estimate," Jenness wrote.

> But mysterious and hostile powers, invisible and incalculable, and therefore potentially all the more dangerous, hem them in, as they believe, on every side, so that they never know from day to day whether a fatal sickness will not strike them down or a sudden misfortune overwhelm them and their families—from no apparent cause, it may be, and for no conceivable reason, save the ill-will of these unseen foes. Young and old, the good and the bad, all alike are involved in the same dangers, and all alike share the same fate. Death rolls back the gate, not of a happy hunting ground, or of a heaven of peace and happiness where friends and lovers may unite once more, but of some vague and gloomy realm where, even if want and misery are not found (and of this they are not certain), joy and gladness must surely be unknown.

Given his own understanding of this system of beliefs, Jenness found the Eskimo persona an unusual mix of sadness and resilient good humor. Though they seemed perpetually melancholic about the possibility of death, they exhibited no dread about it, and showed none of the desperate anxiety that Jenness had come to associate with Europeans. "Generally they lowered their voice and assumed a mournful tone when speaking of dead relatives or friends, though occasionally one heard the remark, half-jest, half-earnest, that 'the foxes have eaten so-and-so,' or 'so-and-so's remains retained no semblance of a man.' "

It was little wonder that the mind of the average Eskimo was deeply tinged with fatalism, Jenness continued. "Life would be unbearable indeed with this religion did he not possess a superabundant stock of natural gaiety and derive a joy from the mere fact of living itself. The future holds out no golden promise, not even the hope of a life as cheerful as the present one; so the native banishes as far as possible all thoughts of a distant tomorrow, and drains the pleasures of each fleeting hour before they pass away forever."[6]

Since shades controlled everything from the weather to the migration patterns of caribou, Eskimos had created rituals to appease them. Neglecting these rituals could bring about catastrophe. Whenever a hunter killed a caribou or a seal, a scrap of the organs or piece of blubber had to be thrown to the spirits. Products of land and sea were never to be cooked in the same pot at the same time, though they could be eaten in the same meal. Any time an Eskimo traded an animal skin to a white man, he had to cut off a small piece and keep it. Otherwise, all animals would leave the country.[7]

As a rule, animals were considered far wiser than men. Animals knew everything, including the thoughts of men. But there were certain things animals needed that they could not provide for themselves. Seals, for example, needed fresh water to drink, but since they lived in salt water they had no way to get it. So seals would allow themselves to be killed in exchange for a dipperful of fresh water from the hunter. If a seal was killed and not offered water, all other seals would hear of it, and no smart seal would ever allow itself to be killed by that hunter. Likewise, polar bears in the afterlife desired tools like crooked knives and bow drills. Since a bear's soul remained with it for four or five days after death, hunters would hang these tools beside a drying skin inside their snowhouse. When the bear's soul was finally driven from the house, it would take the souls of the tools with it.[8]

—

IF MALEVOLENT SPIRITS seemed capricious in their visitations, Jenness learned, they could also be conjured and driven off by shamans, who knew incantations handed down from "men of the first times." The word "shaman" derives from the Tungus people of Siberia, who used it to describe a person who has the power to cross from the human to the spirit world and to make journeys in disembodied form. In shamanic mythology, the line is blurry between good and evil, playful and serious. A ghost becomes a boy becomes a raven becomes a feather becomes a man, Hugh Brody writes. The mystery of the material world is boundless, and must therefore be respected. People must pay exquisite attention, to learn the secrets of the land. There is a profound and intelligent uncertainty. No one knows what is going to happen, or which decisions about any part of life will turn out to be correct. The world defies binary ways of thinking and speaking: there are no certainties, and truth is approximated only with humility. It is for this reason, as much as anything else, that Eskimos feared moving into unknown territory. Since spirits are full of trickery and exquisitely sensitive to disrespect, people had to know the subtleties of the land and the spirits that inhabited it.[9]

Shamans could also enter a trance, during which they were possessed by a "familiar," or spirit guide, who would give the shaman access to the spirit world. Once possessed, shamans could perform extraordinary acts: they could swallow fire, fly through the air, change into animals, sink into the ground or water, kill and restore to life. One man would put his bow over his shoulders and fly like a ptarmigan. Another, during a séance, shrank and shrank until he sank through the floor of the snowhouse, only to emerge through the floor of another snowhouse. A female shaman once swallowed a snowknife all the way to its handle, then stood by as a male shaman pulled it from her stomach. In previous times, they had been able to visit the moon, but recently they had lost that power.

Unlike priests, Jenness found, shamans wore no distinguishing clothes, even when they were performing séances. They could be either men or women, and came to their powers not through appointment but by performance. Although they had a power that other people did not possess, they were not afforded sanctity or social status. To Jenness, shamans more closely resembled physicians than priests, and they gave their services free for any public cause.

The greatest spirit of all was Kannakapfaluk, who lived in a snowhut at the bottom of the sea and was protected by two bears, one brown, one white. Her consort was a three-foot-tall dwarf called Unga, so named because of the cry he issued whenever a shaman dragged him to the surface. In a foul mood, Kannakapfaluk could bring bad weather or cause pack ice to crack beneath the feet of a hunter. If a person broke a taboo—if a woman sewed too much out on the ice or a hunter neglected to offer a mouthful of water to a seal—Unga would call all the seals inside the snowhut. Hunting on the surface would then be fruitless.

To appease Kannakapfaluk, a shaman would gather the people inside a dance house, cut a hole in the ice, and lower a rope with a noose on one end. The people would chant:

> *The woman down there she wants to go away*
> *Some of the young seals I can't lay my hands on*
> *The man he can't right matters by himself*
> *That man (the shaman) he can't mend matters by himself*
> *Over there where no people dwell I go myself and right matters*
> *He can't right matters by himself*
> *Over there where no people dwell, thither I go and*
> *   right matters myself.*

When the chant was done, the shaman would slip a noose around Kannakapfaluk's wrists and haul her up to just below the surface—never closer, for Kannakapfaluk must never be seen by anyone but a shaman. The shaman would then plead the people's case. We are starving, he would say. Please tell Unga to release the seals. Or the shaman might dive down to the snowhut, kidnap Unga under his coat, and return to negotiate at the surface, all the while keeping the spirit out of sight.[10]

One May, with the sun never setting, a group of Eskimos wondered whether to go traveling to find a group of people living near Prince Albert Sound. They asked a shaman named Higilak to conduct a midnight séance to see if their travel would be safe. All the Eskimos, save the small children, got inside one large tent, with Higilak sitting in a back corner. She began with a long speech asking about the wisdom of the excursion, then suddenly gave a piercing cry of pain and covered her face in her hands. The entire tent remained quiet for several minutes, the silence broken only by the low, somber murmur of someone in the audience. Then Higilak began to howl, and growl like a wolf. She raised her neck and, opening her mouth wide, showed two oversized canine teeth. She leaned over to a man and pretended to gnaw his head, then uttered broken, barely decipherable remarks that her audience could not understand, but that they latched onto nonetheless and tried to discuss. Every few minutes, Higilak would reach up and reinsert the teeth. After fifteen minutes of this, she once again cried in pain and hid her face in her hands. She then discreetly dropped the wolf's teeth inside her boot. Now, apparently, the wolf's spirit was fully inside her body. She uttered a few broken words in a feeble, barely audible falsetto, the audience leaning forward to catch every nuance. Two minutes later, it was all over. Higilak cried again as her familiar left her, then gasped. At last, the séance was over. Close to collapse from exhaustion, Higilak claimed to be ignorant of what had just transpired, and had to ask others in the tent what she had said. Later, when Jenness inquired, everyone agreed, without the slightest reservation, that Higilak had not been acting. She had been transformed into a wolf.

If these ceremonies piqued his intellect, Jenness never gave himself over to them. To begin with, he depended on his translator, Patsy Klengenberg, the teenage mixed-race son of an Eskimo woman named Qimniq and a Danish trader named Christian Klengenberg. And he acknowledged that shamans, when under a trance, often spoke in "old or semi-poetical expressions that greatly increased the difficulty of understanding them." Jenness confessed that "it is not at all impossible that I may have missed the correct interpretation in some instances."

"To a critical and unsympathetic outsider it may seem that a seance of this type is simply a case of palpable fraud on the part of the shaman, and of almost unbelievable stupidity and credulity on the part of the audience," Jenness wrote. "A little amateurish ventriloquism, a feeble attempt at impersonation, and a childish and grotesque blending of the human and the animal, all performed in full daylight before an audience incapable of distinguishing between fact and fancy, between things seen and things imagined, or at least so mentally unbalanced that it reacted to the slightest suggestion and hypnotised itself into believing the most impossible things—that perhaps is all there may seem to be in Eskimo shamanism."[11]

Indeed, for all the stories he heard, and all the séances he witnessed, Jenness remained skeptical. He needed physical evidence. In some cases, this standard created interesting results. Once he asked a man to sing into a recording phonograph. When he played it back, the man was convinced a spirit was trapped inside the machine. When a bemused Jenness asked the man to look for himself, the man said sure enough, there the spirit was: a tiny being about an inch and a half high, down in the phonograph, singing. If Jenness could hear with his ears, he could not see with his eyes.

"Hysteria, self-hypnosis, and delusion caused by suggestion are well known to every psychologist and medical practitioner, and everything that I witnessed could be explained on one or more of these grounds," he wrote.

The natives have many tales of far more wonderful phenomena, phenomena which, if true, would be as mysterious and inexplicable as the much discussed walking over red-hot stones that is practised by a certain Fijian tribe. But of these marvels I saw nothing, and until we have the evidence of some more critical eyewitness than the Eskimo himself, it is safest perhaps to attribute them to the over-wrought imaginations of a people whose knowledge of the workings of our universe is far more limited than our own; a people who have no conception of our "natural laws," but in their place have substituted a theory of spiritual causation in which there is no boundary between the possible and the impossible.[12]

Strangely, shamans often considered the God described by missionaries as a new spirit, not a false one. The Christian God seemed to be connected to a glorious life after death. Add him to the mix, shamans seemed to say. The Eskimo religion was a religion of life. The missionaries' religion was a religion of death. "We have to follow Innu ways in order to get our food here on our land, to live," one man said. "But we have to follow the Christians in order to get into heaven. When we die. So we need them both."[13]

Missionaries, of course, also heard stories about spirits and trances and dreams, with shamans able to move through the porous barriers separating man and animal, man and woman, visible and invisible. At best, priests considered this foolishness. At worst it was devil worship. "We must be indulgent toward Eskimo superstition," one priest concluded, "but we shouldn't forget that superstitions are signs of clouding faith, and that the spirits the Eskimos believe in are the last faint glimmers of an extinguished religion. As one shaman put it, 'Since the missionaries came, we are finished.' "[14]

—

CHAPTER FIVE

In the times when that sort of thing happened,
there was so much that was incomprehensible.
Now we know no more that the human mind and human
speech once had mysterious powers. A fancy,
a word, cried out without any intention at all might
have the strangest consequences.

—KNUD RASMUSSEN, *The Netsilik Eskimos:*
Social Life and Spiritual Culture

As ENTHUSIASTIC AS HE WAS ABOUT HIS MISSIONARY WORK,
Father Rouvière could not help worrying about the prospect of spending a
winter in the Arctic. Lake Imaerinik sat at the northern extremity of the
tree line. Beyond it lay nothing but boundless, rolling hills, then the Arctic Ocean. Even the Eskimos, who had accommodated themselves to Arctic winters for thousands of years, still prepared for them with a certain
degree of dread. Though winter offered Eskimos a cozy communality,
with seal-oil lamps lighting festive dance houses and long nights spent
sharing stories with neighbors, there was always the fear of starvation. "Always at the back of their minds there is the lurking dread of hunger and of
cold in those in those dark sunless days," Diamond Jenness would write,

"when the huts perhaps are empty of food, the lamps extinguished for want of oil, and the people, driven indoors by the howling blizzards, huddle together on their sleeping platforms and face starvation and death."

Among the things that most perplexed white explorers of the Arctic was how these northern people managed to survive on a diet consisting almost entirely of animal fat and protein. How could they live without the vitamins found in vegetables? History was rife with stories of British sailors dying of scurvy simply because they had failed to pack any fruits rich in vitamin C. Virtually nothing edible grew where the Eskimos lived. The only vegetable matter that ever entered their diet, in fact, was the partially digested moss they gleaned from inside the stomach or entrails of a caribou. In summertime, people would eat as much of this as they could. In colder months, they relied on the vitamins from seal blubber, or would slice up caribou stomachs that had been allowed to freeze with the herbs still inside. Though the Eskimos preferred to boil their meat when they could find fuel, they frequently ate it raw or dried it in the sun.

Depending on the season, Eskimo meals consisted of multiple courses, usually including frozen caribou fat, frozen caribou meat, dried and moldy fish, and portions of boiled caribou leg. In winter, they ate mostly bearded seal meat, skin, and blubber; strips of blubber were often left out for visitors, who would cut off pieces the size of a sugar cube. Caribou hearts were split in halves and laid out to dry in the sun; seal livers and kidneys were always eaten raw and unfrozen. Seal intestines were a delicacy, as were flippers. Blood poured into a sealskin bucket was used to thicken soup. Unborn caribou fawns were skinned and dried or cooked at once, often for children to eat.[1]

Especially as the weather turned colder, hunters were exceedingly careful to preserve every ounce of fat from caribou and seals. Fat skimmed from the surface of boiled bones was ladled off with a musk-ox horn, poured into a pericardium bag, and left to solidify into a white tallow considered a delicacy.[2]

In midwinter, an Eskimo wife would rise early to light the lamp that had gone out during the night and begin boiling seal meat to warm her husband for the hunt. Children would emerge from their snowhouses and walk about distributing food. Men would gather together, harness their dogs, and set out looking for seals. With their dogs trained to sniff out seal breathing holes, hunters would stalk seals on their hands and knees, sometimes until their wrists were black from frostbite. When a hunter discovered a breathing hole, he would erect a delicate system of fine, knitting-needle-sized bone sticks. Kneeling beside the hole on a pad of bear- or deerskin, the hunter, with astonishing patience, would hold a harpoon aloft, and wait. If a seal did eventually rise, the bone sticks would fall, and the hunter would strike with all his might. Then, often with the help of several men, he would drag the seal to the surface and jab it in the eye with the sharp handle of his ice shovel. After a few years of this, most men had huge rope scars on their hands; many others had lost fingers. One man told of watching a harpooned seal plunge below the ice and drag the hunter with him; off in the distance, the seal could be seen popping to the surface to breathe, apparently still dragging the man behind.[3]

One winter was so severe that people were forced to eat their sealskin boots. Night after night their shamans would interrogate the spirits they believed to control the weather, to try to appease their anger. Whenever the storms did abate, even slightly, every man and youth would sally forth and hunt seals for hours in the bitter cold. There was not a man whose face was not covered with great blotches where he had been severely frostbitten. "Sometimes the natives would recall dreadful tales of years gone by, how, not a generation before, the Kanghiryuarmiut had chopped up the corpses of their dead and eaten the frozen flesh to save themselves from starvation," Jenness wrote. "Away in the East, too, the Netsilingmiut had cut off a man's legs while he was still alive and tried to appease their hunger with his flesh. Fortunately, a change came over the weather about the middle of March. Before the month was out the crisis was over; the huts of the Eskimos were filled once more with meat and blubber, and the dance-house resounded with song and laughter."[4]

—

SOON AFTER their arrival on the shore of Lake Imaerinik, Father Rouvière and John Hornby managed to kill three caribou, which allowed them to concentrate their energies on the urgent work of building Rouvière's cabin. They needed to work quickly. Throughout the fall, the weather remained dull and cold, with temperatures often dipping to twenty below zero. Though he was willing to help build the cabin, Hornby once again got restless. Against the wishes of Rouvière, and long before the cabin was finished, Hornby took off for Great Bear Lake to get his own winter cabin in shape. When he got there, he told the Douglases that he had left Rouvière "on quite friendly terms with the Eskimos and well fixed for food." Though he would always have the option of trekking the fifty miles to visit Hornby and the Douglases, Rouvière nonetheless faced the prospect of spending his first winter in the Arctic by himself. As he had done many times and would do again, Rouvière elected to suffer in order to improve his chances of ministering to his chosen people.[5]

At first, Rouvière's decision seemed to pay off. In September, a group of ten or twelve Eskimo families came and pitched their tents near his cabin. Rouvière was thrilled. Perhaps, in the end, his flock would find him, rather than the other way around. Through the middle of October, Eskimos dropped by every single day. Sometimes it would be a family or two, sometimes four or five families at once. There were repeat visits, which made Rouvière feel he was making headway. Over the course of six weeks or so he figured he saw close to two hundred people. His reputation seemed to be spreading.

Yet there still remained the terrible awkwardness of his not knowing the native tongue. "The language—that's the trouble," Rouvière would write. "I have collected some words, but not as many as I would have liked." Rouvière's struggle with the native language was more than an inconvenience. It was a source of great anxiety. Coming as he did from a country and a landscape utterly different from this vast expanse, Rouvière not only lacked the physical talents for Arctic survival, he lacked, in a way, the intellect. Without the ability to name a tree or a river—let alone a food source like a char or a caribou—Rouvière was deficient in far more than a native vocabulary or a means of social communication. He lacked the very means of navigating the place itself. The inability to call even the simplest things by their name, especially when these things were unique to his new environment, left Rouvière feeling even more alone in the world. This was not Italy, where the language was different but the art and the wine familiar. This was not Spain, where a keen ear might pick up a stray noun or verb. The language the Eskimos spoke was as different from French as ancient Chinese, and the customs of the people and the land they inhabited were, if anything, even stranger. Rouvière was not just shut out from the barest comforts of human conversation. He was also alone in the physical world. Because he lacked words, he was incapable of knowing, or even seeing, the same world as the people whose territory he was hoping to understand.

More pressing, his cabin was nowhere near complete, and Rouvière, with limited carpentry skills, had no idea what the Arctic winter held in store for him. "I must say frankly [it] is Mr. Hornby's fault for leaving me alone for almost a month," Rouvière wrote. "Having to finish the house—or practically to build the thing—I have had only a little time to devote to [the Eskimos]."[6]

ON OCTOBER 20, down at Great Bear Lake, John Hornby hitched up a dog team and packed a big sled he had commissioned from a group of Indians and, with the Douglases dragging a pair of toboggans, set off to convince Rouvière to spend the winter with them near Great Bear Lake. They found the priest "looking well and cheerful," apparently quite glad to have company once again, since the last of the Eskimos had left for the coast just the day before. The Douglases spent the day with Rouvière, taking a hike over the hills to the north of the lake. As it did time and again, the wet, foggy weather limited their view. "That part of the country was bad enough in summer," Douglas reported. "In early winter with the sun only a short distance above the horizon and the air full of frozen mist the outlook was miserable indeed." With the Eskimos gone, Father Rouvière at last agreed to move back to Great Bear Lake for the winter. His decision was undoubtledly wise. Spending the winter alone could well have cost Rouvière his life. And compared to the isolation and loneliness of his cabin at Lake Imaerinik, to say nothing of the mercurial behavior of John Hornby, Rouvière found the atmosphere inside the Douglases' cabin remarkably cheerful.

While the rest of the men had been exploring Eskimo country, Lionel Douglas had spent the time building a fourteen-by-sixteen-foot log house that appeared particularly sturdy and welcoming compared to Rouvière's quarters at Lake Imaerinik. Constructed of spruce logs, it had a floor dug six inches below ground level, composed of wooden blocks pounded in on their ends and grouted with sand. Douglas had chinked the seams between the logs on the walls—both inside and out—with a layer of mud plastered over a stuffing made from moss and caribou hair. The roof he'd built with a lathe of small spruce poles chinked with caribou hair, covered with a layer of dry sand, and then wrapped in a sheet of waterproof canvas the team had brought to make canoes. The two small windows the team had carried all the way from Fort Simpson gave the lodge just enough light to keep it from feeling claustrophobic. One window was placed on the west wall, the other on the south, next to the cabin door. Lionel had papered the interior walls with the illustrated pages of magazines that Hornby had left behind.

As pleasant as the windows and walls were, it was the stone fireplace, diagonally across from the door, that gave the cabin a charm that made the coming winter seem wholly tolerable. Rather than following the regional custom of building a narrow hearth in which logs were burned standing on end—a style he considered both a nuisance and inefficient—Lionel had made his fireplace wide and deep, with a big slab of quartzite for a mantelpiece. The chimney drew smoke beautifully, leaving the air in the cabin's close quarters surprisingly clear. All in all, George Douglas wrote, the fireplace was "a regular triumph."[7]

As the Arctic autumn began to set in, the days became markedly shorter and temperatures began to fall in earnest. Although there was little early-season snow, the Dease River was completely frozen over by October 20. The Douglas party routinely ran into a group of about twenty-five Bear Lake Indians, who would emerge from the woods after a caribou hunt and set up their tepees on the shore of the lake. As the season progressed, the Indians concentrated their attentions on netting fish, which they fed to their dogs.

Situated twenty-five miles above the Arctic Circle, the little house that Lionel built was ready for winter. On November 26, the sun went down. It would not be visible at the house again until January 9.[8]

BY NOVEMBER 1 Rouvière and Hornby had settled into Hornby's cabin near Great Bear Lake, and the Douglas team was in their new house six miles away on the Dease River. By now, Rouvière's hair had grown longer, and his clean-shaven face was covered by a full beard. George Douglas took a photo of Rouvière standing outside in the snow, wearing nothing but his black robe. His face, framed above and below by unruly hair, appears sober, weathered. The priest was beginning to look more and more the frontiersman. In a December letter, Rouvière wrote that he and Hornby had decided to return to Eskimo country in March. Rouvière's plan was to somehow attract the Eskimos as close as possible to Great Bear Lake—perhaps only as close as Lake Imaerinik—to make their tending easier. Once he established himself with the people, the chances of setting up a permanent mission base on the Arctic coast would be vastly easier. Yet his letter also seemed tinged with doubt, and even homesickness. He asked his superiors' advice about his idea, and inquired whether they thought the plan was "useless." If they wanted him to abandon the mission and return to Fort Norman, Rouvière said, he would happily "take up the community life as soon as possible."[9]

The Douglases, as always, did their best to make the winter sociable. They invited Rouvière and Hornby over to play chess and bridge. Rouvière and Hornby had made a lovely chess set out of carved wood, but George Douglas confessed to being unsure about which pieces were which. Pieces would be pawns one day and bishops or castles the next. Playing chess, Rouvière was serious but unskilled. Playing cards, Hornby was brilliant but erratic. He never knew when to stop bidding. With only two packs to play with, the cards got so dirty that the men had trouble distinguishing between hearts and diamonds.

Christmas Day arrived on a Monday, during Lionel Douglas's turn as chef, and he proved as adept cooking in the kitchen as he had been building it. The Douglases had reserved an arctic hare—the first they had ever seen around the Dease River—for Christmas dinner, and to this Lionel added a plum pudding, which he served with blueberry jam he had made the previous summer. This was followed by a round of Teshierpi toddies and a game of twenty-one, with squares of chocolate, divided evenly among all the players, for stakes. By the end of the night, Lionel and Rouvière had cleaned the others out. The evening meal consisted of the region's great delicacy, smoked caribou tongue, which also happened to be a particular favorite of Rouvière's. Outside, after the meal, George Douglas had Hornby snap a photograph of Rouvière standing alongside the Douglas brothers, Sandburg, and a sled dog. The entire day, Douglas wrote, "was really one of the most pleasant Christmas Days that ever I spent."

AFTER CHRISTMAS the weather turned bitter. For five straight days in mid-January, temperatures stayed well into the minus fifties, with high winds and drifting snow. The spruce trees, frozen solid, had lost their previous grace in the wind, and now creaked stiffly, like masts at sea. For drinking water, they kept open a hole in the six-foot ice sheet over the Dease River, in a quiet spot between two rapids.

Most of the talk that winter returned to plans for a spring trip to the coast. The Douglases' plans were firm, but Rouvière felt obliged to wait for the okay from his superiors back at Fort Norman. In March, a letter arrived by an Indian dog team from the mission. Far from giving Rouvière the go-ahead, it instead demanded that he return at once to the mission. Just why he had to leave the Barren Lands, the priest did not say. If Rouvière was disappointed at being unable to join the Douglas trip, the Douglases seemed equally sad to part from their young friend. They gave him a compass and wished him Godspeed. "We were sorry to say good-bye to him," Douglas wrote. "He had added greatly to the pleasure of our life in winter quarters, and it was with sincere regret that we saw him off on his journey back to the mission."

Dutiful as ever, Rouvière set off for Fort Norman. On his way west, he ran into John Hornby heading east, back to Great Bear Lake, and gave him a letter to pass to the Douglas brothers. He wanted to apologize, he wrote. He had lost their compass.[10]

By late July, Father Rouvière was heading back to the Barren Lands for what would be the last months of his life. He had with him something he had never had before: a companion from the church. The prospect of sharing his experiences with another man of the cloth could not have been anything but joyous for Father Rouvière. "The missionary is as human as any other man, and he feels the need of a human companion with whom he can talk of familiar things, with whom he can exchange ideas, share his joys, his triumphs, his anxieties, his failures," another Arctic missionary has written. "That is why the chance to visit with a fellow priest is such an exciting event to the lonely padre off there on the ice. He is all atremble at the prospect of a visit, nervous as a bride."[11]

The priest heading into the wilderness with Father Rouvière was a highly educated man who, early in his life, had been torn between spending his career as a professor of philosophy and serving as a missionary. Born Guillaume Joseph Yves Marie LeRoux on March 30, 1885, in Lanviliau, to Yves LeRoux and his wife, Marie Anne Poudoulec, he had studied at the seminary at Pont-Croix, then entered the novitiate at Bestin, Belgium, in October 1904. He took his formal vows at the Scholasticat at Liège on November 4, 1906, and was ordained as a priest there on July 10, 1910. He ultimately joined Bishop Breynat's Vicariate of Mackenzie, where he managed to learn some of the Eskimo language. He moved first to Fort Resolution, on Great Slave Lake, and had been at Fort Good Hope, north of Fort Norman, since 1911.

Despite his time in the north country, Father LeRoux did not seem terribly happy about his newest assignment. Not long after leaving Fort Norman, he and Father Rouvière crossed paths with the Douglas team, now on its way back to Edmonton after a quick and remarkably efficient run to the coast. The Douglases had not, despite their initial objectives, found a great deal of promising copper deposits; August Sandburg would report that though some Eskimos had fashioned eight-inch knives from the stuff, "in our search we did not find any large slabs." But they had done something that many far more celebrated Arctic explorers had not: they had thrived. George Douglas had to confess that the longer he remained in Eskimo country, the more he admired the people who managed to make their lives there. He had heard stories of whites contributing to the rapid degradation of the Eskimos living near the Mackenzie River delta. But from what he had seen of the kindnesses of Father Rouvière, Douglas was optimistic about the relationships that might develop between Eskimos and missionaries.

This last meeting with the Douglases was also difficult for Father Rouvière. After a warm, if melancholic, greeting, during which the Douglases told of their coastal adventure and Rouvière relayed the news about the sinking of the *Titanic*, the young priest expressed his gratitude for all the Douglases had taught him about Arctic survival. Their departure could only mean more difficulties. Rouvière had not only just missed another excellent chance to get to the Arctic coast, a chance he would not have again for at least another year; he was now also losing his most trusted companions, men who had made his first winter in the north not merely tolerable but a real pleasure. The Douglases had offered a consistency and a reliability that Hornby did not. There was also something about the Douglases' firm adherence to a thoughtfully outlined schedule—explore the Coppermine, winter back near Great Bear Lake, run to the Arctic coast, go home—that stood in marked contrast to the plans of both the itinerant Hornby and Rouvière himself. The Douglas team came to the Arctic for a brief expedition with narrow objectives and comparatively simple desires. They came to look around, then leave. Hornby and Rouvière seemed, by contrast, to be hooked into the place in far deeper ways.

This final encounter with Rouvière and his new companion left a sour impression on the Douglas team. As far as George Douglas could tell, Father LeRoux did not seem pleased to be living outside the relative comfort of the mission at Saint-Thérèse. Rather than deferring to the gentle guidance of Rouvière, a man the Douglases had come to respect and admire through a winter and two summer seasons, LeRoux seemed domineering, even insolent. Though younger than Rouvière and considerably less experienced in Arctic travel, LeRoux seemed intent on speaking as the leader of the team.[12]

Having successfully navigated a journey that had begun a year before with the discovery of the trappers' murder-suicide and reached a climax with the trip to Bloody Falls and the Arctic coast, the Douglases were all too aware of the importance of trust and diplomacy between travel companions. A team in the wilderness is only as effective as the weakest of its members. When conditions are stressful, the breakdown of a single man can quickly put the entire group in danger. The Douglases had come to enjoy Rouvière as much for his gentle demeanor as for his quiet competence in and around the cabin. There was nothing like an Arctic winter to bring out a man's volatility or sharp edges, and Rouvière had not only survived in good stead but had made everyone else's experience more pleasant. This first brush with LeRoux—lasting a matter of hours—seemed ominous. The Douglas party took their leave, doubtless pleased with their own team's successful chemistry but worried for their friend Rouvière. If LeRoux proved to be as volatile as he appeared, the priests' experience in the frozen north could turn out to be trying indeed. And how the Eskimos would react to such a domineering personality was hard to guess. George Douglas took a photograph of Rouvière and LeRoux paddling a heavily loaded canoe. "We saw the outfit get started, thankful now at any rate that we were *not* traveling in the same direction," Douglas wrote.[13]

Sure enough, on their way north, Rouvière and LeRoux were immediately confronted by their own relative inexperience. Windbound for a full week at Fort Franklin, they then spent another full month crossing Great Bear Lake, a trip that had taken the Douglas team just eight days. In all, it took the two priests six weeks to make their way from the mission at Fort Norman to the Douglas cabin. The Douglas team had made the journey in sixteen days.

For the priests, the slow progress was doubly agonizing. The diminishing sunlight meant the onset of another brutal Arctic winter, which in turn meant that the community of Eskimos waiting for them at Lake Imaerinik, fifty miles from the Douglas cabin, would soon begin moving north toward their winter seal-hunting grounds. When they finally reached the Dease River on August 11, the priests found John Hornby waiting for them. Hornby was apparently no more impressed with LeRoux than the Douglases had been. He considered him a scold, and overly controlling for a man with virtually no experience in the Barren Lands. Over time, his dislike of the new priest would fester.

The two priests set up in the Douglas cabin on the Dease River. Though the Douglases hoped to return to the Barren Lands the following summer, they had agreed to let Rouvière use their cabin over the winter, and had left sizable stores of food—flour, bacon, sugar, and beans—at the cabin and in caches on Lake Imaerinik and along the Coppermine. They'd also left rifles, ammunition, blankets, furniture, tools, and winter clothing. George Douglas was well aware of how little the church had given Rouvière to survive, and how little he was likely to receive in the future. But his generosity also seemed certain to cause trouble, now that the cantankerous LeRoux was joining Rouvière and Hornby. How would the trio, with competing interests and complicated personalities, divide up the food, once winter set in in earnest? Granted, two of the three were priests, but as the Douglases had discovered with the unfortunate trappers at the beginning of their journey, starvation and months of sheer darkness could make men do unspeakable things.

On August 27, Rouvière and LeRoux pushed north to see if any Eskimos were still waiting for them at Lake Imaerinik. When they arrived on the first of September, they found that most of the Eskimos had left for the northern coast. Only a handful remained. To Rouvière these people still seemed "very good natured to us and very well-disposed." He was delighted to find that those Eskimos he had taught to make the sign of the cross the previous summer not only remembered it but seemed to have taught a number of others as well. Apparently, given their experiences with Rouvière and Hornby, the Eskimos were slowly getting over their fear of both whites and Indians. Perhaps with the idea of working on his own language skills, Rouvière asked a young Eskimo man to spend the winter with him. He also hoped, come spring, to bring the man to Fort Norman. The young man seemed enthusiastic about the proposition, perhaps in part because Rouvière offered him generous compensation: a .40-44 rifle. Writing a letter to Bishop Breynat two weeks later, Rouvière seemed well aware of the rifle's dear expense. "Since I have only one, I should then find myself without a firearm—a very useful thing, even indispensable at this point; for we still have to count on ourselves, and not much on the others, for food." How Rouvière planned to feed himself without a gun, he did not say.

Even LeRoux, at least at first, seemed to make a positive impression on some of the Eskimos, most likely because of his cursory language skills. He asked for help hunting, in anticipation of the coming winter, and spoke of his desire to reach the coast the following spring. "These two men were telling us about the land above the skies," an Eskimo named Hupo would later relate to the police. "They showed us coloured pictures of Heaven, and they said that after we died we would go there. They used to sing just like the Eskimos when they make medicine. They held our hands and taught us to make the sign of the Cross, and they put a little bread sometimes in my mouth." The Eskimos came up with names for the two priests: Rouvière they called Kuleavik. LeRoux they called Ilogoak.[14]

In fact, LeRoux continued to have difficulties with the Eskimo language. "I was able, Monsignor, to note a few words, see a little into the lan-

guage, but it was very little that I could gather this year," LeRoux wrote
Bishop Breynat. "It is a labour so slow that I can scarcely see if we are getting ahead." LeRoux's difficulties with the language were hardly surprising. For one thing, the Eskimos had a daily vocabulary extending to some
ten thousand words, four times that of Europeans. Human speech has 140
separate pieces of sound. Norwegians use sixty. Eskimos use fifty. English
speakers use forty. The possibilities for error were rife. In one dialect, the
word *uttuq* means "a seal sleeping on ice; *ujjuk* is a bearded seal; *ujuk* is
soup; *uksuk* is "the fat of sea mammals"; *utsuk* is a vagina; *usuk* is a penis.
Vilhjalmur Stefansson, who was surely LeRoux's superior as a linguist, illustrated the differences between Eskimo and English this way: English
speakers used four forms of a noun: man, man's, men, men's. The Greeks
used fourteen. The Eskimos used twenty-seven. The Eskimo language
had evolved to a precision that astonished its first Western listeners and
vividly reflected the subtle relationships they had with the land. There was
no direct translation for "fish," but there were distinct words for "arctic
char," depending on whether the speaker meant arctic char that were running upstream, arctic char that were moving down to the sea, or arctic
char that remained all year in the lake. For Arctic natives, precision was a
matter of survival. What astonished the Eskimos, of course, was how
strangers could expect to survive in this country without such language.
The answer, for quite a few of them, was that they couldn't.[15]

LeRoux's limited language ability could hardly have failed to dismay
Rouvière, who had counted on precisely these skills in his new companion. If LeRoux couldn't communicate with the Eskimos, what exactly was
he doing joining this mission? He plainly did not have the wilderness skills
needed for the job, and his impatient and ornery temperament seemed
particularly ill suited for a life that depended first and foremost on cooperation with native people. In a letter to Bishop Breynat, Rouvière acknowledged that LeRoux already seemed to be wearying of the work, but
managed to strike a determined tone nonetheless. "The devil took a hand
in the game, I suppose, and our visit has probably not produced the results
we hoped for. We will eventually know enough of the language to tell the

Eskimo that we are missionaries. . . . Some day they will know how to render true homage to God."[16]

On September 13, Rouvière wrote Breynat describing the Eskimos the Douglases had met near the Dismal Lakes and near Bloody Falls. He said he hoped to follow in the Douglases' footsteps, hopefully with John Hornby as a guide. Perhaps, he wrote, Father LeRoux could stay behind. "I keep wondering whether it wouldn't be better for one of us to stay. I'm not afraid to undertake the journey myself and go even to Bloody Falls where they spend the spring." Though he did not say it explicitly, Rouvière's implication that he and Hornby ought to undertake the mission without LeRoux was hard to miss. If Hornby was only moderately reliable, he had never been anything but competent in the field and diplomatic with the native people. Apparently, after just a few short weeks, Father LeRoux had already become a toxic presence. He had already infuriated Hornby by refusing to share the stores the Douglas team had left behind — stores that, Hornby maintained, had been intended at least in part for him. Worse, LeRoux had scolded Hornby for his five-year relationship with the Indian woman named Arimo. Hornby had abruptly refused to continue his relationship with LeRoux.

In October, things got worse. Hornby fell seriously ill, possibly with pneumonia, and for a month was barely able to leave his tent. Athough LeRoux took credit for tending Hornby, police testimony would later reveal that most of the nursing may in fact have been done by a small group of Eskimos, who came by every day to see how much weight Hornby had lost. Once again, LeRoux's lack of wilderness skills may have compromised his abilities. One day, on his way to visit to replenish Hornby's wood supply, LeRoux somehow got lost. Hornby had to crawl out of his tent to keep his fire going, and "damned near died as a result."

A short time later, Rouvière found LeRoux in a funk that managed to contaminate even his own genial mood. "The Father is aware of his own quick temper and is striving to subdue it," Rouvière wrote to Bishop Breynat on January 29, 1913. "He has never tried to hurt my feelings. I like to think that our good relations will not be soon disturbed. After all the reports I was given last year, I was afraid there would be some difficulties; but the good God has taken everything in hand and nothing has come about to disturb our good understanding."[17]

Though it is impossible to know just how bad things had gotten between Rouvière and LeRoux, each man seemed to take every chance he got to go off on his own. In mid-March, LeRoux left for Fort Norman to recharge his flagging enthusiasm for remote missionary work. On cue, John Hornby suddenly reappeared. Once again, he wanted to talk to Rouvière about a trip north. Without LeRoux. Hornby and Rouvière could hike to the Coppermine River and, weather permitting, make it all the way to the coast.[18]

Besides the prospect of traveling with Hornby, something else had begun to make Rouvière anxious to get to the coast. A Church of England missionary was reportedly moving quickly toward Coronation Gulf, and the Catholic Church wanted very much to get to the needy souls first. Rouvière wished to establish a mission "in order to arrest a little the zeal of Mr. Fry who comes to sow the bad seed in our fields."[19]

As it turned out, Hornby and Rouvière never made the trip to the coast. A journey that would have been challenging under any circumstances suddenly took on a distinctly dangerous aspect. Out on a fishing jaunt one day, Hornby had a nasty run-in with one of the Eskimos Rouvière and LeRoux had met in the fall. The man, Sinnisiak, tried to steal one of Hornby's sealskin fishing lines, and when Hornby caught him in the act, Sinnisiak threatened to kill him. "Sinnisiak wanted to kill Hornbybenna in the summertime," another Eskimo named Hupo would testify later. "Hornbybenna dropped a sealskin line and Sinnisiak picked it up and wanted to keep it. Hornbybenna saw him with it and took it back from him, and Sinnisiak wanted to kill him. Sinnisiak is a bad man, everyone says so, and he told me lies."[20]

To Hornby, the encounter with Sinnisiak was shocking. Along with most whites who had traveled in the region, Hornby had known the Coronation Gulf Eskimos to be far more more pleasant than the people corrupted by whalers over near the Mackenzie River delta. Perhaps this encounter was a harbinger. Perhaps here too, in three short years, the Eskimos had overcome their initial fear of Europeans. How they would treat white travelers from here on out was hard to fathom. Hornby told Sinnisiak—and, later, any other Eskimos he met—that murdering a white man would result in the extermination of all Eskimos. When he returned to Great Bear Lake, Hornby warned the priests about the encounter with Sinnisiak. Things with the Eskimos were "getting ugly," he said. How other Eskimos responded to Hornby's warnings is hard to know, but the fight over the fishing line plainly left Sinnisiak emboldened. How serious could Hornby's threat be? In all his life, over all the thousands of miles he had walked, Sinnisiak had seen perhaps a half dozen white men.

On July 17, Father LeRoux bid adieu to the mission at Fort Norman for the last time and began, also for the last time, walking into the Barren Lands.[21]

—

CHAPTER SIX

When an Arctic missionary finally falls in his
tracks, he does so as silently as a snowflake
falling from the Arctic sky.

—ROGER P. BULLIARD, *Inuk*

On OCTOBER 8, 1913, FATHERS ROUVIÈRE AND LEROUX LEFT
their cabin on Lake Imaerinik and began walking north, following a group
of Eskimos that included Sinnisiak, the man who had threatened to kill
John Hornby over the stolen fishing line. Their decision to move north so
late in the season seems, in retrospect, to have been foolish, an act of desperation. Perhaps Father Rouvière was exasperated at all his missed
chances to get to the coast. Perhaps Father LeRoux felt a successful reconnaissance trip to the mouth of the Coppermine would allow him, come
spring, to take on a less taxing assignment. Whether they were fully aware
of the sheer difficulties of moving north just at the onset of winter is also

uncertain. What does seem certain is that the two priests were anxious to establish themselves among the Eskimos after so many months of frustration. That they would make such a trip so late in the year, with people they barely knew and with at least one man recently known to have been violent toward a white man, can only have resulted from their fierce determination to move their missionary work forward. Waiting until spring must have seemed intolerable.

Their challenges, as it turned out, did not even begin with the lateness of the season. Physically, both missionaries were in bad shape. In addition to being sick from chronic malnourishment, Father LeRoux had a severe cold and Father Rouvière had recently suffered an injury while repairing the cabin on Great Bear Lake. For their journey, they depended utterly on this small band of Eskimos, who acted as guides, hunters, and protection. Without the natives, Rouvière and LeRoux would never have managed to navigate the vast empty spaces between their cabin and the Arctic coast. They would have gotten lost, or starved, or died of exposure. As it was, the Eskimos considered the idea of the priests traveling without women extremely strange. Were they asking for trouble? Men depended on women as much as women depended on men. Men provided food; women provided clothing. The priests, it seemed, could provide themselves with neither.

Leading a small caravan of sleds, two men named Hupo and Kormik guided the priests across the Barren Lands to the coast. By this time, after just a few months together, the priests were beginning to look scruffy. Rouvière's beard had grown to a full three inches long. Both men wore long black coats, buttoned down the front from their necks to their feet. As they walked, Rouvière and LeRoux discussed their plans, at least as far as they could imagine them: they only wanted to see the coast on this trip, they said. Next summer, once the weather turned warm again, they would return to Fort Norman, catch the Mackenzie River ferry to the coast, and fill a giant ship with lots of supplies. Then they would sail east to the mouth of the Coppermine and set up a new mission post.

The sun, already very low in the sky, would, within a few short weeks, disappear for the winter. November is the month when Eskimos move from hunting on land to hunting on ice. It was a precarious time, since the caribou herds were thin and the ice on the lakes and the sea was not yet thick enough to allow confident fishing or seal hunting. Men dug into their caches of caribou meat, dried fish, and pokes of blubber to prepare for the season of deprivation; women spent their time sewing all the clothes their families would need for six months of darkness. Families that had been scattered during the summer months now began to congregate, there being great strength in numbers when it came to surviving an Arctic winter.[1]

Each night, the group would pitch their collection of eight tents. At first, things seemed to be going well for the priests. Kormik not only invited them to use his sled to transport their things north but asked them to live with him in his tent as well. It took the group twelve days to walk the ninety miles from Lake Imaerinik to the mouth of the Coppermine River. When they reached the coast, the priests looked out on the gray expanse of Coronation Gulf, and for a few moments could imagine themselves the Catholic Church's most northerly pioneers. The landscape itself was hardly inspiring: an endless roll of treeless hills behind them; to the east and west, a gravelly beach extending hundreds of miles, perhaps unbroken by a single human footprint. The wind blew strong and damp, and the sky foretold nothing but months of crushing cold and darkness. The entire picture was so ceaselessly monochrome and flat that the Frenchmen could not have helped feeling physically disoriented. Like Arctic sailors who discover their compasses to be useless so close to magnetic north, the priests felt their own internal gyroscopes muddled and confused. Here, at the very place they hoped to build a mission base, they found their connection to their church and their home as thin as it could possibly be.

Fathers Rouvière and LeRoux were greeted by some other Eskimos who had also just arrived for the winter hunting season, and together the groups set up camp on an island in the mouth of the Coppermine. They remained together for five nights. The sun was very low. An Eskimo named Angebrunna would later report that the ice out on Coronation Gulf "was not yet strong for spearing seals." Hupo's wife, Ohoviluk, fixed holes in the priests' boots and their mittens and sewed up their clothes.[2]

Despite the generosity of some of his hosts, Father Rouvière was beginning to feel real danger, and only some of it was generated by the extreme remoteness of their camp. The priests were five hundred treacherous miles from their closest brethren, a distance that seemed far greater given that, without Eskimo guides, they could not possibly find their way back. The winter was coming on hard, and the priests, remarkably underequipped even back in their primary cabin near Great Bear Lake, had only the most rudimentary clothing and gear. They had virtually no hunting skills, and could not have known how to build a snowhouse. They relied in every sense of the word on the hospitality and skills of their Eskimo hosts. Undoubtedly they were perpetually hungry, perhaps starving. And judging from Rouvière's private journal, not every Eskimo had the best interests of the priests in mind.

"We have arrived at the mouth of the Copper River," Rouvière wrote soon after arriving at the coast. "Some families have already left. *Disillusioned* with the Eskimos. We are threatened with starvation; also we don't know what to do."[3]

The word "disillusioned" was heavily underlined. The sentence it began was one of the last Rouvière would ever write.

To Bishop Breynat, reading the journal entry later, the emphasis on the word "disillusioned" represented "the first occasion on which Father Rouvière ever spoke with anything like bitterness of his flock." But the underlining could have pointed to any number of feelings. Perhaps Rouvière was glimpsing just how complicated Arctic missionary work would be. What, exactly, would he ever be able to teach these people? What did they expect from him, and what would they tolerate? Could he really imagine a time when Eskimos, who were migratory by nature and by necessity, would someday willingly build a Catholic church and attend mass? How could Christian doctrine, its parables sprouted from a world that was both warm and agricultural, ever have a practical relevance to people who lived where nothing edible grew? Where stories about people fleeing oppression by crossing a hot, sandy desert would have seemed utterly abstract? Where lessons about the superiority of man to all other creatures jarred up against an ancient, intricate system of subtle relationships between man and beast? What was Rouvière doing up here?

Perhaps, in addition to physical weakness, Rouvière was at last beginning to understand the magnitude of the task he had undertaken. Here he was, miles from the nearest mission and thousands of miles from his family in France. His partner, Father LeRoux, was by all accounts a difficult man in the best of circumstances. Pushed up against the Arctic Ocean in the middle of October, with weeks of hard travel just to get back to their drafty cabin at Lake Imaerinik, and surrounded by people who spoke a language he could only barely comprehend, LeRoux could not have been in a cheerful state of mind. How LeRoux felt about Rouvière is hard to determine, since he left little evidence. But surely Rouvière, as the only one to whom LeRoux could freely speak, served at least as a cauldron into which he could pour his resentment. As the weeks and miles of travel wore on, and the priests got thinner and weaker, with only cached meat to eat, the intense difficulty of their plight must have begun to seem overwhelming.

Perhaps, given their utter lack of experience with coastal winters, they were already beginning to suffer from the depression-induced madness that the Eskimos understood as a seasonal given. *Perlerorneq.*

The camp at the edge of the gulf, it turned out, offered little relief to the sick and hungry priests. The number of caribou passing through the area was unusually small, and with the ice still too thin for sealing and the fishing season long since past its peak, the Eskimos had already run out of fish to feed their dogs. Most of the men in the camp were forced to spend their days scouring the gulf and the river searching for food. Among the men was Hupo, who just a few months before had seen Sinnisiak threaten John Hornby over the fishing line.

With so little food to spread around, the addition of two more mouths to feed could not have been a welcome fact for the Eskimo hunters. Rouvière and LeRoux holed up for five or six days in a skin tent belonging to the Eskimo named Kormik. What little food they had quickly disappeared. Later, people would say, the food was stolen, probably by Kormik's wife. It may have been that the Eskimos were testing the priests. Perhaps they were trying to assess their intelligence. What skills did they have? What could they contribute to the community? Could they provide food? Could they hunt? Could they build a snowhouse? Would they be a help to the community or a hindrance?

One night, Kormik himself crept over to LeRoux's pillow, removed a carbine hidden beneath, and hid it. Shouldn't the best hunting weapon go to the man most likely to bring food home to the people? Surely neither priest would have been considered even moderately reliable as a hunter, and neither, despite their claims of being representatives of a holy order, would have been considered anything like prominent members of the group.

The rifle's disappearance meant the end of the priests' last vestige of autonomy. They did not have the tracking skills of their hosts. They could not trap. Given the late season, they could no longer rely on fish. The theft of the rifle, to the priests, meant an utter dependence on the Eskimos, who, given the thin food supply and the approaching winter, were dangerously strapped themselves. In another way, the theft of the gun presented a challenge of a different kind. What place did personal property have in a missionary's life, even a piece of property that could mean the difference between life and death? And what would it mean for a priest to forcibly, perhaps violently, wrest a gun away from someone at least nominally a member of his own flock?

Whatever their ambivalences, LeRoux, always the more aggressive of the two priests, acted quickly. While Kormik was outside the tent, he dug around and found his gun. Learning of this, Kormik burst in and, in a rage, hurled himself at LeRoux.

As the two men fought, an elderly Eskimo named Koeha stepped into the tent and, after a struggle, managed to pull Kormik off the priest. Intervening more with unspoken authority than physical strength, Koeha ordered Kormik to stay in the tent and motioned for the priests to follow him outside.

"You are in danger," he said. "Kormik and his crowd are after your blood. You must return to your hut right away. Next year, you will come back in better company."[4]

With that he helped the priests harness a team of four dogs to a sled and agreed to accompany them for a half day's hike south along the Coppermine. Simply navigating the landscape would be exceedingly difficult for two men not accustomed to traveling through the Barren Lands. "There are no trees here," Koeha said. "Go on as far as you can. After that you will have no more trouble. I am your friend. I don't want anyone to do you harm." Koeha shook their hands and disappeared. The priests were on their own, days from their cabin at Lake Imaerinik, with no one to help them make their way across the difficult and confusing ground.[5]

FOR THE NEXT three days, the priests struggled along through soft, early-season snow, never making more than a few miles in a day. The temperature began dropping rapidly, and they had no shelter, no wood to make a fire, and virtually nothing left to eat. They had nothing to feed their dogs. They did have the rifle, but a rifle with no hunting skills is a walking stick.

Sometime during the second night, back at the Eskimo camp, two men grabbed a dog and set off for the south, following the tracks of the priests' dogsled. By midday Sinnisiak and Uluksuk overtook Rouvière and LeRoux and their famished dogs. In three days, the two priests had managed to cover about ten miles.

When Sinnisiak and Uluksuk arrived, they explained that they were an advance party returning to hunt around Great Bear Lake, and that their families would be following shortly. Sinnisiak said he was looking for his uncle.[6]

Since all four men were headed south, Father LeRoux asked the hunters for help pulling the sled. In return, he said, he would pay them in traps.

With that, Sinnisiak and Uluksuk harnessed themselves to the sled and began pulling. Hauling a sled by hand, especially in soft snow, was simply what one did. The dogs could not do it alone, and on long journeys every member of a family might take a turn at the harness, with women up front, dogs in the middle, and men in the rear. But the work was hard, and the foursome did not make much progress.

By late afternoon the weak autumn sun had already begun to disappear. Sinnisiak and Uluksuk built a small snowhouse, about eight feet in diameter. They laid caribou skins inside, and invited the priests to sleep with them.

The next day bitter weather descended fully on the Barren Lands, sharp winds and blowing snow making even minimal progress difficult. For the priests, already nearly incapacitated by hunger and cold, the change in the weather meant desperation. After vainly searching around for the trail that led south, Sinnisiak and Uluksuk gave up. They couldn't find their way in the storm, they said. They wouldn't go any farther. They wanted to return to the mouth of the Coppermine. They brought the priests back to the river and showed them the way to go.

Suddenly, back at the sled, the dogs started barking and straining at their leads. Unharnessing himself, Uluksuk walked over to see what had caught their attention. Peering through the blowing snow, he discovered a cache of gear, apparently left by the priests, and motioned for Sinnisiak to come over and take a look. Amid a pile of gear—traps, deerskins, axes— they could see a bagful of rifle cartridges. The two hunters stood over the gear. Were they going to steal the bullets? It was hard to tell. Rouvière reached for his sled, grabbed a rifle, and handed it to LeRoux. LeRoux ran toward the Eskimos, brandishing the weapon. LeRoux started shouting, obviously furious, but the Eskimos, as was often true, could not understand what he was saying. Seeing the confrontation growing hot, Father Rouvière rushed over and began throwing the cartridges into the river. Why would he do that, the Eskimos wondered? Since they had first met white men, ammunition had become one of the Arctic's most precious commodities, often representing the difference between survival and starvation. Rouvière had given the rifle to LeRoux, an unexpected gesture of aggression for the gentle priest. But his decision to throw the cartridges into the river seemed to represent a change of heart. Perhaps Rouvière, despite his terrifying fear, managed to catch himself. Not so LeRoux, whose quick temper had suddenly exploded. To the Eskimos, all this indecision and anger was confusing. The priests had suddenly become unpredictable. Dangerous. The cartridges especially represented the only hope the priests had of getting food for themselves. Throwing them away seemed foolish to the point of self-destructiveness. What was going on? Was the prospect of another Arctic winter more than the priests could bear? Had the crush of living so far from home, in such trying circumstances, pushed them beyond the pale? To the Eskimos, it seemed clear that something in the priests had snapped.

SOMETIME LATER, Sinnisiak and Uluksuk returned alone to the community at the mouth of the Coppermine. They arrived by the second day of November and went straight to the tent occupied by Kormik, who had first struggled with LeRoux over the rifle.

"We have killed the white men," they said.

PART TWO

CHAPTER SEVEN

—

The literature of Arctic exploration is frequently
offered as a record of resolute will before the
menacing fortifications of the landscape. It is more
profitable I think to disregard this notion—that the land
is an adversary bent on human defeat, that the people
who came and went were heroes or failures in this. It is
better to contemplate the record of human longing to
achieve something significant, to be free of the grim
weight of life. That weight was ignorance, poverty of
spirit, indolence, and the threat of anonymity and
destitution. This harsh landscape became the focus of a
desire to separate oneself from those things and to
overcome them. In these Arctic narratives, then, are
the threads of dreams that serve us all.

—BARRY LOPEZ, *Arctic Dreams*

RUMORS ABOUT THE PRIESTS SWIRLED AROUND THE ARCTIC
like a winter wind. An Eskimo woman named Palaiyak told the anthropologist Diamond Jenness a story about some white men over near the Coppermine River who had been shot but who had come back to life again.
Jenness had heard the story before; it sometimes included a third man
who "flew up a tree." Jenness filed the story away as another bit of Eskimo
mysticism and did not give it another thought. Until February.

In the middle of the month, Jenness visited a band of Coppermine Eskimos camped near Locker Point and met a man sipping afternoon tea.

The man, who had two small cups, two saucers, and tea he had obtained at Great Bear Lake, was in the midst of "regaling himself, his wives, and the assembled company." But it wasn't the teaware—or the plug tobacco, or the American magazine—that struck Jenness as strange; these odds and ends routinely turned up in the possession of Eskimos who mixed with white traders. What intrigued Jenness were the weapons the man possessed: a .22 Winchester rifle and a double-barreled Hollis fowling piece. Even more bizarre, the man had in his possession a series of religious objects, including a Roman breviary in Latin, a French illustrated Scripture lesson book, and a black rosary. Not long afterward, Jenness would see something stranger still. He saw the man wearing a priest's cassock, a small metal crucifix suspended from his neck.[1]

CONJECTURES ABOUT THE priests' fate also circulated among the Barren Land Indians. When a group of Bear Lake Indians asked an Eskimo man and his son if they had seen the priests, the Eskimo boy ran away, terrified. In early spring, some other Indians had gone to the priests' cabin at Lake Imaerinik and found the door splintered by an axe, the fireplace and the chimney smashed, and the windows shattered. Snare wire was scattered over the ice. Soon after, the Indians ran into an Eskimo family and a quarrel erupted. One of the Indians grabbed an Eskimo woman and threw her out of the tepee. When the woman fell, a number of strange objects spilled from inside her clothing, including a communion plate and a pall with a cross on it, used in covering a chalice. The man of the family was wearing a black cassock, cut off at the knee. On the left side, at the heart, was a knife-sized hole. Around the hole there was dried blood.

Like most rumors in the Barren Lands, word of the missing priests also eventually reached Fort Norman. In July 1914, an explorer named D'Arcy Arden reported seeing two Eskimos in priests' cassocks walk into camp as if they had worn such clothes for generations. "My opinion of the missing priests is that, judging by their condition of health when they left their houses (reputed to have been poor indeed), they have become sick and died somewhere on the Coppermine River," Arden wrote. "I am convinced that they were sick and that they should not live with the Huskies as they intended."[2]

John Hornby also refused to believe that his friend Rouvière had been killed. Father Rouvière, he said, was too gentle to invoke such passion. About Father LeRoux Hornby felt differently. "I hardly think the Esquimaux would kill them, unless they had done something to make them afraid," Hornby would write to George Douglas. "Father Rouvière was not of the kind to do so, but Father LeRoux was a little too quick-tempered and not accustomed to handle savages."[3]

Father Ducot, the priest in charge of the Fort Norman church, quickly transmitted his fears to other missionaries, but given the huge distances over which mail had to travel in the Arctic, word that the priests might have perished did not reach the ears of Bishop Breynat until August 1914, just as Europe exploded into war. Breynat was returning from a trip to Rome, where he had been lobbying the Vatican to contribute to his mission's thinly spread resources. Back in Montreal, he received a shocking telegram. A rumor had been circulating for some time that the two young priests working near the Coppermine River had been murdered.

"An Eskimo has announced by signs the death of two whites," the telegram read. "He had had no communication with the band that accompanied the Fathers. Their house was pillaged by Eskimos of a different gang."

In a panic, Breynat rushed off to Ottawa to see Laurence Fortescue, the controller of the Royal Canadian Mounted Police. Finding Fortescue away, Breynat left a note and a copy of the telegram. Fortescue later replied that he had made the necessary arrangements for a thorough investigation by a competent young officer of the Royal North West Mounted Police. He concluded, "Trusting that he will find the priests alive and well and that the rumor of their murder is without foundation, I remain, Sincerely yours, Laurence Fortescue."

Given the number of men signing up to fight in Europe with the Canadian or British armies, police barracks throughout Canada's frontier regions were stretched terribly thin. In 1916, the Royal North West Mounted Police covered hundreds of thousands of square miles with exactly two inspectors, three sergeants, three corporals, ten constables, two ponies, and forty-five dogs.

With only two murders officially reported in the Northwest Territories (and only thirty-three in all of Canada that year), much of the force's work involved investigating horse and cattle stealing. Police found themselves looking into a blotter full of diverse cases: there were six cases of bigamy (one convicted, three dismissed, two awaiting trial) and twenty-six cases of "carnal knowledge attempted" (nine convictions, eight cases dismissed, nine awaiting trial). Police in Alberta handled four cases of "wife desertion"; nine cases of "dogging cattle"; four cases of "keeping savage dogs"; twenty-four cases of swearing and obscene language (twenty-two convicted, two dismissed); seven cases of "buggery" (two convicted, four dismissed, one awaiting trial); forty-one cases of keeping a house of ill fame; sixty-four cases of "frequenters of house of ill fame"; and 218 cases of "insanity" (197 convicted, twenty-one dismissed).[4]

His ranks depleted by men signing up for the war, the region's police commissioner had a difficult decision to make. The investigation of the missing priests would require a man capable of living thousands of miles from home, with no contact or support from police headquarters. There were no reliable maps and, since the priests had disappeared north of more familiar Indian country, no reliable guides. The investigation would require a man skilled in wilderness navigation and survival, possessing diplomatic skills of a kind the police force had not previously had to employ. Just for starters, it would require scouring the Arctic for one of the very few Eskimos who could speak English. Though a tiny handful of explorers, trappers, and missionaries had made contact with some small bands of Eskimos in recent years, no one in the police force had had any experience with the people of the Barren Lands. And this mission north would have a distinctly more aggressive tenor than any of its predecessors. How the Eskimos would react was impossible to gauge.

On May 8, 1915, as one writer put it, "the long arm of the law made ready to reach out over the frozen north." The man for the job was a twenty-five-year-old named Denny LaNauze.[5]

Charles Dearing LaNauze was tall and wiry, with broad shoulders and blue eyes. He had been born in Ireland of French Huguenot ancestry. His father had been a member of the Royal North West Mounted Police in the Edmonton district but had taken the family back to Ireland after inheriting property there. As a young constable, LaNauze had worked a number of assignments in Indian country. He had opened the Fort McMurray detachment, a couple hundred miles north of Edmonton, in 1913. Since July 1914 he had been stationed at Hay River, on Great Slave Lake. But to a man of LaNauze's adventurous demeanor, this new assignment seemed like a dream come true. He had read Stefansson's book, as well as any other books he could find on the Arctic. So far, he had never been anywhere near that far north. He did not speak a word of the Eskimo language. As soon as he was chosen for the investigation into the missing priests he was promoted to inspector, a rare honor for one so young.[6]

Nevertheless, LaNauze felt ambivalent about abandoning the chance to fight in the escalating war in Europe. Both his brothers would join the fight in France, and both would eventually be killed in action. His sister would serve in Flanders as a nurse in a Red Cross hospital. For LaNauze, "the hardest task was to go north at such a time when the Dominion was arming and the Canadian casualty lists already appearing."[7]

In Edmonton, LaNauze and two constables, Corporals D. Withers and James E. F. Wight, outfitted themselves for two years of hard travel. Things had changed in the four years since the Douglas team had begun its journey. Where the Douglases had boarded a stagecoach for Peace River Landing, LaNauze and his men took a train. They made their way to Fort Resolution, on the southeastern shore of Great Slave Lake, where they bought toboggans, snowshoes, sled dogs, and a York boat. Then they boarded the *Mackenzie River* steamer and began hopping up the string of trading posts dotting the Mackenzie. Given the extreme remoteness of the ultimate search area, LaNauze decided to set up camp at Great Bear Lake, 350 water miles northeast, where the Douglases, Hornby, and Rouvière had spent the winter of 1911–12.

As the *Mackenzie River* pulled up at Fort Norman, LaNauze, Withers, and Wight were greeted by the two black-robed priests from the Saint-Thérèse mission, Fathers Ducot and Frapsauce. Ducot, the elder of the two, had been in the Far North for forty years, ever since he had left his native Brittany. Though he had been a regular correspondent with Father Rouvière, and had more experience with the people of the Barren Lands than anyone in the church, he was plainly too frail to join the investigation. He agreed to let his younger colleague, Father Frapsauce, go instead. Speaking in clear English, Ducot told LaNauze that when he had first heard of the Eskimos wearing the priests' cassocks, he had not been concerned. "The Fathers had a change of gowns with them and as strange Eskimos were reported to have come from the East, I think it likely that they stole the Fathers' spare gowns they had left behind them. I still believe that the priests are safe and that they will come back this summer." Frapsauce was less optimistic. "I do not believe that the fathers are alive," he said. "In our work we must report frequently to our superiors and since the priests left we have had absolutely no news of them and this is the reason why I think that they are dead."[8]

If even the vaguest tips about the priests' whereabouts were difficult to come by, finding someone who could eventually elicit information from the Eskimos would prove far more so. Even as far north as Fort Norman, the nearest Eskimos were still perhaps four hundred miles away. Rather than take his chances scouring the thinly populated Barren Lands, LaNauze decided to reboard the *Mackenzie River* and head up to the Mackenzie delta to interview the coastal Eskimos. At least some of them had had contact with Stefansson's expeditions. If there was an Eskimo who spoke English anywhere in the Arctic, the Mackenzie delta was likely to be the place to find him.

Sure enough, after a long steamer trip north and a difficult search once he arrived, LaNauze finally found Ilavinik, a Herschel Island Eskimo who had spent four years working for Stefansson during his first Arctic expedition. Ilavinik had not only served as an expert translator and diplomat but had an unerring sense of direction, on which Stefansson had come to rely. To someone as new to the Arctic as LaNauze, Ilavinik's services would prove even more vaulable.

Ilavinik agreed to come south with LaNauze for forty dollars a month, provided he could travel with his wife, Mamayuk, and his daughter, Nangosoak. If the woman and the girl would hardly add to the speed of the team, they would contribute in other important ways, from cooking to sewing boots to balancing the group in ways that Eskimos cherished and white explorers, often at their peril, usually ignored. As important as any hunting skills the men might possess, the talent required to tailor and maintain the exquisitely effective clothing the Eskimos depended upon could make the difference between thriving in the Arctic and dying in it. LaNauze agreed. His first encounter with an Eskimo proved emblematic: unlike so many white men in the Arctic, he was willing to compromise. More important, he was willing to defer to native experience. He had not only read Stefansson, he had understood him. In the Arctic, LaNauze's humility may have been his most valuable asset.

Back at Fort Norman on July 16, LaNauze immediately began interviewing local Indians to see if they had any news about the priests. There was no shortage of stories. Harry, a teenage Bear Lake Indian whose mother, Arimo, had befriended John Hornby and who had traveled to the coast with the Douglases, claimed to have been the last man to see Rouvière alive. Harry felt certain the priests "were frozen to death somewhere."

Before setting out for the coast, LaNauze agreed to add two civilians to his team: Father Frapsauce, who though he spoke no Eskimo would at least be able to communicate with Bear Lake Indians, and D'Arcy Arden, the itinerant white explorer who had first reported the news of the missing priests to Fort Norman.

LaNauze arranged for the bulk of the team's freight to be sent ahead up the Bear River with a group of Indians, who would tend it by the shore of Great Bear Lake until he and his men arrived. The patrol itself needed to get cracking, and not just to start the investigation. With nearly twenty-four hours of sunlight, daytime temperatures at Fort Norman had hit ninety degrees in the shade. The mile-wide Mackenzie River, LaNauze wrote, "was as calm as a mill pond," and the mountains to the west were shrouded in haze. Ilavinik and his family, who had never been this far south, were suffering terribly from the heat.

LaNauze and his team set out on July 23. Their York boat was heavily loaded with personal gear. Dogs followed on the shore. The team proceeded a half mile down the Mackenzie to the mouth of the Bear River, where they got their tracking lines ready and started the ascent. In constant rain, the team had a hard time making progress. With swift, freezing water careering through countless horsehoe bends, the river made hauling the York boat upstream particularly onerous. The team was constantly scraping up against shallows, dragging the York to shore, transferring all the gear into canoes, and walking miles upstream with the dogs, then back again to retrieve the York. Portaging their gear four miles upriver took hours of unloading and loading and twelve miles of walking. One day LaNauze and his team were up to their waists in freezing water until ten P.M. At another stretch, it took the team four days to move a single mile upstream. The country to the north did not offer any respite. On July 29, an old white trapper named Stohe said he had been held up for fully sixty-three days by a relentless east wind. The ice had left the lake only a week before.[9]

By August 4, the team finally managed to paddle a few miles of open water into a southwestern bay of massive Great Bear Lake. The ninety upstream miles had taken the team two weeks; LaNauze remarked that the entire stretch could be paddled downstream in a single long day. After so many days on the river, the lake harbor was quiet, with few sounds save the splash of a grayling or the howl of an Indian dog. The water was so clear that the men could see the bottom forty feet below. All around them, crimson fireweed bloomed in the hills. Blueberries and red currants were profuse. The forests were primarily stunted spruce, with spots of birch and, more rarely, poplar.

As they had hoped, the gear they had entrusted to the Indians was fully intact. As the team set up camp and sorted through their equipment, they were approached by a number of Indians hoping to trade bales of Bear Lake herring for tea and tobacco. It turned out that the Indians had something LaNauze wanted more than fish: several of the families, he learned, had recently met some Eskimos. With Father Frapsauce translating, an Indian woman who may have been Hornby's companion Arimo said Fathers Rouvière and LeRoux had been seen setting off for Lake Imaerinik, about fifty miles northeast of the top of Great Bear Lake. They had planned to travel to the Arctic coast with a pair of Eskimos named Kormik and Hupo, and apparently had no definite plans to return south. Their determination to move so far north had struck Arimo as a bit odd, since both priests were in visibly poor health.

The last thing the woman said seemed ominous. She told of an Eskimo named Illuga, whom the Indians greatly feared. Illuga was easily identified by two things: he had three wives, and he had a habit of wearing a black priest's robe.[10]

LaNauze hired a few Indians for fifteen dollars each for the trip across the lake. Despite some ferocious gales, the patrol made it to the far end of the lake by early September. To LaNauze, it was immediately obvious why the northeast shore had made such a popular camp for Indians and white explorers alike. Good harbors were plentiful. Fishing nets hauled up endless loads of seven-pound lake trout. Most important, given the advancing season, was the shoreline's position just south of the tree line. The considerable forests, which petered out a few days' walk to the north, offered both protection from northerly winds and plenty of fuel and building material. LaNauze could already see huge flocks of seagulls winging their way south as the frost arrived. The long Arctic winter would arrive soon.

He had his men set up camp on Big Island, a mile's paddle from the shoreline. Ashore on the mainland, they quickly discovered the cabin once used by the priests, and with Father Frapsauce's blessing they decided to move in. There were no clues whatsoever that the cabin had been occupied since 1913, when the priests had last been seen. If Rouvière and LeRoux were still alive, where were they?[11]

Back on the island, a group of Indians arrived "in great excitement." A week before, they told Father Frapsauce, they had been camped over by the priests' cabin when several volleys of stones had rained down on their tepees. The Indians had grabbed their rifles and rushed out to confront the aggressors, but had seen no one. The next morning, they found fresh Eskimo tracks in the mud. Distraught, they had left immediately for Big Island, putting a mile of water between them and the dreaded "Huskies." The Indians told Father Frapsauce that they genuinely missed the priests, but warned him that the patrol "was only going to its death if it visited Husky country."

LaNauze brushed the warning aside. He decided, as Hornby, the Douglases, and Father Rouvière had before him, that this was by far the best place in the region to spend the winter. It would also offer an excellent jumping-off point for the spring journey northward. There was no way the Indians' fear of the Eskimos was going to push the patrol back south. LaNauze ordered the York boat hauled ashore before the lake froze over, and had Withers and Wight build a storehouse. This was where they would ride out the winter.

ON SEPTEMBER 19, LaNauze organized a team of himself, Father Frapsauce, D'Arcy Arden, Ilavinik, and two Indian guides, Harry and Ferdinand, for a seven-day reconnaissance trip to Lake Imaerinik. They hoped to find the cabin, fifty miles to the northeast, that the priests were rumored to have used as a base for their own excursions to Eskimo country. The team took camping gear and five sled dogs, but with the weather bitter and the ground only lightly covered with snow, sledding was impossible. The men shouldered their packs and walked. If the snowfall was not yet sufficient to accommodate a sled, it was perfect for tracking. With every step, they kept their eyes on the ground, searching for footprints. The country they crossed was pocked with small lakes and ponds, all of which, by mid-September, were frozen solid and bordered by stands of white spruce trees shaped like pipe cleaners.[12]

Hundreds of caribou had begun their migration south and east from the frozen Dease River; although the men did not see Eskimo camps, the scattered detritus of caribou bones clearly marked their route as bisecting native hunting grounds. To the north lay a range of bare, purple mountains. LaNauze found the landscape entrancing, especially the fingers of forest that followed the river corridors deep into the Barren Lands. This was an area, he knew, that had provided good campsites for Stefansson's team back in 1910–11. When a couple of moose appeared near the camp one day, Ilavinik, who had never seen such a beast, went off on a hunt with the Indian guide Harry. Three hours later they returned with a giant moose rib. They cached the meat under some heavy stones. "It has been a glorious day," LaNauze wrote. "The setting sun turned the brown of the barrens into a royal purple, and before darkness the pinched face of a great full moon rose over the hills to the East in a turquoise sky."

A couple of days later, the men were treated to one of the Arctic's true blessings: a grand display of the aurora borealis, a celestial light show that, astonishingly, was accompanied by "an elusive low rustling sound as the swishing of silk." With darkness deepening with every step northward and every passing day, the northern lights this night were "singularly vivid," LaNauze wrote. "Its rays appeared to range over every point in the heavens. Glorious rainbow colors grew and radiated as they danced across the moonlit sky. Marshalling in long silver threads, they appeared to hang for a moment as a heavenly candelabra, then suddenly disband and dart away in a maze of flickering, irridescent hues."

When the sun came up, the patrol continued its search. Walking near one stand of trees, Ilavinik called out: he'd found a cache of food, and bootprints, probably ten days old. The Indians had been right; Eskimos had moved this way. You could tell they were Eskimo prints and not Indian, Ilavinik said, by the shape: Indian moccasins left slim prints shaped like a foot, with a recognizable arch. Sealskin tracks left by Eskimos were flat and round. Even if there were no people left, even if they might not see an Eskimo for six months, the patrol was on the right track.[13]

LANAUZE AND his men crossed Lake Imaerinik on September 28. There, on the far northeastern shore, was the priests' cabin. It was "a scene of ruin."

"It was a wild and dreary spot for a Mission, situated as it was on the very edge of the far-flung barren grounds, and surrounded by high, rocky hills," LaNauze wrote. "The main cabin appeared to have been ruthlessly destroyed, half the roof was burned away and the debris from it covered the floor. There was nothing movable left. The door was missing."

Besides the physical damage, there was little to indicate the fate of the missing priests. Father Frapsauce searched through the debris, hoping to find a letter or a notebook that might indicate the priests' plans. He found nothing. The only indications that the cabin had ever been inhabited were a few deer bones, a sealskin Eskimo slipper, an Eskimo copper-tipped arrow, and a single, spent .44 cartridge. Though these odds and ends seemed at least a year old, some fresh wood shavings seemed to indicate that Eskimos had used the shelter more recently.

Worse still, they could find no evidence whatsoever of the priests' whereabouts. Exasperated, and worried about the advancing season and the scarcity of caribou in the area, LaNauze had to make a decision. So far, his journey had been fairly routine, with few anxieties and relatively temperate weather. Suddenly, though, he was faced with the same pressures everyone traveling late in the Arctic season must confront: shortening days, dropping temperatures, and diminishing sources of food. Pushing on toward the coast—even as far as the Dismal Lakes—seemed foolhardy, especially given the complete lack of clues at the priests' cabin. Yet the idea of giving up the search for the winter was frustrating. Sitting inside a lonely cabin for four months was hardly the first choice of a man most comfortable out on the trail. Reluctantly, LaNauze decided to turn back. After a one-day trek of thirty miles, they were well into the trees, and a more leisurely couple of days had them back at Great Bear Lake, arriving in a full snowstorm.

By now, winter had begun to descend in earnest. With Father Frapsauce anxious to return to Fort Norman, D'Arcy Arden and the Indian Harry decided to accompany him back to the mission. Caribou were moving south in large numbers; LaNauze counted four hundred in a single day. The presence of so much game gave LaNauze confidence that his team could survive. No matter how ingenious he and his men might be with hunting and wilderness skills, everything depended on the flow of caribou. They set about stocking up enough meat to last them until spring. Ilavinik, proving to be as good a hunter as he was a translator, quickly filled the team's winter coffers by killing ten caribou. LaNauze's admiration grew daily for Ilavinik and his wife, who was always busy repairing the men's clothes. LaNauze considered Ilavinik "scrupulously honest and conscientious" and always included him in discussions about the patrol's plans. "We were now fast friends," LaNauze wrote. "Eskimo cannot be treated on the footing of master and servant." Ilavinik and LaNauze built a series of caches by digging deep holes, filling them with caribou meat, and covering them with piles of stones so large they were hard to lift. LaNauze seemed quite happy with the new arrangements; he reported himself to be thriving on a diet consisting of "straight meat and tea." Within a month, however, Wight and Ilavinik would discover that every one of the caches had been destroyed by wolverines, who had dug in around the removable stones and dragged away the meat; all that would remain would be the caribou hide and a quarter of the moose.[14]

On October 4, they were blanketed by a heavy snowstorm. This was it. They were locked up until spring. By December, weak sunshine provided just enough light for three hours of scouting per day. Shortly after New Year's, the temperature dropped to sixty below zero—the lowest the thermometer would register—and stayed there for two weeks.[15]

—

ON AUGUST 22, 1915, unbeknownst to Denny LaNauze, another corporal in the Royal North West Mounted Police, Wyndham Valentine Bruce, began moving eastward from Herschel Island with Stefansson's Canadian Arctic Expedition. Stefansson had been working the Beaufort Sea and Arctic Archipelago region while Diamond Jenness and the zoologist Rudolph Martin Anderson were exploring the mainland and adjacent islands. With this expedition already well known to many Eskimo communities, Bruce figured he could learn a lot about the missing priests without revealing his intentions.

On Jenness's recommendation, Bruce began looking for a man considered to be one of the region's most powerful shamans. He was known by several names: Diamond Jenness had called him "Snowknife"; Indians and Eskimos called him Illuga, or Uluksuk Mayuk. But given his unusually large collection of material possessions, to say nothing of his three wives, he was mostly known as "the Rich Man." He was rumored to have buried a cache of goods obtained from the priests, and Frits Johansen, the expedition's naturalist, thought he could help Bruce locate it.

Johnson and Bruce found the cache on a rocky island near the expedition's camp on September 9, 1915. Opening it up, they discovered ten deerskin bags and bundles, several boxes—one stenciled HODGSON but painted over in red with the name Arden—and an assortment of hides, pots, tins, and native sealing and hunting spears. Some of the items—the marked box, a Henry Disston ripsaw, and a Welland Vale lance-tooth crosscut saw—seemed to suggest that the Rich Man had been an active trader with white explorers. But a closer look was more haunting. In the cache, Bruce found a dark blue blanket capote with tartan pockets on the inside, two small rosettes at the back, and a trim of brown braid or tape. Unwrapping one of the bundles, he pulled out a piece of clothing that had clearly not been made locally. It was a black, full-length robe, instantly recognizable as a priest's cassock. Spreading open the collar, Bruce saw a name printed with indelible ink: PÈRE ROUVIÈRE.

CHAPTER EIGHT

—

Like our distant ancestors, no doubt, these people
fear most of all things the evil spirits that are likely
to appear to them at any time in any guise,
and next to that they fear strangers.

—VILHJALMUR STEFANSSON, *My Life with the Eskimos*

LEAVING THE BULK OF HIS DISCOVERY BEHIND, CORPORAL
Bruce took the cassock and a brass plaque and started walking east in
search of the Rich Man. Six weeks later, in late October, he came to a
Copper Eskimo village on an island in Coronation Gulf, where he visited
the snowhouse of an Eskimo introduced to him as Kormik. Kormik knew
well the hunting grounds between Coronation Gulf and Great Bear Lake,
and Bruce hoped that in the course of his hunting trips Kormik might
have run into the priests. Apparently he had. Kormik had an entire box
full of Catholic items, including a book entitled *Psalterium Breviarii Ro-*
mani and two cheap colored prints, one of the Savior and one of the Vir-
gin Mary. Kormik also had several old, apparently discarded notebooks

with little more than a few Eskimo words and their French equivalents, and a set of linen handkerchiefs, initialed with an H in the corner. He said he'd gotten the handkerchiefs from John Hornby. The other things had come from some "other white man."

Two years ago, Kormik told Bruce, he had been hunting near Great Bear Lake with his wife, the Rich Man, and two of the Rich Man's wives. "We met many white men and traded a lot of things from them, the things I have traded to you," Kormik told Bruce. "In exchange, I gave them musk-ox skins, bearded seal rawhide rope, and caribou skins. There were three white men; two, I think but am not sure, wore long black coats and had beards, and were called Kuleavick and Ilogoak. These men had a house where the river flows into the lake. One of these men one day took us across a bay in the lake in a boat. I was afraid. These men went away hunting caribou in the summer, and I did not see them after this."

Kormik said he had also met another man, named Arden, who had given him a rifle. "We stopped with him for a few days and were going with him to get more lead and ammunition but the journey was too far," Kormik said. "The ice was nine inches thick when we left the lake."

Despite the details of Kormik's story, Bruce felt that the man appeared "confused."

"I am convinced that he is lying," Bruce wrote in his report. "Not only that, but I am sure he knows far more than he would say. These natives are in the possession of numerous articles which have not been obtained from the [Canadian] expedition and have no doubt been stolen from the priests cache at Great Bear Lake, and as yet I have only thought it necessary to re- cover what I believe to be the property of the Roman Catholic Church."

If Kormik had things Bruce wanted, Bruce had more than enough bar- gaining power to get them. Though a number of the local Eskimos had ri- fles, which they had received in trades from Great Bear Lake Indians and men like Hornby, they rarely had enough rounds to fill them. In exchange for six boxes of .30-30 cartridges, Kormik gave Bruce a small package of things of far less practical value, which Bruce duly noted in his police re- port: "two white handkerchiefs, initialled G.R.; one breviary; one prayer book; one small crucifix; two tassels; one plain linen surplice; one lace-bound linen surplice; two linen mass aprons; one linen communion cloth; one linen altar cloth (cut and blood-stained); one mass server (carmine and gold); one altar cloth (carmine and gold); one mass vestment (carmine and gold); one stole (carmine and gold)." Bruce snapped a photograph of Kormik and added it to his growing cache of evidence.[1]

NOT FAR FROM Kormik's tent, Bruce found the Rich Man, living in a deerskin tent and in a jovial mood. Following a tradition that Bruce had become accustomed to, the Rich Man offered his guest the best food he had, in this case some pieces of frozen fish and, later, some "very appetizing" caribou-blood soup served in a musk-ox horn. Despite months of travel in the Arctic, and despite the ever-present seal-oil lamps, Bruce never seemed able to stay warm in Eskimo shelters. The Rich Man motioned for him to sit on the sleeping platform at his side.

After a few minutes, the Rich Man got up and hammered a few nails in the wooden supports above the seal-oil lamp hanging above his sleeping platform. He reached up and hung a long black silken cord around the nail. At the other end of the cord was a crucifix. Suspended over the arms of the cross were two rosaries, one of ebony and one of alabaster.

Bruce somehow managed to keep his thoughts to himself. Sometime later, though, he asked the Rich Man's permission to take a closer look at the crucifix, and at the other "civilized articles" in his possession. His host "seemed quite pleased and showed me all that he had with him," Bruce reported, and said he had two more caches, one near the Canadian Arctic Expedition's camp and another somewhere inland. The Rich Man said the crucifix had been given to him by a white man near a big lake. Bruce put his hands together, inquisitively, as if he was praying. The Rich Man nodded.

By November 15, 1915, the Rich Man was back at the Canadian Arctic Expedition's camp at Bernard Harbor, to the west of the mouth of the Coppermine. While there, he agreed to trade the crucifix and rosaries to

Diamond Jenness for two boxes of .44 cartridges. Two weeks later, he handed over a Bible lesson book, illustrated with colored prints, entitled *La Religion en Tableaux*, along with a Latin breviary. On the breviary's fly-leaf was inscribed the name of its previous owner: "G. LeRoux, Oblat de Marie Immacule."[2]

With Jenness acting as interpreter, the Rich Man told Bruce how he had come into possession of the Catholic things. In the summer of 1914, he and two wives had been at Great Bear Lake with Kormik, his wife, and several others. While there, they had met three white people, along with a number of Indians living with them in the house and several Eskimos living outside. Other Eskimos, he said, had seen a different group of white men at the lake, and had traded them musk-ox and other skins for guns, saws, powder, traps, and cartridges. One of the white men the Rich Man met spoke the Eskimo language well. He had hung some necklaces and a metal crucifix around the Rich Man's neck. He told him "to always keep it and to hang it up where I would see it the first thing in the morning, for it would protect me when I died; when I did die it should be placed under my head. He also told me that we were all bad people, but if we became good, when we died we would go up in the sky, and if not we would go down under the earth."

That summer, one white man—presumably John Hornby—joined the Eskimos on a hunting trip. The Rich Man considered him a good hunter who "got plenty of caribou." When the Rich Man invited him to live in his tent, the man "brought a stove with him so he could keep warm while writing." The Rich Man and the others stayed down at Great Bear Lake "until the ice was three feet thick and the snow was deep." When they left for the coast, one of the men gave the Rich Man some books and two black robes—one of which had since been stolen. If he still had the robe, the Rich Man said, he would gladly trade it for a box of cartridges. To the rest of the Eskimos, the man gave some tea and other small things. He said he would be going south the following summer, but would then travel up a big river "in a boat with a stove in it."[3]

Even after hearing the Rich Man's story, Bruce had a hard time figuring out what it all meant. The Eskimos' possession of a breviary and a psalter "seems to me to be inexplicable," Bruce wrote, "although this may be explained by someone more conversant with the ways of the Roman Catholic missions. The other articles, the rosaries, the crucifix, and cassock may well have been given away by the priests, seeing that the cassock is an old one and to my mind it would be impossible for the Eskimo (The Rich Man) to have invented the story that he told seeing that the Eskimos here know so little about the white race."[4]

TWO WEEKS BEFORE Christmas 1915, Bruce organized a party consisting of himself, Diamond Jenness, and Jenness's interpreter, Patsy Klengenberg, as well as a sled, five dogs, and two weeks' worth of supplies for a trip to the Liston and Sutton Islands, sixteen miles offshore and halfway to Victoria Island. The Eskimos called the islands Okallit, for the arctic hare. Jenness had spent the previous summer among the village's 140 people, and Bruce hoped that some of them might know more about the missing priests.

As soon as the patrol pitched their tent, it was constantly full of Eskimos, many of whom entered with gifts of fish, caribou, and seal meat. The white men were invariably made welcome in the Eskimos' houses and at the many village dances. They were also invited to attend frequent rituals — Bruce called them "séances" — performed by the community's seven shamans, who claimed the ability to communicate directly with invisible spirits from both the human and the animal worlds. Their entranced bodies twisting and contorting, their voices rising to a frenzied pitch, the shamans would whirl with such athletic intensity that they would convulse and collapse, utterly exhausted, upon the séance's conclusion.

Bruce found the séances "amusing to watch," he wrote, until the night he was included in one. In a trance, a shaman revealed that Bruce, Jenness, and Patsy would be taken by spirits, thrown over a cliff, and killed. The shaman offered no reason. Another night, some villagers asked a shaman to find out why the seal hunting had been so poor recently. After completing a séance, one shaman reported that the seals objected to the smell of the patrol's tobacco smoke. It took some doing, but Jenness finally convinced the shaman that tobacco smoke actually *attracted* seals. The next day, luckily for Jenness, hunters killed six.

Bruce's opinion about his hosts was gracious, if condescending. "These people were all well, happy, and contented, and did not try to molest us in any way," he wrote. "I personally think that any white man who is at all discreet need fear no danger from them. They seem to be nothing more or less than overgrown children."[5]

In late January 1916, Bruce decided to head south, in hopes of finding Denny LaNauze down at the old Fort Confidence site, near where the priests, John Hornby, and the Douglases had built their cabins on Great Bear Lake. Bruce and the zoologist Rudolph Anderson planned to hike the coastline to the mouth of the Coppermine, then follow the river south. But the weather was awful from the outset, and the dogs were strained under 125-pound backpacks. By the time they reached the mouth of the Coppermine, on February 4, Anderson had had enough. He told Bruce he would stay with the group only until they reached the timberline, then would return to his research. On February 15, they reached the woods. Wolves prowled around the camp all night. Bruce came across a wolf-killed caribou being scavenged by a pair of silver foxes. Four days later, he nailed up a large placard on a tree by the riverbank; to it he attached a tin box with a note inside for LaNauze. Be sure to find me, the note said. I have information about the missing priests.[6]

BY THE MIDDLE of March, down in their cabin at Great Bear Lake, Denny LaNauze and his team began loading up for the trip to the coast. The woods just to the north of Great Bear Lake were so thick that he and his men had to cut a trail just to get their eighteen-foot chestnut canoe through. The Dease River valley opened up to the west, and sent mirages radiating out in the brilliant morning sunlight. North of the woods, the snow on the Barren Lands was still packed hard and afforded excellent sledding, but the country was utterly devoid of game. Six months earlier, in October, the same country had been crowded with caribou. Now there was not even a track. The scarcity of caribou also meant that local scavengers were applying their skills to the caches left by the patrol. One food pit left by LaNauze's assistant Corporal Withers was recovered just in time; wolverines had beaten a path around it and had begun gnawing through its wooden barrier.

Leaving Withers and the translator Ilavinik's family back at Great Bear Lake, LaNauze, Arden, Wight, and Ilavinik began to move north on March 29 with two dog teams. Almost immediately, they left the comfort of the woods and entered the vast, forbidding, coverless reaches of the Barren Lands. "The north wind had driven the snow into hard, packed wavelets, bare and jagged masses of black rock forced their way clear of the enveloping snow," LaNauze wrote. "It was a scene of infinite dreariness and magnitude." On April 1, after a twelve-mile hunting trip, Ilavinik returned to camp with five caribou. He had seen more than two hundred. Just like that, the season had changed. Now, like Arctic hunters throughout time, the men could follow the migration north.

If it improved the men's mood, the sudden glut of deer meat was hardly a guarantee of future plenty. A day after bringing the catch home, Ilavinik led LaNauze on a scouting trip several miles to the north; they returned to find two of the caribou carcasses stripped bare by wolverines. More troubling was the weather, which, now that the team had passed out of the forest cover, had turned considerably colder, the northeasterly winds stinging their cheeks as they hauled their sleds over the undulating hills. Sporadic blizzards made scanning the terrain especially difficult. Discovering a pile of stones marking Eskimo hunting country, the team figured they had reached the Dismal Lakes; five miles farther to the west, they climbed a hill and saw the lakes far off to the southwest. The "lakes" were in reality a single long lake with two distinct narrows, running thirty-five miles generally northwest from the mouth of the Kendall River.

LaNauze estimated the distance between Lake Imaerinik and the Dismal Lakes to be twenty-one miles, a far cry from the distance indicated on their primitive maps.[7]

Since they had once again run out of fresh meat—a couple of arctic hare had provided a tasty but inadequate dinner—LaNauze and his team decided to set up camp and hunt and dry a load of caribou before pushing on to the Coppermine. With hundreds of caribou—most of them cows heading north to drop their young—moving along the Kendal River, Ilavinik led a hunt that netted thirteen. While Ilavinik retrieved and prepared the meat for smoke-drying and LaNauze fed the dog teams for the journey north, Arden and Wight hiked back to Lake Imaerinik to retrieve the rest of the team's gear. By the time they returned, two days later, they were partially snowblind. Even though their eyes had been protected by snow goggles, they had been damaged by the long days of peering into the shocking glare of the Arctic spring.[8]

The team once again set off north on April 15. After a two-day hike, they at long last reached the Coppermine. By the riverbank, LaNauze saw a blaze on a tree: "Canadian Arctic Expedition. Mail party. Fort Norman. R. M. Anderson, Arnout Castel. February 24, 1915. Returned down river March 19, 1915." Though more than a year had passed since the tree had been blazed, LaNauze felt encouraged. He did not know how close he had come to meeting Anderson and Bruce just a few weeks before, but he would soon find out.[9]

Thrilled to set up once again next to a good-sized river, LaNauze and his team decided to spend a few days hunting, not so much to provide for the trip north but to set up a safeguard cache for their return trip. If the men knew one thing about travel in the north, it was the wisdom of taking advantage of every opportunity of plenty to guard against the potential paucity of the future. With fully seventeen hours of daylight, they had plenty of time to track. For the next couple of days, the team shuttled its gear and dried meat over the ten miles from the Kendall River to the Coppermine. April 18 dawned clear and warm. LaNauze and Ilavinik headed north—downriver—to check out the quality of the Coppermine's ice.

They found the river flowing freely in its widest spots, and locked in snow and ice in the narrows. Fox and wolverine tracks were everywhere. Above the budding willow trees, LaNauze spotted the first hawk of the spring. About fifteen miles upriver from their previous camp, LaNauze and Ilavinik made camp in the snow. They awoke the next morning in the midst of a full-blown blizzard; a canoe strapped to the top of the sled swung around and knocked Ilavinik to the ground. With no more hospitable campsites in view, the two men and their dogs, wind at their backs, pushed hard. The river ice grew rougher. Finally, the blizzard abating, they set up a camp on the river's west bank. On April 20, they turned around, followed their tracks, and made the trip back to their original campsite in just five hours.[10]

On Good Friday, with another blizzard blowing from the northwest, Wight and Arden started their own canoe journey north. The ice during their trip remained dangerouly unstable; at one point Wight, his sled, and his dogs fell into a snow-veiled ice crack. Wight could drag the tangled pile out only after hauling everything from the sled and heaving it back to the frozen surface of the river.

On Easter Sunday, the team set out on the trail created by Arden and Wight. En route, they passed a pair of seventy-foot-tall basalt cliffs on which were perched abandoned eagle's nests at least four feet high and three feet in diameter. All along the riverbank, ice had heaved up in huge pressure ridges, making travel along the corridor impossible. On the plateau above the river, the going was easier, at least for most of the men. Arden had developed a serious case of snowblindness and was nearly incapacitated. At last, up ahead, Ilavinik pointed to a range of cliffs he guessed was the coastal range.

The combination of the snow cover and the early spring sunlight continued to be very hard on the men's eyes, but they pushed on, following the river north. With even the few scrawny trees now having disappeared, LaNauze was forced to fire up his Primus stove for the first time on the trip. Setting up camp, the men pitched their tent by lashing it to the toboggans. Finally, on April 30, LaNauze climbed a low ridge and there, off in the distance, was the Arctic coast. "The blue haze over the ocean was unmistakable," he wrote. At five P.M., after twelve months of travel, the team arrived at the delta where the Coppermine dumped into Coronation Gulf. It had taken the team, what with bad weather and constant double-tripping, a full month to cover the 190 miles from Great Bear Lake to the coast.

The river at its terminus was a mile wide; a small island, one of many out in the open water, lay a quarter mile out in the iced-over sea. Following old sled tracks out to the island, LaNauze and his men discovered a group of abandoned snowhouses, apparently built not by Eskimos but— judging by a cache of canned pemmican—by white men. The sled trail continued to the east, and the next day, May 1, LaNauze decided to follow it. With Coronation Gulf still covered by a smooth coat of snow over a deep sheath of ice, the toboggans moved easily, and for the first time in months the prospect of finding an Eskimo village began to seem imminent.[11]

At eight P.M. that night, they came upon fresh sled tracks. A quarter mile later, they saw it: an Eskimo village. As soon as the villagers noticed the strangers approaching their camp, they began jumping up and down and holding their hands over their heads, a sign of welcome meant to demonstrate that they were carrying no weapons. They did not make the low moaning sounds that Stefansson had heard five years before. By this time, the people could distinguish a white man from a malevolent spirit. As soon as LaNauze and his men returned the gestures, the Eskimos appeared relieved, and began advancing toward them. Ilavinik moved off ahead of the others, and, after speaking with the Eskimos, motioned for the rest of the team to follow. The patrol's dogs, apparently unaware of the delicacy of the moment, charged ahead, and soon the entire patrol found itself careening headlong into a group of laughing Eskimos, who instantly grabbed the reins of the sleds and helped the patrol drag their gear into the village. Every resident—fifteen souls—emerged from large caribou-skin tents to celebrate the arrival of total strangers. Once again, Ilavinik's presence made the jovial encounter possible, and LaNauze realized afresh how his translator was perhaps his greatest asset.

The Eskimos had survived another winter, but they showed the ravages of the season. Their skin tents were in good repair, and they still had a full supply of dried caribou meat. Yet the appearance of all the natives LaNauze encountered that spring struck him as remarkable for the evidence of the conditions under which they had spent the previous six months. After the long winter, the Eskimo families seemed "unspeakably ragged looking in their summer dress, which consists of worn-out clothes of the previous year," LaNauze wrote. "During the winter they often suffer privations on the ice during sealing operations, their dogs not being able to smell out the seal holes during the blizzards which often rage for a week on end." Several men had become so hungry the previous winter that they had been forced to eat their sealskin bow cases.

What should LaNauze say to them? He and his men were outnumbered by the Eskimos, and nowhere near as comfortable on this terrain. Their mission was not to trade or to proselytize; it was to investigate the killing of two of their own people. The manner in which he planned to speak to the Eskimos might at some level resemble the way Vilhjalmur Stefansson and Diamond Jenness had spoken to them, but LaNauze was not here just to write down his impressions of the people. He was here, in all likelihood, to take Eskimos out of the country and put them in jail.

The Eskimos, of course, initially figured that the men had come to trade. So far none of these strange parties had treated them aggressively. Perhaps this was just the way white men were.

Through Ilavinik, LaNauze responded gingerly. His approach revealed much not only about his intuitive investigative skills but about his sensitivity to the strange relationship between his patrol team and the people he hoped to interrogate. Rather than speak aggressively—or even directly—about the search for the missing priests, he hoped to elicit information casually, patiently. He had arrived at a time when there were quite a few Eskimos gathered in one place—a fact he knew would work to his advantage. The spring season meant that there would be plenty of caribou, and because of that, together with the full provisions they had left over from their winter hunts, LaNauze hoped to remain long enough in the Eskimo company to gain their trust. He began by telling them he had been sent by the "Big White Chief," that his patrol was part of a group that "looked after the people, and told them what was right and wrong, and that they must not steal or rob caches."

With Ilavinik interpreting, LaNauze quickly learned that a pair of white men had taken up with an Eskimo family in a camp across the bay and that a big ship lay locked in ice four days to the west, its crew set up in a big house right next to it. The ship, LaNauze figured, must be the *Alaska*, back at the Bernard Harbor headquarters of the southern arm of the Canadian Arctic Expedition.

The Eskimos refused to let LaNauze and his men pitch their own tents, instead ushering them on their hands and knees through a ten-foot-long passageway into a roomy deerskin tent, where they were greeted by an elderly man and his wife.

"You have traveled far, no doubt; would you not like to change your footgear? Here is some of mine and my wife will dry yours over the lamp," the man said to LaNauze. "You too must be hungry; everyone is cooking for you." LaNauze was moved by the hospitality. "No civilized hosts could have been more thoughtful than this old couple," he wrote. "They possessed the natural easy manners of travelled people, were genuinely glad to see us, nor were they as yet the least bit curious as to who we were or the object of our visit."[12]

Women began cooking caribou meat in a large stone pot suspended over a seal-oil lamp, but the preparation took so long, and his men were so famished, that LaNauze trotted out his Primus stove. Throughout the meeting, other members of the comunity entered the tent, many of them bearing pieces of ground squirrel meat or caribou fat. At midnight, a large group gathered for a full meal. At last, after midnight, the entire group settled in for supper. Everyone in the village was clothed in caribou skins. Most had a few tin kettles apiece, which LaNauze guessed they had bartered from a previous Arctic expedition. A few carried rifles. Though LaNauze asked Ilavinik to hold off on any interviewing until the morning, the translater was nonetheless overwhelmed with conversation. The talk went on late into the night. When everyone finally began turning in, the hosts offered the patrol places on the sleeping bench built of snow and covered with musk-ox and caribou skins. As they did every night, the white men rolled themselves up in their robes. As they did every night, the Eskimos removed all their clothes. Soon, they were all fast asleep. Thus ended, LaNauze wrote, "our first experience with the Coronation Gulf Eskimos."

The next morning, following Ilavinik's advice to speak modestly to the Eskimos—and his urging that LaNauze not interrogate them directly—LaNauze began his questioning softly. "The big white chief that lives far to the South, where people are as thick as mosquitoes, had only just heard of the people living on the ice," LaNauze said, speaking through Ilavinik. He explained that the team "had not come to trade, or to collect things, or to teach them of the land above the sky, but simply to visit them." As a gesture of respect, the patrol traveled with "a mouth-piece, one of their own people, Ilavinik." Given the dignity with which LaNauze treated Ilavinik, the Eskimos could tell that he meant what he said.

After this, LaNauze asked Ilavinik and Wight to remain in the village to learn what they could from their hosts. He, Arden, and a pair of volunteer guides set off to look for the white men's camp. An eight-mile crossing brought them to a camp that had only recently been broken. Following the fresh sled tracks west to the Dolphin and Union Strait, they quickly caught up with K. G. Chipman, a topographer with the Canadian Arctic Expedition who was mapping the Arctic coastline as far west as Point Barrow. Traveling with Chipman, LaNauze was delighted to discover, was Corporal Bruce of the Royal North West Mounted Police. Two arms of the investigation, operating independently, came together at a tiny camp on an island off the coast. LaNauze had had no idea there were any other Mounties in the region; all along he'd been under the impression that he was working alone. Bruce, for his part, had heard that LaNauze had begun his investigation, but had figured, after two unsuccessful attempts to contact him, that the priests had somehow turned up safe at Great Bear Lake, and that LaNauze had gone home.[13]

THOUGH HE HAD collected plenty of stories and gathered odd pieces of clothing and religious articles that undoubtedly had belonged to the priests, Bruce had no news of the priests themselves. Perhaps they had returned to Great Bear Lake. Perhaps they had perished.

They aren't at Great Bear Lake, LaNauze said. I just spent the winter down there.

LaNauze mentioned that he had heard of two brothers named Home and Hebo who had apparently accompanied the priests on their voyage to the coast. Bruce said he knew these men. "Hupo," he said, correcting LaNauze's version of the name, was in fact one of the men who had been seen with the priests's articles. When LaNauze asked about the priests' rifles, Bruce replied that he had no idea where they might be. The Eskimos, he said, had a number of .44-caliber rifles in their possession. Bruce told LaNauze about the Rich Man, who had taken possession of a priest's cassock. The Rich Man had been quite happy to show off the priest's things, but he had revealed little about how they had made their way into his tent. How well he knew the priests was still a mystery, largely because Bruce had not then been traveling with an interpreter and had been unable to question him in any depth.

To LaNauze, this was by far the biggest break in the case. He and Ilavinik immediately decided to scour the coastline in search of the Rich Man. LaNauze set up a base of operations at the southern headquarters of the Canadian Arctic Expedition at Bernard Harbor, in the Dolphin and Union Strait.

On May 3, an arctic blizzard blew in that was so severe, LaNauze wrote, that "one could not stand up." The next day, anxious to continue explorations apart from the police investigation, D'Arcy Arden left the patrol and joined Chipman, who was heading east. Corporal Bruce took his

place beside LaNauze, and the two Mounties set up a camp near Coronation Gulf. They pitched their own tent and "found it much more satisfactory than camping with the Eskimos, in spite of their hospitality."

Ilavinik, it turned out, had spoken with a number of Eskimos and reported that each one, interviewed independently, had offered their opinions voluntarily. The only thing Ilavinik was unclear about were dates, of
which, LaNauze wrote, the Eskimo mind seems to have "very little conception."

For the next several days, which varied from warm and clear to brutally
cold and windy, Corporal Bruce led the team off to the northwest, sledding across the gulf. Their course took them through a chain of low-lying,
rocky islands, half of which were not described on any of LaNauze's
charts. At five P.M. one afternoon, the team pulled up at another Eskimo
village on the ice between two small islands, six miles north of the mainland's Locker Point.

Once again, the residents, upon seeing their visitors, jumped up and
down and waved their arms. Once again, the meeting was entirely hospitable. A group of some forty Eskimos carried both seal meat and driftwood—an especially rare commodity at that time of year—on which to
cook it. Some of the people had known Stefansson, they said. The Eskimos offered to trade LaNauze as much caribou meat as he could carry for
a handful of matches. Shortly after the patrol's arrival, several hunters returned to camp after a successful bearded seal hunt. Two had been
speared that day. The meat was divided.

Once they had pitched their tent, LaNauze entered the dwelling in
the village. Inside, he met Kormik, a taciturn man who, over sealskin soup
served in musk-ox horns, said he had been with Stefansson when the explorer had brought Indians and Eskimos together. Kormik also claimed to
have heard of D'Arcy Arden, but said he knew of no other men on Bear
Lake, and certainly did not know any priests. Thankful for the meal,
LaNauze nonetheless went to bed that night sure that Kormik knew more
than he was telling. "I felt convinced that this man knew something about

the priests, but I did not like to excite his suspicions," LaNauze wrote. It would not be long before LaNauze discovered the truth.

ON THEIR WAY again on May 7, the patrol passed Locker Point, then three deserted snow villages, one with twenty-seven houses. At five P.M. LaNauze came to the mainland at Cape Krusenstern, where he organized a two-mile portage over the neck of the cape that saved his men a seven-mile detour around it. At eight P.M., they arrived at a pair of large Eskimo villages on the ice beneath Cape Lambert, in the Dolphin and Union Strait. More than three dozen people greeted them; more than a hundred lived in the village's numerous caribou-skin tents. The village's men were busy caching their seal meat before the villagers moved south for the caribou-hunting season.

Ilavinik learned that this group of Eskimos hunted near Great Bear Lake every year. The previous year, however, they had gone to look for white men "but could not find any." By eleven P.M. Ilavinik had started getting acquainted with a man named Nachim and wife, Kanneak.

Even LaNauze could tell from watching Ilavinik's excitement that the conversation was beginning to turn. Ilavinik learned that Nachim and his brother Ekkehuina had met Stefansson and an Eskimo interpreter named Natkusiak somewhere in the Dismal Lakes region back in 1910. Nachin and his wife had once nursed Natkusiak after he had suffered a bad powder burn while hunting near the Dismal Lakes. In passing, Natkusiak had told the brothers of a great friend of his named Ilavinik—and here he was!

Enjoying an intimacy they had not experienced at the previous village, Ilavinik and LaNauze continued their conversation with the villagers, and ended up with an invitation into one of the men's snowhouses, in the middle of the village. Inside the surprisingly warm shelter, a seal-oil lamp burned off to one side, under the watchful eye of Nachin's wife. LaNauze and Ilavinik took their places on the skin-covered sleeping platforms. LaNauze asked his hosts if any of them knew of any white man who had been to Lake Imaerinik. Oh yes, came the reply, they had met several.

Startled, LaNauze glanced at Ilavinik, then sat back and let his interpreter do the talking. Ilavinik turned to LaNauze.

"Inspector, I will talk straight now."

Ilavinik leaned closer to the men in the icehouse, and his questions grew more intense.

"Did you ever see two white men who lived at Lake Imaerinik, who came here to live with you people?" Ilavinik asked the brothers. The Eskimos spoke long and carefully. When words failed, Ilavinik used sign language to explain the appearance of the priests, their long cassocks, their beards, and the cross they always wore.

Suddenly, the Eskimos started visibly trembling, and covering their faces with their hands and sobbing. LaNauze, oblivious to the content of the questions as well as the replies, checked his anxiety and remained silent. Finally Ekkehuina spoke.

Within minutes, Ilavinik leaned over to LaNauze and broke the case.

"I got him, Inspector," Ilavinik said, the igloo now otherwise completely silent. "I got him now this time. The two fathers were killed all right. Husky kill them. These men very, very sorry. Now I am going to find out all about it."

Stunned, LaNauze whispered to Ilavinik to continue talking to the men, while he went outside and collected Corporal Bruce. When the two men returned, Ilavinik told LaNauze to pull out a pencil and paper. "Now you write down these two names, Uluksuk and Sinnisiak, you got that? Now I find out some more."

As Ilavinik turned back to the conversation, a number of other village men entered the igloo and began excitedly talking over one another. Over the din, Ilavinik asked a question of Ekkehuina: "Did anybody see two white men with beards? Long coat they wore. They had crosses hanging from neck."

"Yes," came the answer. "He come down mouth of Coppermine River, the two white men. Husky kill him."

Before Ilavinik could translate this news to LaNauze, the cacophony hit a peak. The Eskimo named Hupo told of the day he had returned from fishing to find the village in a clamor with the news of the priests' killing. Hupo had been so upset by the news that he was unable to sleep that night. He had disliked Sinnisiak since the summer when Sinnisiak had gotten into a fight with John Hornby over the sealskin fishing line. When he awoke the next morning, Hupo went to Sinnisiak's tent. "Why did you kill the two white men?" Hupo demanded.

"They were going to kill me," Sinnisiak had said. "Ilogoak had his hand on a knife all the time. I was afraid and I killed him."

Hupo's anger had continued to surge, and for a moment, while he was wrestling for the gun that had once belonged to the priests, he thought he would kill Sinnisiak. "I took it from him by my strength. I would have killed him if I had not got it from him," he said. "Then I thought I would not kill him as someone would kill my brother. I did not like to see this man with the good white man's stuff. I talked to him and I made him cry."

As he was speaking, Hupo showed LaNauze a number of things he had taken from the priests' cabin. Although he had waited until "after my heart felt better," he had long since traded away the rifle, he said. Hupo added that he and other Eskimos had often seen the priests writing in small notebooks, but since their deaths he had not seen any sign of their diaries.[14]

Ilavinik asked that only one man speak at a time. As if on cue, a stout elderly man named Koeha shuffled into the igloo and raised his voice above all the others. Rather than try to shout him down, the others in the snowhouse yielded. They said that Koeha had better speak, "as he knew all." Without a moment's hesitation, and with his audience rapt, Koeha began to talk. He would not stop until four A.M.

Koeha spoke very slowly. Throughout the testimony, Ilavinik, LaNauze, and Bruce did their best to keep Koeha on track. This proved difficult. Koeha found the interrogation exhausting, especially when he was asked to recall the past. Such intense questioning, he said, made him sleepy. To break the tension and the monotony, Corporal Bruce—knowing the Eskimos' taste for a joke—would croak and call like a raven, imitating its bell-like note to perfection. This invariably caused a great deal of laughter, and managed to keep the conversation going.[15]

The priests, Koeha said, had initially left their cabin at Lake Imaerinik to travel north to the mouth of the Coppermine with a group of Eskimos that included Kormik, Hupo, Uluksuk, Sinnisiak, Angebrunna, and Adjuna; all told, the group filled eight tents. They arrived at the coast, Koeha said, "when the sea ice was not strong" (probably late October, LaNauze figured). After seeing the coast, and with late-season food supplies so short, the priests decided they would return to their base camp near Great Bear Lake. Perhaps, they said, they would come back the following summer "in a big ship and build a big house on the coast."

The priests stayed with the Eskimos at the mouth of the Coppermine for five nights, sleeping in Kormik's tent. One day, Kormik took a rifle the priests had been carrying and hid it in the corner of the tent. When LeRoux discovered this, he exploded. "Ilogoak found the rifle and got very angry with Kormik," Koeha said. "Kormik got very angry and I watched him, he wanted to kill the white man. I am speaking the truth and not talking foolish. I did not want to see the good white man killed, and I helped them to get away."

In a flurry, Koeha grabbed Kormik as he tried to rush out and continue the argument. When Kormik's mother appeared, Koeha demanded that she get control of her son. Koeha then rushed from the tent to help Rouvière and LeRoux load their sled. The priests were clearly unnerved by the sudden violence; they were talking rapidly to each other, Koeha said, and were very anxious to flee south.

The days were dark, the sun was low and nearly gone, and the snow was still soft when the priests left the Coppermine with a sled, some dogs, and no guide, for the two-hundred-mile journey south. They were exhausted and clearly in poor health. Father LeRoux had a bad cold, and Father Rouvière was still nursing an injury he'd sustained working on his Great Bear Lake cabin. They both suffered from inadequate nutrition. Certainly they were anxious about this violent turn of events with the Eskimos. Certainly they also feared what the coming winter would mean to their frail bodies, especially now that they had essentially been kicked out of the only community of people they knew for hundreds of miles around. They had no idea how to build an igloo, and they carried no tents. How they planned to make camp was unclear. They had a pair of rifles, but neither was an expert hunter.

Perhaps because he sensed the difficulties the priests were sure to encounter on their way, Koeha gave them a pair of dogs to add to their own two, and personally helped haul the sled over the first few miles back up the Coppermine. Koeha went with them "as far as I could see the tops of the tents behind." He then turned to them and spoke his final words before leaving them on their own. "There are no trees here and you go as far as you can. After that you can travel easy," he said. "I like you and I do not want anyone to hurt you." Rouvière was driving the sled, Koeha said; LeRoux was running up ahead. Rouvière stopped to shake hands with Koeha. "The sun was very low when the white men left, and there was not much daylight at that time."

Two nights after the priests left, Sinnisiak and a man named Uluksuk started off in the same direction. They told their fellow villagers they were hoping to rendezvous with a group of Eskimos moving north from the Dismal Lakes. Beginning their trip in the evening, they traveled fast and light, taking dogs but no sled.

SEVERAL DAYS after they had left the coast, Sinnisiak and Uluksuk returned, alone. They were not accompanied by the group of Eskimos they said they had hoped to help move north. However, in addition to the few things they had set off with, they were now carrying two things they had not had before: the priests' rifles.

They told the villagers they had killed the priests near Bloody Falls. Uluksuk did most of the talking. After he and Sinnisiak had stumbled upon the priests' cache, LeRoux had exploded in anger. He kept putting his hand over Uluksuk's mouth. Rouvière had handed LeRoux a rifle, and

LeRoux had brandished it. LeRoux and Sinnisiak had scuffled. Sinnisiak stabbed Father LeRoux in the back. When the priest was found still breathing, Sinnisiak demanded that Uluksuk finish him off. Seeing this, Father Rouvière began to run. Was he lurching for his sled, where there was another gun? Or was he running because he didn't want to fight? Rouvière had never been as aggressive or unpredictable as LeRoux, but nothing, at that moment, seemed predictable. Uluksuk grabbed the gun himself, and gave it to Sinnisiak. Rouvière kept running, Sinnisiak shot him in the back. On Sinnisiak's command, Uluksuk stabbed Rouvière in the side. Sinnisiak smashed his neck with an axe. They cut both priests open, and ate a small part of their livers to protect themselves from being haunted by the priests' spirits.

"Sinnisiak and Uluksuk each took a rifle and came back to the mouth of the Coppermine; I saw them with the rifles," Koeha said. "I asked Uluksuk 'what did you kill the white men for?' and he said 'I did not want to kill them; Sinnisiak told me to kill them.' I asked him if he eat any part of the man, the same as he would do if he killed a caribou, and he said 'I eat some of his guts.' "

In telling his story, Koeha once again recalled the complex emotions he had felt at the time of the killings. He also showed a remarkable knowledge of the history of the one thing the priests had that the Eskimos needed most: their rifles. "After this the people did not like to see Uluksuk and Sinnisiak with the good white men's stuff," he said. "Kormik took the rifle away from Uluksuk. The rifle was traded many times. I do not know where the rifle is now.

"I look for a long time to tell this to some one, for some one to speak for me, and now I speak," he said. "The two men that killed the good white men do not belong to my people. All the Coppermine River people are very, very sorry."

Koeha's wife, whom LaNauze considered highly intelligent, confirmed her husband's testimony. She had helped her husband stop Kormik from killing the two priests, she said, and had watched as the two white men had loaded up their sled and fled south.[16]

Even after hearing Sinnisiak's tale, Koeha had had a hard time believing that the priests were dead. Despite a taboo about visiting places where men have died violently—Eskimos feared they would be cursed by the dead men's shades—Koeha, Kormik, Toopek, and Angebrunna decided to travel upriver to see the bodies for themselves. They covered the ground quickly, arriving at the spot Sinnisiak had described in a single long day of walking. "I was very very sorry that the two white men had been killed, and I wanted to go and see them," Koeha said. "I wanted to go and get my dogs which the two men who had killed the priests had left behind."

When they arrived at the spot to the south of Bloody Falls, on the west bank of the river, they saw, next to a sled, a body lying on its back, its face covered in snow except for the nose. As they got closer, then removed the snow, they recognized the body as LeRoux's. Koeha started to cry. The body had been eviscerated. "The man that had killed him had cut up his breast and all inside was cut up with a knife," Koeha reported.

"I saw the dead man Ilogoak lying by the sled," Angebrunna said. "There was blood on his body. I did not look very close. There was snow on his body."

Rouvière's body was nowhere in sight. Uluksuk had said Rouvière had run away before he had been shot, then dismemberd, by Sinnisiak, but which way he had run they were unable to tell. Inspecting the sled and the gear around it, Koeha and his companions discovered some of the priests' food and ate it. None of the priests' gear had been removed, Koeha saw, except for the guns and ammunition. Sinnisiak and Uluksuk had even left the dogs harnessed to the sled. Koeha unstrapped the dogs and helped himself to a small pot about five inches high, a pair of "white man's boots," and a short fishing line, which he put inside the pot. Angebrunna took two small pots and some matches from the sled. They also grabbed what shirts and pants they could find. "Kormik told me I had better take some more stuff, [but] I was afraid," Koeha said. "I liked [Rouvière] very much. I was afraid of the white men finding this out. The white men were very good to us and gave us ammunition, cod line, and gilling twine." The priests were dead now, and had no need of these things. A year after the killings, Koeha told LaNauze, he had returned to the site and come across not only the sled but scattered bones. He had taken Rouvière's lower jaw and placed it near a rock.

Koeha told LaNauze that he could take the investigator back to the spot where they had left the sled. "I do not think the bodies would be there—some animals might have taken them—but I know the place well and I will take you there."

LaNauze, Koeha warned, should be wary of Kormik—not just because of his well-known temper but because of his tendency to distort stories. "Kormik has two tongues," Koeha said. "I will go with you when you go to see him, and listen if he speaks the truth. He speaks lies."[17]

Even with thirty months gone by since the priests' disappearance, the men in the village were still aghast at what had happened. "The lapse of two and a half years had not weakened their horror," LaNauze wrote. "The acts were evidently greatly deplored by all, and in their simple words they paid tribute to the dead priests. 'We have carried this in our heads a long time.' "

When LaNauze asked why Koeha and the others hadn't spoken of the killings in all the time that had passed since the priests had been killed, Koeha said the villagers had been afraid. They had wanted to tell Arden, but there had not been a translator present. Also, John Hornby, who had had a run-in with Sinnisiak himself, had said that if an Eskimo killed a white man, white men would come north and kill them all.[18]

As far as LaNauze could tell, the Eskimos had not punished Sinnisiak and Uluksuk for their crimes. They had no courts, judges, or chiefs. Indeed, they did not seem to have any formal laws at all, save their time-honored customs of shame and excommunication. Crimes in Eskimo communities were typically punished only if a majority of the people decided that the act had been a threat to the community as a whole. Such direct disciplinary actions were rarely taken, Diamond Jenness had discovered, since Eskimos had neither judicial councils nor official leaders to translate judgments into action. In fact, in contrast to the emphasis in European-based justice on protecting individuals and punishing deviants, Eskimos were far more concerned with maintaining communal peace and stability. In European cultures, murder was a crime against the state. For Eskimos, murder was a private wrong, typically resolved by the victim's family. Blood feuds among families were commonplace, but they were never allowed to endanger a community as a whole.[19]

Rouvière and LeRoux, of course, had been traveling on their own. Their families were thousands of miles away, in France. Denny LaNauze considered finding their killers his job. If he was successful, it would be the first time in history that an Eskimo would face European justice.

Koeha said he would help LaNauze with the investigation, but only after he returned from a seal hunt. He would take the patrol to the site of the killings, he promised, "when the sea-ice could no longer be lived upon."

Writing some years later, LaNauze could not help but wax operatic about his mood at learning of the priests' deaths. Their deaths had not been marked by organs in a cathedral, or choirs, or solemn recitations. Their bodies, for a time, had lain beneath the northern lights. "Then come the great white wolves of the Barren Lands, and the voracious wolverines, hungry for the feast, to snarl and fight over the spoil; and before the sun disappears entirely and the long Arctic winter sets in, there is little left to show that another tragedy has been enacted on this far away Coppermine River."[20]

CHAPTER NINE

—

Although shamans and missionaries alike attempted
to cure the ill, shamans were at a disadvantage,
especially as epidemics of exotic diseases such
as smallpox struck. Shamans were unsuccessful
in their attempts to cure patients of these new
diseases, and they lost the confidence of the
people as curers, especially when shamans
themselves died in epidemics.

—WENDELL H. OSWALT, *Eskimos and Explorers*

O N MAY 9, THE PATROL CAME TO A GROUP OF FORTY ESKIMOS
living near the Dolphin and Union Strait. That night, the people gathered
in a huge tent, with a dancer and a man beating on a drum that was ten
feet around. People crowded around the dancer and began singing in chorus. Among the people in the tent was the Rich Man. LaNauze asked
Ilavinik to take him aside.[1]

The Rich Man said he had heard of the patrol's movements months
ago, from members of the Canadian Arctic Expedition. He had tried to
tell his story to Corporal Bruce the previous fall, but he had been unable
to make himself understood. This time, with Ilavinik present, he would
tell all he could.

The Rich Man said he had known the priests quite well. During the year before they were killed, they had asked him to go east and bring back some musk-ox skins for them. When he returned that winter, with a load of skins, he learned that the priests had been killed. The following spring, "when the sun was high up and the snow was a little wet," he, his wives, and his father had traveled south to the priests' cabin near Great Bear Lake. The Rich Man knew the priests had been traveling with two .44 rifles—one with an octagonal barrel, since stolen by Sinnisiak, and one with a round barrel, which had not turned up. Since the Rich Man had traded his own rifle some time ago while on a trip to the east, he decided to see if the round-barreled Mauser might be somewhere in the priests' cabin. It was. The Rich Man found it with a broken bolt—probably the reason it hadn't been looted before—but managed to fix it. He also found some loose cartridges, quite a bit of clothing, and a few boxes of matches. For an Eskimo, in other words, a gold mine. His decision about whether to take the things was easy. "I thought that if I did not take it some other Eskimos or Indians would take it," he explained. He still had the rifle, and said he would give it to LaNauze.

Later in the season, "when the hair of the caribou falls out," the Rich Man and his family went back to the Dismal Lakes, where he met Kormik, who had a kayak, and then returned once again to Great Bear Lake, where he had met D'Arcy Arden.

The Rich Man had wanted to tell Arden about the priests. Later, he had wanted to tell R. M. Anderson, the zoologist with the Canadian Arctic Expedition. He could not make them understand. Arden said he wanted to travel to the coast, but, the Rich Man related, "I did not want him to go as I was afraid he might be killed too."

"I never told anyone about this before, although I was asked," the Rich Man said. "I was afraid. I am not afraid of Anderson, but I was afraid if I told him he would tell the other white men and they would kill us all. Hornby had told me once that if the Eskimos killed one white man, the white men would come and kill every one of the Eskimos."[2]

On their way back to the coast, the Rich Man and his family spent a long time looking for the place where the priests had been killed. When at last they stumbled upon the priests' sled, they were startled to find, lying close by, a human jawbone. "My father was very sorry and put it away in a high place," the Rich Man said. Not far from the sled, they discovered Rouvière's body, still covered in tattered, muddy clothing, lying in a creek.

The Rich Man not only knew Sinnisiak, he disliked him. Sinnisiak had once threatened to kill him. The Rich Man said he would happily take LaNauze to find him. He had recently seen Sinnisiak, far out on the ice, through a telescope he had obtained from the Canadian Arctic Expedition. He also knew Uluksuk, and could help find him as well.

LaNauze was overwhelmed. The Rich Man's testimony "entirely clears up the theft of priests' effects at Great Bear Lake," he would write. The Rich Man "is about the smartest of the Eskimo. This man is useful and will speak when he knows it will pay him, as his business instincts are more strongly developed than the other Eskimos."[3]

Armed with the Rich Man's testimony, LaNauze and his patrol arrived on May 10 at Bernard Harbor, twenty-five miles west of Cape Lambert, opposite Liston and Sutton Islands. The Canadian Arctic Expedition's ship *Alaska* was wintering there, its members living in a small house made of sod and lumber. LaNauze and his men were greeted by Frits Johansen, a naturalist, and Captain Sweeney, who had taken charge of the expedition in the absence of R. M. Anderson, who was on a surveying trip to Bathurst Inlet. The Canadian Arctic Expedition still had plenty of seal meat to feed the patrol's big Mackenzie River dogs, but LaNauze, fearing they needed more sustenance for the coming journey, fed them caribou meat instead. With small herds of caribou migrating north, Ilavinik and the Rich Man had little trouble killing a half dozen.

In this tiny outpost of Canadian civilization, Corporal Bruce formally laid out the charges against the suspects. Sinnisiak, he wrote, "did on or about November, 1913 A.D. at or near the Coppermine River, willfully murder one, The Rev. Rouvière, a Roman Catholic Missionary of Fort

Norman, NWT, by shooting him with a rifle." A similar charge was laid against Uluksuk, and then a second charge against Sinnisiak for killing Father LeRoux "by stabbing him with a knife."

The following day, with the Rich Man serving as guide, the team went northeast across the gulf to Liston and Sutton Islands. The Rich Man wanted to find a deserted snow village where he had seen Sinnisiak during the winter. The patrol would try to pick up some tracks and take it from there.[4]

As always, the weather proved relentlessly unpredictable. Clear days were followed by such heavy snow and fog that a man couldn't see the dogs pulling his own sleds. With little chance of reaching landfall, LaNauze ordered the patrol to pitch its tents in the middle of the Dolphin and Union Strait. Tense with the prospect of an imminent solution to their investigation, LaNauze and his men were beginning to lose patience. Where was Sinnisiak? Was he fleeing? Perhaps word had leaked out about the investigation. Rumors had a way of traveling around in the Arctic, despite the vast distances and the few messengers.

At last, though, the fog lifted. Ilavinik, always adept at discerning the subtleties of the infinite swaths of white arctic space, discovered old sled tracks leading north. Following these, the patrol found two clusters of abandoned snowhouses, then a third. To LaNauze, it seemed that, for the first time since they had encountered Eskimos, people were fleeing their approach.

The next day, their luck changed. A few miles north of their camp, the giant landmass of Victoria Island came into view, and by one P.M. the trail took them to a series of caribou-skin tents just off the island's shore. To LaNauze, the coastline looked woefully bare and stony, with rocky hills rolling inland and expanses of deep, hard-packed snow. Spring, this far north, was still a long way off.

As they approached, they saw the village's men and women quickly separate into two groups, the men gathering up whatever weapons they could find. There was none of the ritual signs of peace, even after LaNauze and his men offered them first. No one ran out to meet them.

Perhaps word had reached Sinnisiak and his people. Perhaps they were arming themselves for a fight. If so, LaNauze and his men would not fare well. True, they had rifles, but so, most likely, did a few of the Eskimos. The patrol was outnumbered and could hardly expect to survive even a modest assault. Their only hope was diplomacy. LaNauze ordered his men to pack their rifles in their sleds, out of sight.

With the team's sleds practically pulled up on shore, a group of forty Eskimos approached. This was it, LaNauze could tell: the moment when the investigation would prove either a success or another chapter in an ongoing tragedy. Once again, and in a way he might not have predicted, LaNauze's foresight and demeanor paid off. The Eskimos instantly recognized the Rich Man, who in his own way and for his own reasons had come to trust the white men. The tenor of the moment changed in an instant. LaNauze and his men were welcomed as friends. Once again, LaNauze's deference to his well-chosen Eskimo guides probably saved his life.

After offering their greetings, the people inspected the strangers' gear. They seemed most taken with the design of the team's toboggans and the size of their dogs. Many of them had never seen a white man. Among this group, LaNauze could not help but notice, were some of the strongest and healthiest Eskimos he had yet seen. The men were preparing to set off to hunt and fish on the island's interior, but they could not leave until they had cached enough seal blubber. A few of them had rifles; the others offered "everything they possessed" in exchange for one of LaNauze's.

The Rich Man asked if one of the villagers had seen the man called Sinnisiak.

"No, but I have seen his wife," the man replied.

Ilavinik shot LaNauze a glance, and said that he and the Rich Man would take a look around the village. If they could find Sinnisiak's wife, the man himself could not be far away. A few minutes later, they motioned for LaNauze to follow.[5]

While Corporal Wight engaged the villagers with talk about sleds and dogs, LaNauze and Bruce followed Ilavinik and the Rich Man to a large tent at the far edge of the village. A man and a woman were seated inside. The man was carving a bow. The Rich Man turned to LaNauze.

"This is Sinnisiak."[6]

IF THERE IS something ritualistic about the confrontation between a police officer and a suspected murderer, the encounter between the Royal North West Mounted Police patrol and the Eskimo hunter showed just how different rituals can be. At first, Sinnisiak was "absolutely paralyzed with fear," LaNauze reported; he was convinced that the police had come to kill him on the spot. It had been fully thirty months since the killing. Were these visitors spirits, come back to torment a killer? Sinnisiak's tent instantly filled with other villagers, all of them speaking at once. With so many other villagers in and around the tent, LaNauze worried for a moment that his investigation might suddenly spin out of control. Showing considerable confidence, given his distance from home and his surroundings, LaNauze managed to keep his cool. He told Sinnisiak he would not be killed; he had "nothing to be afraid of," but he must "come quietly."

Ilavinik, again serving as a mediator, quieted the people. He told them the patrol had not come to make trouble. He related what the patrol had learned—from other Eskimos—about the hunter Sinnisiak.

"My mouth is that of the white men who stand beside me, my tongue speaks for them," Ilavinik said. "We have learned of Sinnisiak's killing the two priests from our own people, your own flesh and blood, who live across the straits. For a year we have followed this, and now we know that Sinnisiak must come with us before the Big White Chief, for we are not going to leave this camp until he does."

The people in the tent were silent.

"I will not go," Sinnisiak said, never getting up from his seat. He turned to his villagers for support. Again they began to chatter. An elderly man who had been silent till now spoke up.

"What Ilavinik says for the white men is right. We have not seen many white men, but we have always heard that the white man speaks straight, and not with two tongues. What our people told you of Sinnisiak is true, and when the white men say he must go with them, he will have to go and none of us will put out our hand to stop him."

Sinnisiak darkened. "I will come with you next month," he offered, his eyes flashing from one member of the patrol to the next. Still he refused to stand up. His tone grew more desperate. He threatened the patrol in the most intimidating way he could conjure.

"If the white men kill me, I will make magic," he said. "Their ship will go down in the ice, and they will be covered up."

Once again, LaNauze assured Sinnisiak and the villagers gathered around him that the patrol had not come to kill him. Once again, the other Eskimos inside the tent told Sinnisiak to go with the white men. Perhaps this was because Sinnisiak was not part of their village; perhaps they feared stirring the ire of an armed white man; or perhaps they felt that Sinnisiak's arrest was long ovderdue and important to resetting the balance of justice.

Bruce leaned over Sinnisiak and formally arrested him. With LaNauze's help, Bruce lifted Sinnisiak from his seat. Beneath him, hidden under a set of deerskins, were two large knives and Father Rouvière's .22-caliber rifle.

LANAUZE AND his men did their best to lead Sinnisiak away from the village as quietly as possible. Sinnisiak said he wished to take his wife, a sled, and his few possessions along with him. LaNauze agreed to the request and asked Bruce and the Rich Man to help him get ready. The patrol, with their prisoner in tow, finally left the village at five P.M. At first, they were accompanied by another Eskimo couple who also wanted to cross back to the mainland, but this proved such a drag on the team's progress that LaNauze ordered Sinnisiak to separate from his wife and possessions and push along faster. This made Sinnisiak furious.

"This was not to his liking, but we were masters then," LaNauze reported. The two groups traveled all night, the patrol in front and the slower Eskimos to the rear. Especially after being separated from his wife, Sinnisiak was very nervous. He stopped the sleds several times and, perhaps to emphasize his own harmlessness, asked to shake hands all around. He repeatedly asked Ilavinik to assure him that he would not be killed on the ice.

Leaving the village, the patrol continued to follow the lead of the Rich Man, who said he had a hunch about where to find another piece of the puzzle: the .44-caliber rifle that had been taken from Rouvière and used to kill him. The Rich Man said the rifle had been traded around among a group of hunters since the killings, and that it almost certainly had landed, for the moment, among a group of people living on the ice south of Victoria Island. A quick series of questions turned it up, in the possession of an Eskimo named Kirkpuk. The short-barreled, .44-caliber octagonal-barreled rifle, serial number 42551, exactly matched the description given months ago by the Indian guide Harry. The Rich Man said he had no doubt it was the right weapon; he even knew its recent history. "It was traded for by the Eskimo Ikpukkuak on behalf of Kirkpuk, his adopted son, to the Eskimo Kormik for a telescope that came from the east," he said.

Grabbing a shotgun he had picked up from the Canadian Arctic Expedition, LaNauze exchanged the weapons, one for one. It was a good trade. The shotgun was a superior hunting tool, and LaNauze was now certain the rifle was the gun Sinnisiak had used to kill Rouvière.

The matter-of-fact manner in which the Eskimos traded things they knew had been taken from the hands of murdered men unsettled LaNauze. The Eskimos "made no secret about taking the stuff either from the unfortunate priests' sled or from the houses on Bear Lake," he wrote. "They produced the stuff they had left and showed it to me; they simply said, 'The men were dead, we took their stuff before someone else would get it.' "

In the Barren Lands, people routinely starved to death because hunters were unable to provide for their families. Leaving a gun in the snow, regardless of how it got there, would not just be foolish, it would be immoral.

Although he spoke firmly to Sinnisiak, LaNauze shied from admonishing the other Eskimos; rather, he offered oblique warnings about future infractions, telling them that "this would not be tolerated in the future." The Eskimo response—"We know now that we must not steal any white man's stuff"—seemed as tepid as LaNauze's reprimand. Once this moment passed, they all seemed to say, the true law of the land would return.

Whether or not any lessons had been learned, LaNauze had, in fact, accomplished a great deal. In less than twenty-four hours, he had both apprehended a suspect and secured a murder weapon. All he lacked was Sinnisiak's accomplice. And a motive. The evidence he had gathered told him only the barest outline of the priests' final days. Clearly, once they had decided to leave Coronation Gulf, they had left quickly. Was this because they were afraid for their lives? That seemed possible. Although they had apparently made a number of warm acquaintances among the Eskimos over the months they had spent with them, they had run dangerously afoul of at least one man, Kormik. And Sinnisiak was considered by many people to have been an unpredictable and even a dangerous man. Or, on the other hand, were the priests in a hurry simply because the season was getting very far along, and the days left to travel in daylight were growing fewer and fewer? It appeared clear that Father LeRoux had quarreled over a rifle with the Eskimo Kormik; a half dozen people had described an enraged Kormik bent on killing him for it, and it was Kormik who'd taken the rifle away from Uluksuk once he had returned from Bloody Falls. Since Kormik had developed a reputation for aggression among his own people—and since Bruce had discovered most of the missing church property in his possession—LaNauze seemed inclined to believe this part of the story. If Sinnisiak and Uluksuk had committed the murders, the aggressiveness of the act had started in Kormik's house.[7]

LANAUZE AND his men led their prisoner through the night and got back to Bernard Harbor at seven A.M. on May 16. They were greeted by Diamond Jenness and his sixteen-year-old interpreter Patsy Klengenberg.

Patsy spoke conversational English and from the beginning had impressed Jenness. Patsy was "strong and hardy, an excellent traveller and a skilful and fearless hunter," Jenness wrote. "Probably no better interpreter could have been found anywhere along the Arctic Coast." Even better, for LaNauze's purposes, Patsy claimed to know Uluksuk well enough to identify him.[8]

Sinnisiak and his wife were given bunks in the camp kitchen. The camp cook said he would watch them for an hour while LaNauze and his men got cleaned up. A short time later, LaNauze heard a commotion and ran to investigate. The cook's four butcher knives had disappeared.

LaNauze confronted Sinnisiak, retrieved the knives, and relieved the cook of his guard duty.

That night, Sinnisiak, fearing he would be killed in his sleep, refused even to lie down. He and his wife "sat up in their bunk and licked each other's faces in their affection," LaNauze reported. At last, exhausted, they both fell asleep.

The next morning, LaNauze opened a formal hearing. He swore in Ilavinik as official interpreter in the proceedings, and Corporal Bruce as the reporting officer. "Since coming into Coronation Gulf, I have found numerous articles in the possession of the Copper Eskimos, and the property of the Church of Rome," Bruce said. "They were the mass regalia of the priests, obtained from one Kormik on March 24, 1916; two brevaries from one Hupo on March 27, 1916; one large crucifix from one Uluksuk in December 1915; and numerous other articles."

Bruce went on to detail his meeting, two weeks previously, with LaNauze, Wight, and Ilavinik near Coronation Gulf, and their subsequent trip to Cape Lambert, where they heard Koeha's description of the killings. The hearing lasted for over three hours. When it had been completed, Sinnisiak and the absent Uluksuk were formally committed for trial on two charges of murder.

Throughout the proceeding, LaNauze followed the traditional legal script. "And the said charge being read to the said Sinnisiak, 'Copper' Eskimo of Coronation Gulf, is now addressed by me as follows: 'Having heard the evidence, do you wish to say anything in answer to the charge? You are not obliged to say anything unless you desire to do so; but whatever you say will be taken down in writing, and may be given in evidence against you at your trial. You must clearly understand that you have nothing to hope from any promise of favor, and nothing to fear from any threat which may have been held out to you to make any admission or confession of guilt, but what ever you now say may be given in evidence against you upon your trial, notwithstanding such promise or threat."

Considering their surroundings, these formal legal rituals must have seemed odd even to Denny LaNauze. To Sinnisiak, they must have been unfathomable. What was going on here? How had these white men found him? What were they going to do to him? Sinnisiak motioned to LaNauze, indicating, "I want to speak."

LaNauze asked Ilavinik, once again, to act as an intermediary. He needed to get Sinnisiak's statement down as accurately as possible. One day, it would provide the most credible evidence in a trial, when the Western legal rituals would take over in earnest. If Sinnisiak thought this was strange, wait until he saw all the men in court. Once again, he would face the scrutiny of men wearing black robes.

Sinnisiak spoke at length. Ilavinik translated. LaNauze wrote. The unembroidered testimony left LaNauze transfixed. It came out in a rush, with no prodding, and seemed utterly without guile. Sinnisiak said that he and Uluksuk had felt threatened. They had been held at gunpoint by a man who was plainly angry and desperate. They had killed the men they feared. To Denny LaNauze, Sinnisiak's confession made the killings seem a clear and necessary action. It had been winter. The priests were clearly desperate. A crisis had arisen, and the Eskimos had decided to act before they were acted upon.[9]

LaNauze was torn. Was what he heard the truth? Every word had come through a translator. What subtleties, what prejudices had been lost? It was not up to him to debate the merits of a suspect's arguments. In a way, his position was not unlike that of the priests. The priests had been religious pioneers, leading the way into uncharted territory for a church whose tentacles reached all over the world. LaNauze's job, as the point man atop a vast pyramid of British justice, was to bring the suspects into the system. Their fate would be up to lawyers and judges, sitting comfortably in a warm and secure place where there *was* time to negotiate, to argue, to persuade.

WITH ONE SUSPECT in custody, LaNauze left Corporal Bruce and Ilavinik in charge of Sinnisiak and set off with Corporal Wight and Patsy Klengenberg to find Uluksuk, whom Patsy thought would be hunting near the mouth of the Coppermine. If things went according to plan, the patrol would return with the second suspect and ship both men out on the *Alaska*, first to Herschel Island, then to Nome, Alaska. From there, the Eskimos, presumably, would be taken south for trial.[10]

LaNauze and his team left Bernard Harbor on May 18 and camped at Cape Lambert, where they managed to kill a caribou but then got caught in a blizzard. The weather, as the season began to change, was mercurial: the very next evening, the temperature stayed high and the sun did not set. The arriving spring meant that the patrol would need to travel quickly to find Uluksuk, since the Eskimos had already starting moving off the ice. Soon they would cache their winter clothes and seal-hunting gear along the northern islands and begin their annual migration south, back toward the hunting grounds near Great Bear Lake. If the patrol missed them, the search for Uluksuk could stretch out for months. Another entire season—complete with the acute challenges of hunting for food just to keep the patrol alive—could be spent looking for him.

The warming temperatures also made the patrol's movements more laborious. The snow was turning to slush, which made hauling the sled that much more difficult. Gear, and particularly boots, got wet in the morning and rarely dried out. Tents were packed—and, at the end of the day, set up—still soggy. Finally, at ten P.M. on May 21, the team arrived at the same island at the mouth of the Coppermine where the priests had started their final journey south. There were no Eskimos camped on the island,

and none visible anywhere out on the ice. For a time the team wondered if they were too late. Perhaps the Eskimos had already left. Perplexed, LaNauze found a patch of dry ground, set up camp, and hung his sopping clothes out to dry. With the ice melting along the fringes of Coronation Gulf, and the water flowing hard from the Coppermine, the sound of running water was everywhere. Overhead, geese were flying north; their calls were matched by those of seagulls and hawks. Little snow buntings twittered. Spring had come to Coronation Gulf in a rush.

With the sun still high in the sky late into the evening, LaNauze and Patsy decided to hike around the island in search of a high vantage point from which to look for any Eskimo camps far out on the ice. Pulling out a pair of binoculars at eleven P.M., Patsy scanned the ice to the north of the island, stretching out toward the mass of Victoria Island. Sure enough, he managed to pick out six dogsleds in the distance, slowly traveling toward them. Whether Uluksuk would be among this group was anyone's guess, but surely this group would know where he was, or where he was heading.

For six hours, the men stood watch. The Eskimos moved agonizingly slowly over the softening ice. At five A.M. they disappeared behind a large island some ten miles to the northeast, just as another sled appeared in the east. After a long night, LaNauze and Patsy turned in, serenaded by the sound of brant geese flying overhead.

Finally, at five P.M., twelve hours after they had vanished behind the island, the Eskimo Angebrunna and his wife arrived with their two dogs pulling a sealskin sled. Angebrunna, one of the men who had gone with Koeha to see the murder site after learning of the killing, said six sleds were camped out on the island. One of the men, he said, was Uluksuk.

Once again, LaNauze had caught a break. At nine P.M. on May 22 he and his men loaded up their sleds and set out for the island out on the ice. Long before they arrived, they could see, high on the rocky edge of the island, a group of two dozen Eskimos dramatically raising their arms in a gesture of peaceful greeting.

As the patrol got closer, it seemed that every one of the Eskimos was jumping up and down and making the peace sign. Plainly, the arrival of this strange group of white men had caused them considerable anxiety. What could the white men want this time? Their anxiety did not abate until LaNauze and his men returned the greeting in kind. Relieved, the Eskimos ran down from their perch on the high rocks and greeted the patrol; many in the group had met LaNauze's group on their way out to arrest Sinnisiak. As the Eskimos approached LaNauze and his men, only one man remained behind. Patsy immediately identified him as Uluksuk.

As LaNauze and Corporal Wight walked past the group, Uluksuk suddenly sprinted toward them. Rather than acting aggressively, however, he held up his hands and repeated two words: "Goanna! Goanna!" Patsy Klengenberg translated his statement: "Thank you, thank you, white men. I am Uluksuk. I will do whatever you want. Are you going to kill me now, as I am ready? I have carried this in my head a long time. I am glad you have come."

Taken aback by the greeting, LaNauze, through Patsy, asked if Uluksuk had any idea why the patrol was there. Oh, yes, Uluksuk said, he knew very well. Did they intend to kill him? The other two white men had hit him over the head—did LaNauze intend to do the same?

In his usual calm voice, LaNauze replied that Uluksuk had nothing to fear. He sensed that Uluksuk was a very different character from Sinnisiak, gentle, less suspicious, and far less confrontational. Indeed, compared to some of the more aggressive men, like Sinnisiak and Kormik, Uluksuk seemed almost passive. His entire set of material possessions consisted of a polar bear–skin sled, a small caribou-skin tent, and his bow and arrows. The rifle he had taken from the priests had been appropriated by Kormik almost as soon as Uluksuk had returned from the scene of the killings.

LaNauze felt certain that this suspect would be far easier to handle than the first. Relieved, almost congenial, Uluksuk agreed to go wherever LaNauze planned to take him. He had one request: his wife was in the middle of making him a new pair of boots. Before setting out on a long walk, would the patrol mind waiting until the boots were finished?

The presence of Uluksuk's wife—who was visibly pregnant, and extremely upset at the prospect of losing her husband—troubled LaNauze.

He did his best to calm her down with gifts. He spoke to others in her group, promising that they would be rewarded someday if they helped her. To the woman herself, he gave a small silk tent, a cup, and a box of matches. Later LaNauze would learn that Uluksuk's wife found a new husband just two weeks after Uluksuk's departure.

Wight formally placed Uluksuk under arrest, and LaNauze committed him for trial. He read the charges against him. "Having heard the evidence against you, do you wish to say anything in answer to the charge?" LaNauze asked.[11]

Like Sinnisiak, Uluksuk offered a vivid and detailed description of the killings. The details he provided were for all practical purposes identical to those offered by Sinnisiak. He and Sinnisiak had set out from the mouth of the Coppermine to rendezvous with their people. They had not set out to kill the priests. They had not followed them in order to steal their guns. They had simply crossed their path and become tangled up in a drama that was already well under way by the time they arrived. As he unwound his tale, Uluksuk seemed "very nervous and was shivering and shaking," LaNauze reported. He wrote down every word.[12]

A year after beginning his investigation, Denny LaNauze finally allowed himself to feel pleased. Within three weeks of arriving at Coronation Gulf, he had not only solved the mystery of the missing priests but had captured both of the men suspected of killing them. His efficiency in carrying out the investigation, under the most trying conditions, was extraordinary.

HIS SLEUTHING WORK done, LaNauze still had to figure out how to get his prisoners home. He was six hundred miles from the coastal police station at Herschel Island, and nearly two thousand miles from any semblance of an actual judicial system. Getting back to civilization meant either a return trip over the Barren Lands or a long sea voyage around the Alaskan coast. The overland route would allow the patrol to look for the spot upriver from Bloody Falls where the killings had taken place. Perhaps, even two and a half years later, they would find some physical evidence to support the testimony they had collected from their prisoners and others.

But the overland route also presented a number of problems, beyond the simple exhaustion and unpredictability of food supplies any long journey would present. Given the distance and the terrain, transporting the prisoners overland would not be a simple matter of putting them in leg irons and forcing them to march. Also, were they to take the inland route, they would surely attract—as explorers always did—the interest of any groups of Eskimos along the way. Who could say how they might respond to seeing two of their own being forcibly removed from the homeland by strangers? There was also the problem of Indians. Like most Eskimos, Uluksuk and Sinnisiak dreaded their neighbors to the south; the blood feuds that had been boiling for years spooked them sufficiently that LaNauze considered it an unnecessary strain even on his own men.

Given the unprecedented circumstance of the arrest—the incredible distances over which all the witnesses were spread and the distance between the Arctic coast and Edmonton—LaNauze had to assume that the government would decide to complete the proceedings against Sinnisiak and Uluksuk by somehow sending a judge north. What kind of judge would be willing to take on this assignment he did not bother to conjecture.

THE PATROL and Uluksuk walked west all night. The breaking ice created a number of difficult moments for the team, as deep-water fractures began to open up along the coast. After shooting a seal, the patrol portaged over Cape Krusenstern, which by now was almost completely bare of snow. As the weather continued to warm, migrating waterfowl—swans, geese, cranes—flew continuously overhead. On May 25, they camped once again at Cape Lambert, where they saw hundreds of eider ducks floating out on the open water and countless caribou—mainly bulls, their antlers already starting to grow—crossing the straits from the mainland. "This was indeed a land of plenty at this season of the year," LaNauze wrote. How Uluksuk must have felt, leaving the country at the easiest time of the year, he did not say.

As the patrol approached Bernard Harbor, the going got particularly rough. The patrol spent the last five miles wading through the knee-deep water of opening creeks. They finally arrived at seven-thirty P.M. on the May 26, and were greeted by members of the Canadian Arctic Expedition and some twenty Eskimos, who, their sealing season at an end, were beginning to move back to the mouth of the Coppermine, where they would join some one hundred others on their journey south. One Eskimo LaNauze expected to see was not there. Corporal Bruce and Diamond Jenness, LaNauze learned, had "tactfully shipped Sinnisiak's wife back to Victoria Land with a few small presents."

For the patrol, getting back to Bernard Harbor with their second prisoner offered considerable relief. Once again, they were in the company of their own countrymen, which must surely have relieved them of the anxiety of traveling through a land inhabited by people who greatly outnumbered them and whose language they could understand only through the good graces of their hired interpreters. Yet their experiences with the Eskimos they had met, LaNauze would later write, had been consistently and almost unfailingly pleasant. At every turn, the natives had treated him and his men with courtesy and grace. In fact, without fail, as soon as one person began to tell a story about the killings, others would crowd around the teller and add their own details. The tale of the missing priests became a tale told by a community, rather than by a single storyteller. Sometimes this was frustrating—as it was before Koeha was granted the floor in the snowhouse—but more often than not it led to a fuller picture of the whole. "Amongst these people, what one knows is known by all," LaNauze wrote. "Once we got the story of the murder everyone seemed to know about it. In getting information they all crowd around and listen attentively and help the speaker along with his story."

As it turned out, public opinion seemed to weigh heavily against Sinnisiak in particular; the willingness of the Eskimos to speak about his role in the killings, LaNauze began to think, seemed designed to purge him from their community. "As I have only been a month among the Eskimos of Coronation gulf I cannot give an expert opinion of them," LaNauze wrote, "but I find them intelligent, straightforward, and hospitable, and I went about my business in the usual manner and did not try to deceive them as to our motives. I believe, and it is the belief of others that know the Eskimos better than I do, that the murderers fully expected to be killed by us on the spot and that the others would not have raised a hand to stop us. Public opinion in Coronation gulf is against the murderer Sinnisiak; all say he is a bad man, and that the other man Uluksuk was led by him."

In the end, the Eskimos' cooperation made the investigation infinitely easier. Indeed, it made it possible. Absent the help of his two interpreters, LaNauze would almost certainly have returned home empty-handed. In addition to his invalubale interpreting, Patsy Klegenberg had managed to identify a suspect. Ilavinik had proved an exceptional hunter and navigator. Diamond Jenness, who had spent all of the previous summer living with the Eskimos on Victoria Island, told LaNauze he was very lucky to have found Sinnisiak, since typically he would have been hunting a long way inland. Uluksuk, who was from Bathurst Inlet and had been living far to the east since the killings, might just as well have been on the Kent Peninsula, a hundred miles to the east, as along the Coronation Gulf coastline. Perhaps most critically, Ilavinik had virtually eliminated the tension implict in every encounter the white men had had with the natives. Writing to his superior officers sometime later, LaNauze made his admiration for Ilavinik clear. "Ilavinik's work on this case is worthy of the highest praise," he wrote. "We have secured one Eskimo out of a hundred in him. I give him all credit for his painstaking and straightforward interpreting."

Back at Bernard Harbor, LaNauze, once again, got a lucky break. The leaders of the Canadian Arctic Expedition, who had always been helpful, offered to help transport Sinnisiak and Uluksuk south aboard their ship.

LaNauze gratefully accepted. Now he would not have to worry about conveying the prisoners thousands of miles across their own country. They'd be packed safely away on the *Alaska*.

LaNauze also decided to split his team up. He would send a brief report on the investigation south with Wight and Ilavinik via Bloody Falls — where they would look for the site of the killings — and, from there, by York boat to Great Bear Lake, Fort Norman, and south on the Mackenzie River. Ilavinik and his family would split from the group at Fort Norman and return to their community at Herschel Island by heading north on the Mackenzie.

LaNauze and Patsy would help load the prisoners onto the *Alaska* and take them to the police outpost at Herschel Island to await trial either there or, perhaps, at a makeshift courthouse near the mouth of the Coppermine. The latter possibility seemed difficult in the extreme. True, holding a trial at Coronation Gulf would make it easier to gather witnesses, but it would also almost certainly require getting a judge on board a ship and having him spend a winter on the Arctic coast. Almost as an afterthought, LaNauze wrote, "If on the other hand the case could be tried without witnesses the matter would be simple."

This suggestion must have seemed somewhat absurd to LaNauze, given his by-the-book approach to every other aspect of the investigation. A trial without witnesses would have flown in the face of every bit of legal training he had ever had. But convincing a judge to take a steamer down the Mackenzie River for a trial at Herschel Island seemed a lot easier to imagine than risking his spending a winter in a snowhouse on Coronation Gulf.

LaNauze also allowed himself a moment to comment on the next stage of the prosecution. "The depositions show that both of the prisoners plead 'guilty' and I have absolutely no doubt that they will ever change their plea," he wrote. "Their own defense of being ill-treated is their strongest point, and the prosecution has no witnesses that will deny this." This was as close as LaNauze would come to offering an opinion on the passions involved in the crime. His tone was neutral, professional, cool. Months down the road, in court, these words would come to carry surprising weight.

NOW ALL THAT remained was waiting for the ice to thin out enough for the *Alaska* to leave Bernard Harbor. Though LaNauze never felt the need to put his prisoners in handcuffs or leg irons, the Eskimos nonetheless grew increasingly agitated by their confinement. Sinnisiak particularly became "very nervous" when LaNauze tried to take the edge off by allowing them to move around the camp and perform chores. While they waited, Uluksuk was given his own formal preliminary hearing. As he had with Sinnisiak, LaNauze laid out the charges against Uluksuk in the clearest way he could. Over and over, he reported, he made every effort to explain what was happening to the two prisoners. Reading the transcripts of the proceedings, one cannot help but sense LaNauze's awareness of the strangeness of his, and the Eskimos', predicament. Even seen strictly from his own perspective, that of a man trying to walk through a rigidly proscribed series of investigative and legal steps—gathering evidence, hearing testimony from witnesses, laying out charges—the case was full of practical problems. Even without the confessions, LaNauze had come to feel he had compiled a strong case. Yet since the Eskimos had no tradition of writing, he was, of course, unable to get any testimony from witnesses— let alone the actual confessions—down in their own hand. "As these people have no conception of writing, I did not get them to make their marks on papers," he wrote. "What they told me was the truth, and they all told me the same story and said 'We will always speak the same.' "

Such evidence, gathered in a typical murder case, might not stand up in court; anything reported to the judge would simply be the word of the police officer. Here again, LaNauze was faced with a dilemma. He was forced to depend on the honesty and accuracy of the very people he was investigating. What if Uluksuk and Sinnisiak arrived in court and, called to the stand, completely changed their story? Wouldn't it be simple for them to claim they had been wrongfully hauled out of their snowhouses, that they were not only innocent but completely unaware of the charges against them? If it came to their word against that of a courageous and honest police officer, surely a jury would side with the police officer. But it would be embarrassing to have to convict men who, once they were pulled wholly out of their native context, would appear utterly alien to the system of justice trying to convict them of murder.

For LaNauze, then, the only solution was to play his role as straight as he could. Even his references to his legal superiors seem to have been imparted to reassure himself that he was acting within a framework that made sense. And for someone who claimed to have so little knowledge of the subtleties of Eskimo life, he was at least conscious of some fundamental differences in their social structures.

"I have not deceived the murderers in any way," he wrote. "I have had it carefully explained to them that it is not for me to judge them but that the Big White Chief must decide what he will do with them. But it is hard for them to grasp the meaning of this. In their life they have no chief. Everyone is equal, and their word 'Ishumatak,' for chief, literally translated means 'the thinker'—the man who does the deciding or thinking for the party."[13]

As he finished writing up his report on the investigation, LaNauze allowed himself some space to think about what might have happened back there near Bloody Falls. Even at this moment, having just completed his remarkable arrests, LaNauze seemed fully open to two very different scenarios. As he had from the beginning, he did his best to suspend his own judgments in the case. Even when they had completed collecting evidence, indeed, even when they had "solved" a crime, he knew that police officers rarely had the bird's-eye advantage of full context. LaNauze and Bruce had collected a great deal of raw data—testimony, material evidence—that would hopefully one day help prosecutors compile a case. But the circumstances were so strange, so unprecedented, that LaNauze felt humility was the best approach to the evidence. Who could really say what had happened out there on the snow on the terrible day in October 1913?

"The priests may have been the victims of a premeditated murder for the possession of their rifles and ammunition, or may have brought on the crime by their own untactfulness," LaNauze wrote. "We have only the murderers' own statements as to the latter, and the unfortunate victims will never tell on this earth of the former."

THE REPORT COMPLETED, Corporal Wight and Ilavinik returned to the mouth of the Coppermine to join Koeha, who would guide them to the crime scene near Bloody Falls. Once there, they would walk overland to the patrol's base at Great Bear Lake, then travel from there to Fort Norman by York boat. A whaling ship would be waiting at Fort Norman to bring Ilavinik and his family north on the Mackenzie River, back to Herschel Island.[14]

On the coast, the snow did not leave until the middle of June. Wildflowers bloomed all over the rolling hills. As the ice in Bernard Harbor at last began to crack apart, thousands of eider ducks sat out near the open water. Bearded seals basked in the sun. At midnight, the sun hung on the horizon for three hours, a cool breeze blowing in from the northwest. With winter conditions finally on their way out, members of the Canadian Arctic Expedition began returning from their travels. By the end of June, Eskimos started arriving in larger numbers to fish a nearby creek for the massive spring salmon run. Using stone fish traps and spears, they managed in short order to land several thousand fish averaging eight pounds each.[15]

The last of the ice did not leave Bernard Harbor until the first week of July. At last, the crew of the *Alaska* began preparing for its trip out west. The ship had a full load of zoological, ethnological, and geological specimens, along with a year's worth of food and supplies. On the calm evening of July 13, the *Alaska* set out, pushing through ice cakes in the harbor's mouth, and began steaming west through a lead close to shore. Three miles later, the ship's progress was halted by pack ice. A strong overnight wind opened up another lead, and the ship once again pushed forward. "It was a fine sight to see the huge masses move slowly past, leaving the open ocean behind them," LaNauze wrote. Sure enough, behind the ship, huge ice floes began clogging the entrance to the harbor almost as soon as the *Alaska* left. At last, the ship entered the open ocean.

Now they had other challenges. Given the expedition's proximity to the magnetic pole, the ship's compass became increasingly unreliable. Visual navigation, using either landmarks or the sun, became the navigator's only options. With the weather still shifting violently, this was hardly optimal. Sure enough, one night a thick fog rolled in and stuck for several days. Neither the coastline nor the sun was visible. Captain Sweeney had no choice but to read his compass heading and hope it stayed at least moderately accurate. When the sun came out for a few moments the morning after the fog first set in, Sweeney discovered he had gotten turned completely around. He was off the coast of Victoria Island and heading east, back into Coronation Gulf. The ship had spun around 180 degrees. Perhaps Sinnisiak's curse—that the white man's ship would disappear under the ice—was coming true.

The *Alaska* finally pulled into harbor at Herschel Island on July 28. "It was a great relief to have our prisoners at last at a police post," LaNauze wrote. "Their conduct had been excellent, and it was indeed surprising how quickly these primitive people have adapted themselves to our ways." LaNauze briefed the station constable on the investigation, and also spoke to a surgeon who had just arrived with the mail—none of it for LaNauze— from Fort McPherson.[16]

LaNauze's good humor did not last. To begin with, the Eskimos at Herschel Island, who had been interacting with white people for years, were in the throes of a terrible influenza epidemic. "We had left behind us a strong and healthy race of people who lived a strenuous though independent life in the hitherto unexploited Arctic regions," LaNauze wrote. "At Herschel Island we were confronted with a people both physically inferior and entirely dependent on the supplies of civilization. Dr. Doyle had many patients on his hands."

Far more personally depressing was an order from headquarters. LaNauze had been reassigned. Rather than return home triumphantly with his prisoners, he would stay up north and take over the Mackenzie River subdistrict. LaNauze could barely contain his disappointment. He had already been away from home for sixteen months. The new assignment, while perhaps a vote of confidence from his superiors, nonetheless meant an extension of an already extremely trying tour of duty. The language he used in a note to his commanding officer revealed, albeit with professional tact, his frustration.

"I was of course greatly surprised, not to mention disappointed as well," he wrote to his commanding officer,

> but I would not feel justified in continuing my journey, as I am confident it is your wish for me to remain here. I fully expect to be able to tell the story of the country and its strange inhabitants to you personally. I now possess a thorough knowledge of the conditions of those parts, and if by any chance headquarters would wish to question me upon the many important points I must have omitted to mention I will only be too willing to return in February by the Dawson patrol. I was very anxious to apply for leave this coming Christmas, as my family affairs, owing to the war, are very sorrowful. However, in these stirring times duty is always first, and you may rely upon me for any duty, as I presume you are shorthanded.

LaNauze asked Anderson, the zoologist, to send a wireless message from Nome, Alaska, reporting the results of the patrol. He also put together all the documents he had written about the investigation and sent them off with Anderson as well. "I trust it will reach you safely," LaNauze wrote in a covering letter. "I have endeavored to make my reports as clear as possible regarding this important case. I will make the usual patrol to

Vilhjalmur Stefansson,
Canadian Arctic Expedition, summer 1914.

Guillaume LeRoux

Gabriel Breynat

John Hornby reading near his cabin at Great Bear Lake.

The Roman Catholic
mission at Fort Norman,
in a photo by a
member of the Douglas
expedition, 1911–12.

John Hornby and
Bear Lake Indians

George Douglas in his cabin
near Great Bear Lake.

Father Rouvière (left), in a photo by a member
of the Douglas expedition, 1911–12.

Father Rouvière and Father LeRoux
on the Bear River, 1913.

COURTESY OF NATIONAL ARCHIVES OF
CANADA/PA 120593

The Bloody Falls of the
Coppermine, in a photo by
a member of the Douglas
expedition, 1911.

A Christmas party, with (left to right)
Lionel Douglas, Father Rouvière,
August Sandburg, and George Douglas.

Copper Eskimos fishing, June 1916.

Copper Eskimos
near Coronation
Gulf (Canadian
Arctic Expedition,
1913–18).

Group of Copper Eskimos, Victoria Island
(Canadian Arctic Expedition, 1913–18).

Copper Eskimo hunters (Canadian
Arctic Expedition, 1913–18).

Inspector Charles Dearing
LaNauze of the Royal North
West Mounted Police.

Corporal Wyndham Bruce

The New Zealand
anthropologist
Diamond Jenness.

The RNWMP patrol moving through the Barren Lands.

Denny LaNauze with
Sinnisiak (center) and Uluksuk.

Wyndham Bruce with
Sinnisiak (center) and Uluksuk.

Denny LaNauze and
the RNWMP patrol.

COURTESY OF ROYAL CANADIAN MOUNTED
POLICE/NORTHWEST TERRITORIES
ARCHIVES/G-1979-034-0009

Judge Horace Harvey

COURTESY OF ALBERTA PROVINCIAL
ARCHIVES/P5265

C. C. McCaul

COURTESY OF ALBERTA PROVINCIAL
ARCHIVES/PR1973.199/1A

Back row: Patsy Klengenberg, Koeha, Ilavinik.
Middle row: Wyndham Bruce, Denny LaNauze, Constable James E. F. Wight.
Front row: Sinnisiak, Uluksuk.

Courtesy of Royal Canadian Mounted Police/Northwest
Territories Archives/G-1979-034-0008

Fort McPherson in January to meet the patrol, and will wait there for more orders."

He ended on a note that was both professional and plaintive. "The case of the missing priests is now practically out of my hands, and I have a competent staff here to guard the murderers." Since leaving Great Bear Lake, LaNauze noted, his patrol had covered, on foot, dogsled, and ship, approximately fourteen hundred miles.[17]

On September 4, a few short weeks after LaNauze had arrived, Ilavinik and his family pulled up in the whaling boat, completing the last leg of a long journey that had taken them across the Barren Lands and north via the Mackenzie River. Ilavinik had left the two corporals, Withers and Wight, at Fort Norman. As it had from the beginning, the patrol had worked like a clock. It had taken a while, but they had come across the scene of the killings.

The corporals and Ilavinik had left for the mouth of the Coppermine in late May to await the arrival of Kormik and the Rich Man, who were returning from hunting on the ice. A week later, their Eskimo guides arrived, and they quickly covered the long day's walk up the Coppermine River. As it had throughout the expediton, the volatile Arctic weather— this time in the form of a heavy rainstorm—initially prevented them from exploring the murder site. When they finally arrived, the patrol found the spot just a hundred yards from the banks of the swollen river—and fully three miles from the trail the priests should have been on in their hike to the Barren Lands. The snowstorm the day of the killings had gotten the priests and the Eskimos seriously off course.

The rising water forced the patrol to camp half a mile west. They returned the next day and quickly discovered two five-foot-long heavy timber sleds that Kormik said had belonged to the priests. Three feet from these lay part of a human jaw. The Rich Man told Wight that the jaw and the sled had been placed there by his father, who had found them closer to the river. The jaw belonged to Father LeRoux, he said.

The Rich Man then took the corporals twenty yards closer to the river.

This, he said, was where Father LeRoux had died. The spot, Wight noted, "was easily recognizable as a place where some body had been chewed by animals, as there were numerous very fine bone splinters strewn about."

As he examined the area, Wight stooped over and collected a buckle with part of a canvas belt and pieces of what appeared to have been a blanket, three pairs of pants, and a sweater. He also found a weather-worn diary, its last entry made in mid-October 1913, some French literature, and three empty rifle shells from a .44 Winchester. In all, a substantial cache of evidence.

The corporals and their guides tried, and failed, to dig a grave. The ground was still frozen solid, and they had no shovels. Instead, they marked the spot with a two-foot-high cross, a heavy sled runner stabilizing it at the base. Wight took a picture of the grave, then asked to be shown where Father Rouvière had been killed.

The Rich Man took him a hundred yards up the river to a large clay hole and said Rouvière had been laid in the bottom of it. The body was still covered in six feet of snow. Wight marked the place with another cross, snapped another photograph, and led his team south.[18]

WITH THE SEPTEMBER sunlight rapidly slipping away, it became clear to Denny LaNauze that there would be no conclusion to the case before spring. Once again, the little wheels of justice were being turned by the big wheels of Arctic weather. LaNauze and his charges settled in for another long Arctic winter.

With so many months of travel under their belts, and so few weeks of good weather ahead, waiting at Herschel Island proved exceedingly dull. Sinnisiak and Uluksak grew especially restless; they hated idleness and viewed the "Christianized" Eskimos around them with deep suspicion. As the weeks went by, LaNauze gave them plenty of work to do around the settlement, and found that physical work immeasurably improved their demeanor. As the weeks at Herschel Island turned to months, news from other parts of the world began to trickle in. LaNauze, who had been loath to forgo frontline military service in Europe, chafed at hearing of the Battle of Jutland, the evacuation of the Dardanelles, and the Irish Rebellion.

But as it had many times before, LaNauze's luck changed. In February 1917, mail arrived by police patrol from Dawson, five hundred miles away in the Yukon Territory. Among the letters was a note asking LaNauze to bring his prisoners south for trial as soon as weather permitted. Although the murder had occurred more than two thousand miles from Edmonton, the Canadian criminal code stated that crimes committed outside a province could be tried wherever it was considered convenient. LaNauze would get to see the investigation through to trial after all.

The journey to Edmonton took five months. LaNauze, Ilavinik, and the patrol packed up and headed south on the Mackenzie River. The watershed, he wrote, was "athrill" with bird life. By July 7, the patrol had left Fort MacPherson by steamer. At Fort Norman, they were greeted by Corporal Wight, Koeha, and Patsy; Koeha and Patsy had traveled overland, accompanied by D'Arcy Arden, from Coronation Gulf. Both interpreters said they would be willing to make the trip "outside."

The presence of so many Eskimos on board a white man's ship caused a minor sensation among the steamer's traditional passengers. White travelers were delighted to hear the Eskimos referring to the steamer lights as "moonlight." Koeha asked if the ship's auxiliary pump was a "pup" of the main engine. But there was also discomfort. When some passengers asked Koeha to show how he would kill a caribou, Koeha cheerfully grabbed his rifle. The white audience scattered in a panic, convinced they "were about to share the priests' fate."

As word of the patrol's impending approach reached Peace River Crossing, people turned out in droves to see the Eskimos for themselves. As the steamer *D. A. Thomas* pulled into port, a crowd strained to see LaNauze and his men, wearing their scarlet tunics, and the Eskimos, who arrived "without handcuff or chain."

"The whistle of the *D. A. Thomas*, long and loud, resounded through the valley and announced to the expectant waiting inhabitants at the village who, armed with a battery of cameras, flocking from every direction to the landing that she had at last arrived," one newspaper reported. Another article quoted a well-known local Arctic traveler, who praised LaNauze's team. "No other force of police could have done it," the man said. "Had they sent three American detectives after these men there would have been three graves up north."

If LaNauze and his men had proved remarkably adaptable in the Far North, no one could guess how the Eskimos would respond to their impending plunge into white civilization. For a people who counted on a remarkably subtle language to navigate their environment, the Eskimos had no words for what now lay before their eyes. They called the train for Edmonton "a ship that runs on dry land." Peering out the windows on the way south, they dubbed a horse a "big dog," cattle "big caribou," and an automobile a "sled that runs without dogs." On the train, the prisoners and members of the patrol dined apart from the other passengers. LaNauze noted that the Eskimos' table manners "were perfect and they quietly watched and copied our use of serviettes."[19]

As word of the Eskimos' arrest trickled back to western Canada's population centers, local newspapers quickly recognized a story with plenty of eccentric drama. At first, the coverage focused on the heroics of LaNauze's investigation. "After Journey of Two Years Police Come from Far North with Their Eskimo Captives," trumpeted a headline in the Edmonton *Morning Bulletin* on August 8, 1917. "Great Interest Taken by People of Hinterland in Famous Trip of Red-Coated Guardians of the Law—Prisoners Trust Their Captors and Follow Them Anywhere—Expected Here Thursday Night."

Initial descriptions of the prisoners and the Eskimo interpreters varied from smug to bewildered. The Eskimos were "fat, smiling, and as happy as children on a holiday," the *Morning Bulletin* reported. "The prisoners were dressed in brown overalls, grey shirts and common caps and not in their picturesque fur costumes of the north. In fact, the only evidence that they had come from a cold climate was the fact that they had their mittens on."

Sinnisiak and Uluksuk, a reporter noted, were already beginning to suffer from the heat of the south, which they complained about with "course grunts." He added, "The well-known fact that Eskimos quickly droop and die when brought within the bounds of civilization was one of the topics under discussion at the barracks following the arrival of the prisoners." To help them cope with the heat, the prisoners were given electric fans, and they were frequently seen "cooling themselves in the breeze from the machine."

Arriving in Edmonton on August 8, the prisoners followed LaNauze around "like faithful dogs, and would no more leave them than a child would leave its parents or protectors. All who have come in contact with the Eskimos as a race speak very highly of them. They say they are industrious, thrifty, hospitable, happy, clean and not envious, and in every way they are superior to the Indians."[20]

The nature of the crime, and of the men accused of committing it, also quickly became a central preoccupation. "They are governed by the same natural laws as the animals and to kill is not a crime," the Edmonton *Morning Bulletin* reported. "It is all part of that great natural law, the survival of the fittest. It is not known whether they will have any defense."

The article then cobbled together a collection of rumors and received wisdom about Eskimo culture, including their "custom" of abandoning newborn babies and leaving the elderly to die in the snow. "These Eskimos are brought down to civilization and are being tried for the crime of murdering two priests. The Eskimos, it is said, after they had cut open their victims and each had taken a bite of the liver of each of the dead men, decamped with their possessions and left the bodies to the mercy of the wolves."

This selection of ethnographic facts about the Eskimos—as a people who routinely abandoned defenseless members of their own families on one hand and killed and cannibalized holy men on the other—seemed an ominous overture to the upcoming trial, which would, after all, draw its jury from the newspaper's readers. The article predicted that the trial was "bound to attract world-wide interest—the trial of uncivilized aborigines, living in an unexplored part of the North American continent, by a jury of their 'peers'—city dwellers of Edmonton."[21]

Despite the drama of the case, newspaper editors had far more pressing news to transmit, and the story of the Eskimo killings quickly fell back into the inside of the papers. Day after day, the Great War in Europe dominated the news, with as many as a half dozen articles a day spread across the front pages alone. Indeed, had the Eskimos been able to read the papers, they would have gotten a vivid impression of the news dominating the minds of their new hosts. "Ground Heaped with German Dead Around Glencorse," screamed a headline in the Calgary *Daily Herald.* "Enemy Is Absolutely Reckless of Losses and Is Striving Vainly to Retain a Hold on Westhoek Ridge." Fighting units from Edmonton were suffering heavily. The Eskimos could be forgiven for failing to comprehend the stories. They did not have a word for war.[22]

PART THREE

CHAPTER TEN

—

As in all great narratives, history, geography,
personal adventure and mysteries intertwine.
There are misadventures, murder, and starvation,
to be sure, but spiritual powers and every kind of
humor mean that even the worst is part of being in
the best possible place, in one's own land.

—HUGH BRODY, *The Other Side of Eden*

WITH SINNISIAK AND ULUKSUK IN CUSTODY IN EDMONTON,
and Koeha, Ilavinik, and Patsy Klengenberg free to wander the city's streets,
the regional press had plenty of opportunities to observe these strange men
at close hand. A reporter for the Calgary *Daily Herald* remarked on "these
representatives of a pre-historic race" who were "clothed in their native ha-
biliments of cariboo skin trimmed with rabbit skin."[1]

To the Eskimos, the city hosting the trial was unfathomably large. The
seventeen-year-old Patsy said he had never dreamed that so many people
could exist in one place. Where did they hunt enough food to feed all
these people? Indeed, two days after they arrived, the Edmonton *Morning*

Bulletin boasted in a headline that the local phone book now had eleven thousand names—fully six hundred more than the year before. Another front-page article quoted a local professor extolling the benefits of graded "earth roads," made of clay mixed with ash and sand, which, he argued, would cost $150 per mile to build and $30 per year to maintain.[2]

The prisoners told their captors they were amazed by the white man's technology. Police officers took them one day to see a "moving picture." Another day, Ilavinik was taken to see a ballet at the Pantages Theater. Reporters focused their attention not on the performance but on the Eskimo's reaction to it. Ilavinik "evinced a lively pleasure in the performance until the ballet came on, upon which he modestly put his head down on his arms," one paper reported, "the sight of the naked limbs of the damsels offending his ideas of what a Christian Eskimo ought to look upon. Whether he did the Peeping Tom act or not can only be conjectured."

Denny LaNauze, who by now was all of twenty-eight years old, could not help but notice the precipitous drop in the self-confidence of his charges. These were people who could survive months of thirty-below weather on little more than seal meat, and here they were in an urban center, surrounded by extravagant amounts of food and shelter, and they were virtually helpless. "It was almost pathetic how they would stick to the patrol as if it was their only connecting link between their past and present life," he wrote. "Their confidence in us was childish; in us who had brought them so far on our stern errand of justice."[3]

AS THE CITY prepared for the trial, newspaper reporters scoured the city looking for "experts" to help make sense of the Eskimos. "Death Is Only Penalty Eskimo Knows; Most Primitive of Races," ran one headline. A man named William Thompson, credited as an author, traveler, and famous ethnologist, offered this: "More primitive than any race of people to be found in darkest Africa, less touched by civilization than any other humans, the Eskimos offer to ethnologists the most fertile subject for study.

If treated well the white man is as safe with the Eskimo as he is anywhere on earth. But anyone who plays them false must expect to die. Death is the only penalty the Eskimo knows. One tribe decapitates its victims. Three such cases are known."

Thompson went on to note that Eskimos brought into society did not do well on a white man's diet. Eskimos, he said, had a particular aversion to pepper and salt. "Living perilously on nothing but fish and cariboo they soon got to like soup, potatoes, beans and bread, and I can hardly see how they will ever be content again with the food they existed on before."

Moving quickly from his observations of the people of the north, Thompson then told the reporter—in apparent contradiction to what the Douglases had found—of the "limitless quantities" of copper near the Coppermine River. Thompson also said he was "enthusiastic about the great northland as a place for the tourist."[4]

AT NINE A.M., on Tuesday, August 14, a full hour before the trial began, the corridors of the Edmonton courthouse were packed with crowds eager for a seat inside. At five minutes after ten, the doors to the oak-paneled courtroom opened. People streamed in, packing the benches to their limits. Spectators who couldn't find seats squeezed onto window ledges. Prominent local attorneys lined up against the rear wall. *Rex v. Sinnisiak* was about to begin.

As soon as the principals in the case were led into the courtroom, the spectators knew they were in for some unusual theater. The players were all dressed in the outfits befitting their professions. Denny LaNauze wore a dark blue tunic and light blue breeches; his corporals wore scarlet tunics and blue breeches. In the audience, several Oblate priests wore long black cassocks with large silver crucifixes hanging from neck chains. The prisoners were dressed in caribou skins adorned with ptarmigan feathers and trimmed with white fur at the neck and waist, and sealskin boots. Lawyers for both sides wore black silk gowns and white socks. The jury wore drab gray business suits. Sinnisiak and Uluksuk, a reporter noted, had dark brown skin and eyes shaped like almonds. "The entire appearance reminds the observer immediately of that of a Japanese."

As the trial progressed, the summer temperatures in the courtroom became plainly oppressive to the Eskimos. The court provided them with buckets of ice to keep their feet cool. Even the usually staid apparatus of the courtroom reflected the strangeness of the case. The lawyers' tables were littered with books about Eskimo life, written by explorers and scientists, in case either side needed to corroborate the opposition's anthropology. On the evidence table, the audience could also see a variety of priestly accoutrements: a bloodstained cassock, several breviaries, a surplice, a crucifix, a paten, an old yellow diary half weathered away. They could also see a rusted .44 Winchester rifle and the lower half of a human jawbone. Its teeth were intact.[5]

The six members of the jury sat beyond the far end of the evidence table with their backs to the side wall. All of them were white. Their names—James E. Mould, R. B. Ferguson, John Kenwood, Alfred F. Fugl, John Harrold, H. Milton Martin—were printed in the newspaper the first day of the trial. Two prominent Catholics had been summoned for the jury, but were successfully challenged and excused. Both sides agreed that each court session should last just two hours, since, as one reporter noted, "the prisoners' constitutions would not stand a more enforced stay in the hot courtroom."[6]

Over in the oak-paneled prisoner's box, just behind the lawyer's table, Sinnisiak sat alone. Clad in his caribou skins, he began sweating the moment he entered the courthouse. The spectators could not take their eyes off him. "The scant black beard on his chin and the close-cropped black hair accentuated the pallor of his erstwhile swarthy skin," an observer named Edmund Broadus wrote. "His heavy bullet head, with its high cheek-bones, was tilted slightly forward. His narrow-set, protruberant eyes, with their small pupils and abnormally vivid whites, were fixed in an unblinking stare. What was he thinking of as he sat there, understanding no word of the lawyers' pleas and counterpleas?"[7]

The chief justice of Alberta, the Honorable Horace Harvey, made his way to the bench. "Underneath a crown of white hair, his face showed round, smooth, without a wrinkle, delicately flushed, and remote, the face of a man who had spent his life in the serene contemplation of the law," one observer reported. Here, indeed, was one of the Great White Fathers the Eskimos had heard so much about.

The prosecuting attorney was Counsel for the Crown Charles Coursolles McCaul. Denny LaNauze considered him "one of the most prominent men of the Alberta bar," but in his way, C. C. McCaul had been almost as itinerant in his chosen profession as John Hornby had been in his. McCaul was the third son of the Reverend John McCaul, the president of University College in Toronto. After graduating from college and being admitted to the bar in Ontario, McCaul had left the East in 1883 and settled near Fort Macleod to help run the 100,000-acre North Fork Ranch, one of the biggest ranches in western Canada. An avid rider and fisherman, McCaul had reportedly developed a passion for climatology, geology, and other natural sciences.

McCaul moved to Calgary in 1891 and joined the city's bar association, where he became heavily involved in revising the ordinances for the Northwest Territories. By the turn of the century, he had moved to the Yukon's Dawson City, then to San Francisco, Europe, Vancouver, back to Europe, back to San Francisco, and back to tiny Fort Macleod. "Whether his restlessness was due to domestic difficulties, or to a latent desperate need for change, or to recurrent ill health, is a matter for conjecture," a McCaul biographer wrote. "Suffice to say that on Sept. 16, 1907 he was admitted to the Law Society of Alberta and at the same time he settled down in Edmonton."[8]

BEFORE THE TRIAL began, McCaul had decided to file four separate murder charges: two against Sinnisiak for the murders of Rouvière and LeRoux, and two similiarly against Uluksuk. As the trial opened, however, and to the great surprise of the chief justice, McCaul decided to present only the charge against Sinnisiak for the murder of Father Rouvière. Sinnisiak, he argued, was both the instigator and the perpetrator of the crime. Plus, Father Rouvière was both unarmed and running away when Sinnisiak shot him. Though he didn't explicitly say so, McCaul was also hedging his bet. If he somehow managed to lose this case—but how could he?—he'd simply present charges against the Eskimos for the murder of Father LeRoux and try again.

McCaul turned to face the accused. "The Big Chief of this country says that you, Sinnisiak, killed Father Rouvière at Bloody Fall in November, 1913 in the north country," McCaul charged.

James Wallbridge and Frank Ford, the attorneys appointed by the Department of Indian Affairs to defend Sinnisiak, did not object to McCaul's decision. They entered Sinnisiak's plea.

Not guilty.[9]

As McCaul stood to begin his opening address to the court, the rumble of streetcars poured through the open courthouse windows. Taking the jury step by step through the massive police report compiled by Denny LaNauze and Wyndham Bruce, and gesturing at maps of the Barren Lands, McCaul tried to convince the jury that convicting Sinnisiak would strike a dramatic blow not only for justice but for the safety of all white men traveling through Eskimo country. Indeed, his sometimes operatic rhetoric seemed directed well beyond the walls of the courtroom. His opening statement would go on for two full hours, a performance that astonished even veterans of the Edmonton courthouse. During his address, particularly as he described the hardships the priests had suffered during their mission work, McCaul "was completely overcome by emotion," a reporter covering the case wrote. "Tears furrowed their way down his face and he was obliged to stop for several minutes, wipe his eyes and gain control of himself before he could proceed."[10]

The jury would be asked to decide "a trial which is really historic, a trial which is absolutely unique in the history of North America," McCaul said. "The long arm of British Justice has reached out to the shore of the Arctic Ocean, and made prisoners of two of the aboriginal inhabitants of the Arctic Shore." Police officers had traveled nearly three thousand miles to bring the accused before a jury of Canadian citizens. He said, "You will have before you a thrilling story of travel and adventure in lands forlorn, and I am quite sure that after you have heard all the story you will agree with me that too much credit cannot be given to the young police officer who is here, Inspector LaNauze, for his discretion and for his splendid courage in effecting their arrest."[11]

LaNauze and his men had begun their trek across the Barren Lands at Fort Norman, then made their way to the shores of the Arctic Ocean, Mc-Caul continued. Just three weeks after arriving at the coast, they not only learned the whole story of the murders but discovered the names of the Eskimos who had killed them, arrested these men, and had them committed for trial.

"I have said this is an extraordinary trial," McCaul said.

It is extraordinary in this particular way: the arrest by two or three policemen—peace officers—not soldiers—peace officers—of the two particular individuals only out of the whole tribe of the Eskimo, among whom Father Rouvière and Father LeRoux had been working and extending their missionary efforts. Contrast that with what would have happened if white men elsewhere had been massacred by a tribe of savages: there would probably have been only one or two who had effected the actual killing—let us say in Central Africa, in Borneo, in the Phillipines, or in Mexico or in (a few years ago) the Western States of America. Contrast the different methods, I say. Here, with us, British Justice reaches out to the shore of the Arctic Ocean and has picked out of the offending tribe two individual men. It says: You two men are responsible for these deaths; we do not want anything to do with the rest of the tribe; we have picked the two individuals who we hold to be responsible. What would have happened in the other cases I referred to? Retributory justice would have dispatched a military force, a punitive force, against the tribe. Retributory justice would have sent a punitive expedition and the tribe would have been decimated as a result, possibly exterminated. This appears to me an extraordinary instance of the fairness of British Justice and of the peaceful instead of the warlike methods in which it operates.

McCaul then praised the effectiveness of British justice in teaching the law to other natives in Canada: the Indians of the Plains, the Blackfeet, and the Crees, and the Chipewayans and the Sarcess and the Stoneys. "They have been educated to know that justice does not mean merely retribution, and that the justice which is administered in our Courts is not a justice of vengeance; it has got no particle of vengeance in it; it is an impartial justice by which the person who is charged with a crime is given a fair and impartial trial, and it is only after a judge—in this case, the Chief Justice—learned in the law, presiding, a jury chosen with care among representative citizens with expert counsel assigned to the prisoner, that we attempt to urge a conviction for the crime charged; and it is only after a conviction by such a trial that punishment can be awarded."

Given the pioneering nature of both the priests' missionary work and the police investigation that followed it, McCaul said, the court had little choice but to instill itself on the only remaining section of North America yet to feel the touch of British justice. His voice rising with emotion, and his eyes tearing, he moved on:

These remote savage, really cannibals, the Eskimo of the Arctic regions, have got to be taught to recognize the authority of the British Crown, and that the authority of the Crown and of the Dominion of Canada, of which these countries are a part, extends to the furthermost limits of the frozen North. It is necessary that they should understand that they are under the Law, just in the same way as it was necessary to teach the Indians of the Indian Territories and of the North West Territories that they were under the Law; that they must regulate their lives and dealings with their fellow men, of whatever race, white men or Indians, according to, at least, the main outstanding principles of that law, which is part of the law of civilization, and that this law must be respected on the barren lands of North America, and on the shores of the Arctic Ocean, and on the ice of the Polar Seas, even as far as the Pole itself. They have got to be taught to respect the principles of Justice — and not merely to submit to it, but to learn that they are entitled themselves to resort to it, to resort to the law, to resort to British Justice, and to take advantage of it, the same way as anybody else does.

The code of the savage, an eye for an eye, a tooth for a tooth, a life for a life must be replaced among them by the code of civilization. They must learn to know, whether they are Eskimo or not, that death is not the only penalty for a push or a shove, or a swear-word, or for mere false dealing; that for these offenses our civilization and justice do not allow a man to be shot or to be stabbed, to be killed or murdered. They have got to learn that even if slight violence is used it will not justify murder, it will not justify killing, and they must be made to understand that Death is not 'the only penalty that Eskimo know' or have got to know. If that is their idea, their notion of justice, I hope when the result of this trial is brought back to the Arctic regions that all such savage notions will be effectively dispelled.[12]

Given the passion of his discourse, and the difficulty in translating it, much of what McCaul said was apparently lost on the prisoners. Both Sinnisiak and Uluksuk were by now fast asleep, whether from the heat of the courtroom or the length of McCaul's discourse was hard to tell. They were shaken awake and admonished to pay attention.

Pointing to a large map, McCaul described the vastness of the Barren Lands. For reference, he also pointed out Hudson Bay and Greenland, then moved west, naming geographical features: Here is the Arctic Ocean. Here is Victoria Island. Here is Great Bear Lake. Here is Coronation Gulf. Here are the Dismal Lakes. Here is the Coppermine River.

Here is Bloody Falls, scene of the gory spectacle Samuel Hearne witnessed in 1771, when his Indian guides slaughtered a group of Eskimos "to the last man, woman and child." This, he said, is near where, 140 years later, Sinnisiak and Uluksuk murdered the priests. "It was whilst struggling to extend the Gospel to these Eskimos that these priests, Roman Catholic missionaries, Father Rouvière and Father LeRoux, met their death: a homicide with which the prisoners are charged. It was there and under those circumstances that they became martyrs to their faith."

Given that so little was known about the culture from which the suspects had emerged, McCaul felt obliged to teach the jury a few things about Eskimo culture. "You do not get any fresh vegetables in that country; every man lives by his rifle," he said. "Every white man carries his rifle, whether he is priest or sinner, ordinary citizen or policeman.

"The great importance of this trial lies in this: that for the first time in history these people, these Arctic people, pre-historic people, people who are as nearly as possible living day-to-day in the Stone Age, will be brought in contact with and will be taught what is the white man's justice," McCaul said.

They will be taught that crime will be swiftly followed by arrest, arrest by trial, and if guilt is established, punishment will follow on the guilt. You, gentlemen, can understand how important this is: white men travel through the Barren Lands; white men live on the shores of Bear Lake; white men go to the shores of the Arctic Ocean; and if we are to believe the reports of the copper deposits near the mouth of the Coppermine River, many white men more may go to investigate and to work the mines. The Eskimo must be made to understand that the lives of others are sacred, and that they are not justified in killing on account of any mere trifle that may ruffle or annoy them.

Just as it is possible to-day for any white man to travel through the country of the Blackfeet, or the country of the Crees, or the country of any of our own Indians, under the protection of the aegis of justice, so it becomes necessary that any white man may travel in safety among the far tribes of the North.[13]

Fighting off any notions that Eskimos were merely a tiny band of nomads, McCaul then launched into a discourse about their wide settlement in the North. "If any persons are under the impression that the Eskimo of Canada are a small and insignificant tribe, it is important that the jury and every other person should have that notion dispelled," he said. Outside of Greenland, where they had become "civilized" by the Christianity brought to them a thousand years ago, thousands of Eskimos could be found from the shores of Labrador and Newfoundland through Hudson Bay, on both sides of Davis Strait, all through Baffin Land, and the Arctic passages and gulfs, all along the Arctic shores of North America, "extending clear across and around the North of Yukon Territory, around to Alaska, to the Bering Sea. I myself have seen the Eskimo in their kayaks, seventeen hundred miles up the Yukon River at Dawson City."

In other words, Eskimos were a grave and gathering threat that white men would ignore at their peril. "History, gentlemen, is repeating itself," McCaul declared.

Hard on the footsteps of the explorers of North America have always followed the Roman Catholic missionaries. Our own Canadian history furnishes us with many examples of their courage, their fortitude and martyrdom. The Jesuits, in the early days of North America, and of Canada, were conspicuous for their missionary zeal, and to us in the West the names of Père Nicolet and Père Hennepin who were tortured and burned to death at St. Anthony's Falls where Minneapolis now stands, are household words. But there were others—the Sulpicians, Recollets, Ursulines—who labored among the savage tribes of Canada, and many of them were put to death by the Iroquois among the Hurons on the shores of the Great Lakes, at Michilmackinac, at Detroit, of which you all are doubtless more or less familiar.

These two unfortunate Roman Catholic missionaries go off
into the barren wilderness a thousand miles or so from their base
into the wilds alone among these savage tribes. They entrust their
lives to the good faith of the tribes among whom they are working.

McCaul told the jury he would be introducing the letters Rouvière
and LeRoux had written during their last days, as well as Rouvière's
"weather stained and wind blown diary."

"Gentlemen of the jury, whether we agree or not with the dogmas and
tenets of the Roman Catholic Church, all good Christians must acknowl-
edge and respect the zeal and fervour, the courage and fortitude of these
Catholic missionaries," McCaul urged, "and we can at least all agree that
they were sincerely anxious to spread among the remotest tribes of the
North the knowledge of God, and the divinty of Christ, and the fellowship
of the Holy Ghost. It was for the cause of Christianity, the cause of the
Kingdom of God, that Father Rouvière and Father LeRoux laid down
their lives. It is in this Christian community, and before a Judge and Jury
both sworn in the name of God to render justice, that the men charged
with their cruel and dreadful death will have to be tried."[14]

Once again, Sinnisiak had fallen fast asleep. Once again he was
awoken. McCaul picked up Rouvière's diary and offered to read.

By now, James Wallbridge, one of the defense attorneys, had heard
enough. He raised an objection. McCaul put the diary down. He would
read it later, he said. Instead, he launched into a detailed description of
the priests' final days. Anticipating another Wallbridge objection, he said
he would not, for now, provide all the details from LaNauze's massive police report. He pointed to Koeha, sitting in the audience. Upon their return from Bloody Falls, the murderers "told the whole revolting details to
the assembled crowd, including this witness who will speak of it. They
told, gentlemen of the jury, how, after they had killed these men, they
ripped them open, tore out their livers and each ate a portion: this is the
cannibalism to which I referred."

McCaul described the epic police investigation, then the "thrilling story of the arrests." He told of the suspects' trip on the *Alaska* and their arrival in Edmonton. At last, after taking up the entire morning session, McCaul sat down.

WALLBRIDGE, ASTONISHED at the length of McCaul's opening statement, stood up and demanded a new jury. Such an epic display of rhetoric left little chance for a fair trial. "I must take great exception to my learned friend's address to the Jury," Wallbridge said. "The address has been unfair, and, calculated to prejudice the Jury by reason of the inflammatory remarks of counsel and it seems to me it would be hardly right to proceed unless you empanel a new jury. He made remarks to the jury which I think were very, very unfair."[15]

Defending his rhetorical burst, McCaul explained that he needed to provide an impression of the region's geography and atmosphere. "I tried to get the jury into a properly sympathetic frame of mind at the very beginning," he said. "I am quite willing to leave myself in your Lordship's hands. I think there is no inflammable language. I put the case quite simply, stating no facts not practically admitted; not common ground."[16]

Judge Harvey rejected Wallbridge's request for a new jury. Although the opening statement was unusual in its length, he said, there was nothing in its language that could harm the case of the Eskimos. But the judge nonetheless scolded McCaul for being so long-winded, and implicitly seemed to question McCaul's experience in murder trials. "It is quite unusual to deal with such matters at the opening," he said. "Generally counsel merely outlines the case to show what evidence he is going to present. However, I think you can trust the jury on these matters. The procedure you have adopted of laying the charges separately may prolong the case for some time."

McCaul replied that he considered the case important enough that "I would be quite derelict in my duty if I did not to the best of my ability take pains and great care to open the case to the Court and Jury, even if at more than usual length."

McCaul then asked Judge Harvey for a recess. The Eskimos, he said, were suffering from the heat.

Court was adjourned until two P.M. As the prisoners were led from the courtroom to the holding cell in the building's basement, "a huge crowd of curiosity seekers eddied and surged about the building."[17]

CONTINUING HIS objections that afternoon, Wallbridge sought to derail McCaul's approach. When everything in McCaul's opening statement described two men killing two other men, why was only one suspect being tried on one count of murder? Perhaps McCaul was playing poker. If Sinnisiak was proven innocent in the murder of Father Rouvière, McCaul would have the chance to try him again for the murder of Father LeRoux. The same, apparently, would hold true for Uluksuk. This was absurd, Wallbridge argued. There should be one trial, and one trial only.

You should have raised that point long before now, McCaul retorted. The trial is already under way. Besides, it is the right of the prosecution to charge suspects individually.

Judge Harvey agreed that such an objection should have been raised during the pretrial hearing. He let the trial continue but, looking pointedly at McCaul, "urged that no unnecessary time be taken."

McCaul agreed. He had just one more thing to introduce before completing his opening statement. He produced Rouvière's damaged diary and read the short passage describing the priests's disillusionment with the Eskimos, which he hoped would set the stage for dramatic evidence he would soon present. Then McCaul sat down.[18]

RISING, WALLBRIDGE offered his own opening statement. He would be brief, especially compared to the astonishing performance the jury had just received from McCaul. By the time they heard all the evidence, he argued, the jurors would surely conclude that the killings had been justified. But before they even considered the evidence, he urged, the jury should be reminded of the unprecedented difficulties of trying the case at all. Quoting from the Magna Carta, Wallbridge acknowledged that an Eskimo could not possibly, in civilized Canada, be judged by his "peers." The best the jury could do would be "to understand his point of view."

He described the priests' final moments once again. "Any man, whether he is white or black, civilized or uncivilized, is justified in killing another in his own self-defense," Wallbridge said.

And I ask you to find that what these men did was nothing more than any of you would have done if the cause in your minds had been the same. I will not suggest that you would have come to the same conclusion, knowing your fellow beings as you know them, that the priests were going to kill you. But with these Eskimos, these primitive men, savage men of the stone age, were they not justified in the conclusion which they came to; were they not justified in believing that these men were going to kill them? Was it not reasonable, considering the extent of their mind, the little knowledge they had of the white race, the two greatest fears they had—fear of the spirits and fear of the white man, the stranger— were they not justified in believing that their lives were in danger?

Wallbridge sat down, and McCaul began calling witnesses.[19]

McCaul's first witness was Father Duchaussois, a balding, bespectacled priest who had taught the classics for ten years at Ottawa College. Duchaussois had studied in Belgium with Father Rouvière from 1901 to 1903 and had taught with him in Ottawa in 1907, prior to their assignments in the Far North. Duchaussois examined a number of photographs from the investigation and identified Rouvière's vestments, a collection of items used for conducting a mass, a diary, and a handful of letters that Rouvière had received from his superiors in the church. Duchaussois testified that Rouvière "was a gentle man but of giant strength and able to suffer enormous hardship." When Wallbridge asked him for more impressions, Duchaussois said he regarded Rouvière as "very calm, very quiet. Not very brilliant, but pretty good for theologists all the same. Docile, very, very humble. Obedient."

Wallbridge objected that not all the items produced had been found in Sinnisiak's possession, but McCaul persuaded the judge that the diaries, for example, should be considered official church documents, and were thus relevant to the case regardless of where they were found.[20]

From the pile of books on Eskimo life, McCaul handed the jury a copy of *Lands Forlorn*, the book George Douglas had recently published about his trip to the Coppermine. Inside the book, McCaul said, jurors could see a photograph of the murdered priest sitting in a canoe with Father LeRoux. McCaul elaborated from the black-and-white image. "The two were calmly floating on a blue northern lake while at the back of the picture the sun was seen half at rest."

McCaul called Corporal Bruce. Closely following the details he had provided in the police report, Bruce described his journeys along the Arctic Coast in the winter of 1915–16. With McCaul marking Bruce's progress on a map of the Arctic coast, Bruce told how he, Diamond Jenness, and Patsy Klengenberg had been welcomed into an Eskimo village. As a rule, he said, white people had nothing to fear from Eskimos. Bruce did, however, mention the séance during which he and his party had been told they would be thrown over the cliffs by the spirits and killed.

Bruce described finding some of the priests' possessions in the hands of the Rich Man, Hupo, and Kormik. He identified the octagonal-barreled .44-caliber rifle that was lying on the evidence table. Such a gun could kill a caribou at five hundred yards, he said. Fewer than ten of the 170 Eskimos he had met had possessed such weapons.

Bruce described the .22-caliber rifle the patrol had discovered in Sinnisiak's tent. He described leading Sinnisiak back to Bernard Harbor. McCaul asked him to describe Sinnisiak's confession.

"My lord," Wallbridge interrupted, accusing McCaul of leading his witness. "I might just as well state now that I intend to make an objection to this man, who doesn't understand the Eskimo language, stating what the prisoner said. Mr. McCaul can obtain whatever statements were made, if they are admissible in evidence, from the Eskimo interpreter."

McCaul said he only wanted to know the circumstance of the confession, whether Bruce had in fact heard LaNauze warn Sinnisiak about how the statement might be used. He altered his question, and Bruce said indeed LaNauze had made the warning clear. "He was told very clearly and very emphatically, not once, but if I recollect right, about three times, that he need not make any statement whatever."

DURING HIS CROSS-EXAMINATION, Wallbridge allowed Bruce to comment more fully on the subtleties of the Eskimo mind. Pointing to Sinnisiak—"the placid creature in the box," the *Morning Bulletin* called him—Wallbridge tried to show "the futility of dispensing justice by trying members of a stone-age tribe according to the principles of modern law."

"What manner of people did you find them?" Wallbridge asked.

"Very simple, kindly as a rule," Bruce responded.

"What about their intelligence?"

"Well, they are very clever in their work, but their minds don't work like ours."

"They compare more with children, don't they, than with grown up people as far as we are concerned?" Wallbridge asked.

"As regards our ways, it is a hard question to answer."

"That is what I say, as regards our ways, our methods of doing things, they are simple like children?"

"Yes," Bruce said. "They want to examine everything. They are very curious to find out about things, how it is made and how it is done."

"Would you call them primitive?"

"Yes, they are primitive."

Bruce said that he had read Stefansson's books and that he agreed with Denny LaNauze that the Eskimos were "men of the Stone Age." It was true, as Stefansson had written, that they feared strangers, but that was simply because they had met so few of them. As soon as they recognized a newcomer's good intentions, Eskimos were unfailingly hospitable. "They never feared me, because strangers are always in the minority," Bruce said.

"You gave them no cause to be afraid?"

"No."

"None whatever?"

"No."

"You were very careful not to give them any cause to be afraid?"

"Yes."

"Did you carry your gun around with you?"

"No."

"Why didn't you carry your gun?"

"I wasn't afraid of them."

"And you didn't want to arouse their enmity or suspicion?"

"No."

"You were better without it?"

"Oh, undoubtedly."

"The man who is taking a gun to go hunting creates no suspicion?"

"No."

"But the man who takes a gun to back up his dealing with the Eskimo creates more or less suspicion and distrust?"

"Yes."

Theft was not common, Bruce said. Thieves were looked down on. Over all the long months that Bruce and LaNauze had conducted their investigation among the Eskimos, very little of their gear had been stolen. Indeed, given the opportunities the Eskimos had for theft, far less had been stolen than if a white community had been living in the same vicinity.[21]

Bruce said he believed that Eskimos treated their children very well, but that child mortality rates were high—and not, contrary to stories propagated by whites, from infanticide. In the summer of 1913, he had been told, fifteen children had died from an unknown disease, possibly contracted from their white or Indian trading partners. Though some babies were "exposed" to the elements at birth, the practice was in fact rare, he said. "The natural affection of the mothers prevents this."

Murder, Bruce reported, was not common. From what he had learned from Diamond Jenness, murder was committed only during a fit of rage. Most acts of violence were handled by the murdered man's relatives, and even the impulse for revenge seemed to dissipate after a few years had passed. When asked whether the Eskimos practiced any form of punishment, Bruce replied, "Not that I know of, except they have blood feuds there."[22]

BETWEEN COURT SESSIONS, Denny LaNeuze took his charges around Edmonton, where they were observed looking "with childish interest" at city buildings. People pushed cigarettes and candy at Sinnisiak; they told LaNauze they wanted to make Sinnisiak's stay in Edmonton "one to be remembered." While in the city, newspaper reporters noted, the Eskimos "are eating the same food as their guards, and contrary to belief, would just as soon have a nice dish of ham and eggs as the cariboo and blubber of their native country."[23]

During the evening, McCaul invited Koeha and the two Eskimo interpreters over to his house for supper. They were joined by a couple, the Hendersons, and their two-year-old girl. McCaul seemed tickled by the affair. The guests laughed heartily and seemed to enjoy a good joke; better yet, he reported, all three Eskimos "had really quite respectable table manners and behaved with the utmost discretion and politeness to everybody." As Koeha prepared to leave the house, he persuaded the little girl to shake his hand, and he laughed jovially when she said, "Bye-Bye, Koeha."

Despite these expressions of collegiality, McCaul did not seem to hold Eskimos as a group in very high regard. He confessed to being impressed with native physiology, noting that "on the whole they appear to be big men, not all the stunted little chaps that one had a notion of before." One man, whose photograph was reproduced in the 1916 police report, had a face like "a handsome Roman emporer or senator."

Despite Corporal Bruce's firsthand tesitmony to the contrary, McCaul had apparently firmly made up his mind about Eskimo morals. "Eskimos seem to have no religion at all, being of the few tribes of savages who have no idea of the Supreme Being," he wrote. "They apparently place very little value on human life, and do not seem to think much more of killing a strange Indian or a white man than they would of shooting down a cariboo or musk-ox. Neither prisoner displayed the slightest compunction or regret for the murder. They are inveterate thieves, and the testimony of all travelers among them is that they will steal anything that they can lay their hands on. To get an article that is very difficult for them to procure and is of great value, such as a rifle, I do not think that some of them would hesitate to commit murder. This is probably true of the majority of the tribe."

On the manuscript on which he composed this paragraph, McCaul crossed out the last sentence.[24]

—

CHAPTER ELEVEN

Chronological sequence is of no importance to the
Aivilik. They are interested in the event itself, not in
its place within a related series of events. Neither
antecedents nor consequences are sought, for they
are largely unconcerned with the causal or telic
relationships between events or acts. They have a
capacity for recounting brief, minutely detailed legends,
but they show little interest in organizing such accounts
into wholes with a significant meaning. The details are of
interest for their own sake, rather than as part of some
larger pattern. When we inspect this mythology, we find
no emphasis on past, present or future, but a unity
embracing complexity. *Everything* is in mythology,
and everything in mythology *is*, and is together.

−EDMUND S. CARPENTER, "THE TIMELESS PRESENT IN THE
MYTHOLOGY OF THE AIVILIK ESKIMO"

THE NEXT MORNING, THE ODDITIES OF THE FIRST DAY'S
sessions were given prominent placement in the local newspapers. "Blood
Stained Cassocks, and Robes and Bibles Produced in Evidence Against
Eskimo," blared a headline in the Edmonton *Morning Bulletin.* Though
it hardly seemed possible, the coverage brought out an even larger crowd
for the second day of the trial. To accommodate the extra spectators, many
of them women leading children by the hand, additional folding chairs
were brought in and placed in front of the railing and to the side of the

judge's platform. When the commotion grew too loud, Judge Harvey issued a warning from the bench and ordered several women to take their
children outside. A second crowd formed outside the courtroom to watch
the Eskimos exit when court was adjourned for lunch.[1]

For the second day of the trial, Sinnisiak and Uluksuk traded their native clothing for blue denim jumpsuits. McCaul picked up where he had
left off. He entered into evidence a piece of a priest's robe stained with
blood. The director of the provincial laboratory, Dr. H. C. Jamieson, testified that it was in fact human blood. McCaul called Constable James
Wight, who corroborated much of what the jury had heard about the investigation, from its departure from Fort Norman in 1915 to its comple-
tion in the spring of 1916. Wight described visiting Bloody Falls, and he
identified photos from *Lands Forlorn*, George Douglas's book about his
trip. He spoke about finding a pair of spent .44-caliber rifle cartridges, bits
of wool clothing and a belt buckle, and a human jaw, its teeth "strong and
compact."

Cross-examined by Wallbridge, Wight said he made the trip from the
mouth of the Coppermine to the site of the murder in a single day—and
that they had not been making very good time. Apparently trying to compare this to the nearly three days it had taken the priests to cover the same
distance, Wallbridge asked if the miles between the river mouth and the
murder site had been easy to walk.

"Anybody could have made that on one day's travel from the mouth of
the river?" Wallbridge asked.

"Yes."

"With comparative ease?"

"Yes, quite easy."

Like Corporal Bruce, Wight said he never traveled with a gun in his
hand. "We didn't want to cause any fear among them," he said.

McCaul offered to read the statement Sinnisiak had given to Denny
LaNauze during the makeshift preliminary hearing up at Bernard Harbor.
Wallbridge fought this move aggressively. How could Sinnisiak possibly
have understood the notion that whatever he said could be "used against

him"? Judge Harvey agreed that the statement should not be called a "confession," but he said he would allow it to be read as long as it was corroborated by further evidence. Harvey asked McCaul to call Ilavinik first, so that he could describe the circumstances under which the statement had been given. On the stand, Ilavinik said he had told Sinnisiak how the police patrol had traveled a great distance to learn the fate of the missing priests and that the patrol wanted to hear what Sinnisiak could tell them. If Sinnisiak didn't want to speak, Ilavinik had said, he didn't have to. Ilavinik said he had repeated this twice. The third time, after Ilavinik had asked Sinnisiak to "speak straight, and not with two tongues," the suspect had finally answered. "I want to speak," he had said.[2]

When Denny LaNauze corroborated this story, Judge Harvey ruled that Sinnisiak's statement was admissable. As the jury and the audience in the courtroom prepared to hear the ghastly story, reporters scrambled to take down every word. Some papers printed Sinnisiak's statement in its entirety.

"I was stopping at the mouth of the Coppermine river and was going fishing one morning," the statement began.

A lot of people were going fishing. When the sun had not gone down I returned to camp and saw that the two priests had started back up the river. They had four dogs; I saw no other men.

I slept one night. Next morning I started with one dog to help people coming from the south. All day I walked along and then I left the river and travelled on land; I was following the priests' trail. I met the priests near a lake; when I was close to them, one man came to meet me.

The man Ilogoak [Father LeRoux] came to me and told me to come over to the camp. Ilogoak said 'If you help me pull the sled, I will pay you in traps.' We moved off the same day I arrived, to be near wood. Uluksuk was with me and we pulled the sled. We could not make the trees; it was hard work, and we made camp.

The next day we started back and the priests were going ahead;

it started to storm and we lost the road. After that the dogs smelt something and Uluksuk went to see what it was, and I stayed behind. Uluksuk found that it was a cache of the priests and told me to come over. As soon as we came there the priests came back. Ilogoak was carrying a rifle; he was mad with us when we had started back from their camp, and I could not understand his talk.

I asked Ilogoak if he was going to kill me, and he nodded his head.

Ilogoak said "Come over to the sled," and he pushed me with his hand.

The priests wanted to start again, and he pushed me again and wanted me to put on the harness and then he took his rifle out on top of the sled. I was scared and I started to pull.

We went a little way and Uluksuk and I started to talk and Ilogoak put his hand on my mouth. Ilogoak was very mad and was pushing me. I was thinking hard and crying and very scared and the frost was in my boots and I was cold. I wanted to go back, but I was afraid. Ilogoak would not let us. Every time the sled stuck, Ilogoak would pull out the rifle. I got hot inside my body and every time Ilogoak pulled out the rifle I was very much afraid.

I said to Uluksuk, "I think they will kill us." I can't get back now. I was thinking I will not see my people any more, I will try and kill him. I was pulling ahead of the dogs. We came to a small hill, I took off the harness quick and ran to one side and Ilogoak ran after me and pushed me back to the sled. I took off my belt and told Ilogoak I was going to relieve myself, as I did not want to go to the sled. After that I ran behind the sled, I did not want to relieve myself. Then Ilogoak turned round and saw me; he looked away from me and I stabbed him in the back with a knife. I then told Uluksuk, "You take the rifle." Ilogoak ran ahead of the sled and Ulusuk went after him. The other white man wanted to come back to the sled; I had the knife in my hand and he went away again.

Ulusuk told me, "Go ahead and put your knife in him." I said to Uluksuk, "Go ahead you. I fixed the other man already." The father fell down on his back. Uluksuk struck first with the knife and did not strike him; the second time he got him. The priest lay down and was breathing a little, when I struck him across the face with an axe I was carrying; I cut his legs with the axe; I killed him dead.

After they were dead I said to Uluksuk, "Before when white men were killed they used to cut off some and eat some." Uluksuk cut up Ilogoak's belly; I turned around, Uluksuk gave me a little piece of the liver, I eat it; Uluksuk eat too.

We covered up both bodies with snow when we started to go back.

We each took a rifle and cartridges. We took three bags of cartridges each. We started back in the nighttime. We camped that night. Next morning we got back to camp as soon as it was light. I went into Kormik's tent. Kormik was sleeping and I woke him up. I told him I kill those two fellows already. I can't remember what Kormik said. Kormik, Koeha, Angibrunna [sic], Kallun, Kingordlik went to get the priests' stuff. They started in the morning and came back the same night. I can't tell any more. If I knew more I would tell you. I can't remember any more.

McCaul paused for a moment, to let the power of the testimony trail off. As rapt as Denny LaNauze had been when he'd heard these words on the Arctic coast, the jury and the audience were more so in the formal setting of a courtroom. Sinnisiak's words were devastating. But how they would affect the jury's decision was impossible to tell.

At last, Denny LaNauze took the stand. Methodically, and with little melodrama, the young police officer described the long investigation and told of meeting Corporal Bruce on the Arctic coast in the spring of 1916. He went over many of the details the jury had already heard several times. He told of Sinnisiak's arrest. "The first thing I saw was a man sitting at the far end of the tent," he said. "He was engaged in the manufacture of a bow, and he sat there trembling. In fact, he was shaking all over."

LaNauze said the Eskimos around Sinnisiak had been remarkably circumspect about the arrest. "I simply explained our mission, and rather curious to relate, the people were all on our side. They turned around [to Sinnisiak] and said 'You must do what the white man tells you; you have got to go with them,' and after that we got quietly away from the camp."

During cross-examination, James Wallbridge saw an opening. Like the other officers, LaNauze said he always kept his gun hidden away on his sled, and that without exception the Eskimos had treated him with civility. Of all the people he had met, only Kormik had ever tried to hide anything from the investigation. Wallbridge asked LaNauze to tell the court what he could about the probable mindset of the Eskimos in the moments before the murders. What became clear, especially by comparison to McCaul's hyperbolic oratory, was that LaNauze had pursued his suspects with no preconceived notions about their guilt or innocence. He had not sought them to broadcast a message to Eskimos generally. He was not an ideologue. He was a peace officer. And contrary to what those in the urban judicial system might expect, he had developed a great admiration for the skills, resilience, and generosity of the people among whom he had come to live. Moreover, despite the patrol's expressed intent of arresting two of their own people, the Eskimos had never treated the white men with anything but respect and dignity. Exactly what their relationship had been with the priests was up to the lawyers—and the jury—to decide.

"The story you got from all of them," Wallbridge asked, "as well as the story you got from the prisoner, the information you got, was that these men had killed the priests out of fear?"

"Out of fear?" LaNauze repeated.

"Yes."

"No," LaNauze said. "I don't know."

"Your report says that they had killed them in self-defense," Wallbridge pressed.

"I said they might have, I think," LaNauze said.

"They might have?"

"They might have."

Questioned about Sinnisiak's arrest, LaNauze said that Sinnisiak was sure he would be killed "on the spot." He said Sinnisiak had been so afraid that he would be killed that he had refused to sleep for forty-eight hours.

"And it was only by gradual persuasion and kindness you persuaded him to come to any different conclusion?" Wallbridge asked.

"We just used a little—"

"You used kindness?"

"We didn't urge him at all."

"You used kindness and a great deal of tact, I think, Inspector, is that right?"

"We just carried out our duty ordinarily as I would in making any arrest."

Wallbridge then reached for a copy of Stefansson's *My Life with the Eskimos*. He read long sections of it, mostly describing Stefansson's groundbreaking "discovery" of the Copper Eskimos in 1910. " 'Their existence on the same continent with our populous cities was an anachronism of ten thousand years in intelligence and material development,' " he read. Sinnisiak is not a descendant of a Stone Age race, Wallbridge said. He is a Stone Age man himself. He continued reading. " 'Like our distant ancestors, no doubt, these people fear most of all things the evil spirits that are likely to appear to them at any time in any guise, and next to that they fear strangers.' "

Wallbridge asked LaNauze if this was a fair statement. Once again, LaNauze demurred. At every turn, it seemed, he refused the offer of a rhetorical burst.

"Well, Stefansson is an authority," LaNauze replied.

The Eskimos first saw a white man in 1910, Wallbridge reminded the jury, and could not be expected to make the jump from the Stone Age to the twentieth century in the three short years it took for the priests to arrive. They were being brought to account for the murder of the priests, while back in the early history of Canada the Iroquois had killed numerous missionaries, traders, and trappers "without being hauled off to England to answer for their deeds."

Wallbridge then asked LaNauze about a comment from his own report: "Their own defense of being ill-treated is their strongest point, and the prosecution has no witness that will deny this."

"You were unable to find any?" Wallbridge asked

"No."

"And if a white man, a stranger, holds a gun on an Eskimo, the Eskimo hasn't any other notion but that it is going to be used? There is no doubt?"

"No doubt."

Wallbridge then read another line from the police report. " 'The unfortunate priests may have been the victims of a premeditated murder for the possession of their rifles and ammunition, or may have brought on the crime by their untactfulness.'

"I want to know whether you had any information that would suggest this untactfulness," Wallbridge demanded.

"Yes, I thought so possibly by the prisoner's statements," LaNauze said. Wallbridge sat down.[3]

McCaul called Koeha to the stand. The Eskimo, one reporter noted, "presented a most fantastic appearance, with long straight hair hanging down to his shoulders, and a stiff beard and moustache." Another account said he looked "not unlike a Japanese." Koeha had been watching the proceedings with an intense curiosity since they began, and now that he was striding onto the stage he began imitating the gestures he had been seeing. He walked to the witness stand, placed his hand on the rail, and cast his eyes dispassionately on the jury. He wiped his brow with a handkerchief. The clerk administered the oath to both Koeha and the interpreter, Ilavinik. Neither one, it appeared, could make sense of the legal rhetoric being read to them. Though he could not read English, Koeha did not hesitate to place his bare hand on the Bible. With Ilavinik translating, he promised not to "speak with two tongues." Both Eskimos bent over and kissed the Bible.

Koeha seemed amused when McCaul asked his age. What difference did it make? he asked. He said Stefansson was the first white man he had ever seen. Asked for his impressions about white man's civilization, Koeha told McCaul he "was rather in doubt as to whether a horse was a big dog or a big caribou."

Sitting among the spectators, a young American lawyer raised his eyebrows. Edwin Keedy, who would go on to become a professor and later dean of the University of Pennsylvania's law school, was taking close notes. Imagine how difficult it would be to present a story in such a formal setting when you didn't even speak the system's language, Keedy thought. Forget about understanding the British judicial system; Koeha couldn't even understand the English language. How odd, he thought, to have a man swear on a Bible that he could not read, let alone comprehend. Keedy's mind immediately flashed back to a Canadian trial in 1904, when a Chinese prisoner named Lai Ping had written his name on a piece of paper and, burning the paper, said his soul would burn similarly if he did not tell the truth. His method of swearing was held to be valid. Two years earlier, in 1902, another Chinese had been on trial for murder, and a witness named Chong Fon Fi had offered to swear by the burning-paper method, but his lawyer had objected, saying there was an oath even more solemn: "the chicken oath."

Once the witness signed his name, a cock was procured. Then the court and jury adjourned to a convenient place outside the courthouse, where the witness read an oath: "Being a true witness, I shall enjoy happiness and my sons and grandsons will prosper forever. If I falsely accuse [the prisoner], I shall die on the street, Heaven will punish me, earth will destroy me, I shall forever suffer adversity, and all my offspring be exterminated. In burning this oath I humbly submit myself to the will of Heaven which has brilliant eyes to see." The witness wrapped the oath in joss paper, laid the cock on the block, and chopped its head off.[4]

Securing testimony from an Eskimo would have its own difficulties. As everyone from Vilhjalmur Stefansson and Diamond Jenness to Corporal Bruce and Denny LaNeuze knew, Eskimos tended to tell stories in a meandering, complex manner that often frustrated Western listeners wishing they would just get to the point. Their stories wandered back and forth in time, slipped easily off onto tangents that to white ears sounded irrelevant, and would often tumble into and out of strong emotions during the telling. Men were known to spontaneously start weeping in the middle of a sad story and then, when the emotion passed, carry on with the rest of the tale. When a man wept, his audience would often weep with him. Eskimos "have very little of the stoicism so characteristic of the American Indian," Jenness had written. And British courts were hardly known to encourage emotional outbursts. If anything, the entire system was designed to examine moments of passion with supreme, highly formalized disinterest. Dry intellect was favored over visceral display; direct, unembroidered fact was given precedence over loose or meandering storytelling. Answers from witnesses were best when they were limited to a single word: yes or no.

But in a court, where jurors relied more than anything on a vivid portrayal of events they had not themselves seen, who could say which was a more accurate method of description? What in life actually unfolded in a linear manner? What crime, especially one as complex and violent as this one, occurred apart from a long chain of events, independent of a complex web of causes? In a courtroom, where testimony was spoken and not written and read, which would provide a more reliable story: the strictly linear Western convention or a more flexible oral tradition? True, oral histories tended to blur experience and metaphor, myth and fact, but people steeped in the tradition had no trouble navigating these tales. How did the priests come to such an end? How long do you have? Truth be told, the story of the priests' murder could spin back in time to include the whole history of colonization, of everything leading up to that one terrible moment. What of that was relevant, and what wasn't? In one later case, a court had to sit and listen to native testimony for 243 days. The court transcript filled 126 volumes.[5]

From the beginning of his testimony, Koeha's tendency to veer from McCaul's questioning frustrated both the prosecutor and the newspaper reporters trying to get their stories straight. Koeha took five full minutes to tell the court how long ago the crime had occurred, and even then he arrived at the right year only by counting on his fingers. The Eskimo, one reporter concluded, "appeared to have an exceptionally simple mind."

"Do you remember the time the priests were killed?" McCaul asked.

"Mr. McCaul, I suggest that you don't refer to them as 'the priests,' " Wallbridge interrupted. "He doesn't refer to them by 'priests.' He mentions them by name."

Good suggestion, McCaul said. "Do you know who killed them?" McCaul asked Koeha.

"Just a moment," Wallbridge said. "I think that is a very unfair question, my lord. If he saw somebody kill them, or perhaps if somebody told him that he killed them there might be something to it, but supposing he heard it from some other Eskimo, that it came indirectly, perhaps from three or four people, that a certain person killed another person, and he is asked that question in the form of which Mr. McCaul asks it he immediately says yes, so-and-so did it, and when he is asked, how do you know, well, so-and-so told me. That, my lord, would be a very improper way of getting at the evidence. My learned friend knows a method of getting at it which is not objectionable."

"With a witness of this mental calibre it is very difficult," McCaul replied.

"It is very much worse, because a witness of that calibre is more apt to give an answer in the form of the question," Wallbridge said.

"I think I should be allowed to lead this witness to a certain extent," McCaul said.

The questioning continued. McCaul asked that questions be translated first into pidgin English by a member of the Royal North West Mounted Police, then given to Ilavinik for translation. Koeha described hearing of the murders, and of the tense moments with Kormik before the priests started their final journey south. Ilavinik, who had translated successfully for Stefansson and LaNauze for years, was perplexed by McCaul's formal rhetoric, and by the aggressive tone in his voice. What, exactly, was he supposed to translate? The words or the emotions behind them?

"Did you see Kormik take the rifle?" McCaul asked.

"I saw Kormik take the rifle, this rifle, and Kormik give Uluksuk old rifle .44," came the response.

"At that time where was Sinnisiak when Kormik take the rifle from Uluksuk?"

"I saw him at the same place, Sinnisiak."

"At the same time?" Wallbridge interrupted.

"That was the question," McCaul said.

"My lord, I direct that question to be answered whether or not Sinnisiak was there at the same time," Wallbridge said. "He said he saw Sinnisiak at the same place, but he didn't say he saw him at the same time."

By now, Ilavinik's head was spinning. The speech was too fast, and too strange, for him to understand. He turned to Koeha. They spoke in low, guttural tones. Ilavinik tried again to translate. Again he had no luck. To at least one of the spectators, Ilavinik's mind "seemed to have lost the pliancy which both Stefansson and LaNauze attributed to it. The poor fellow was sadly muddled by the complex sentences of those who, through him, sought to question the witness."

Perhaps things weren't quite so simple. As the Catholic priests and the constables alike had discovered, translating one language into another is never simple; indeed, some linguists doubt whether meaning can ever be fully understood by someone who hasn't been steeped in a language's subtleties since birth. How could an Eskimo understand the centuries of Christian ritual behind the image of the cross? How could an Eskimo comprehend the bottomless body of case history defining the difference between murder and manslaughter? If the Eskimos had developed a vast vocabulary to help them grasp the intricacies of their world, so had these white men. Translating a language as subtle as the one spoken by the Eskimos into a language as formal and stylized as that used in a courtroom would have been trying even to a scholar with decades of experience. Over by the defense table, the only other person in the room able to understand both languages was seventeen-year-old Patsy Klengenberg. He leaned over and whispered something to James Wallbridge.

"My lord, the interpreter Patsy informs me that this interpreter is putting [the witness] through the third degree, is accusing him of lying, and trying to get him to give an answer which the Eskimo doesn't want to give."

Judge Harvey reacted gruffly. "Ilavinik, just ask him the question that counsel give you," he said. "Do not say any more to him. Just get him to answer that. You can explain that to him, but do not ask him anything else, and do not say anything else to him."[6]

Exasperated, the court finally asked Ilavinik to let Patsy Klengenberg take his place. Patsy's eyes darted across the courtroom. Turning to Koeha, he managed to make himself understood. The questioning continued.

"Had the priests been pretty good to the Eskimo, to the Huskies?" McCaul asked.

"Yes, they had been good," Koeha replied. Kuleavik (Rouvière) had taught the people to fish with nets.

"Did you look at Ilogoak's [LeRoux's] body to see how he had been killed?"

"I didn't look. I only saw the cut here." Koeha gestured lengthwise along his chest. "It was snowed up. I couldn't see much."

Koeha told of the things he had taken from the murder scene: a tin can, a pair of scissors, spoons, a pair of boots, and a cod line. Kormik and Angebrunna took everything else, he said.

McCaul sat down. Wallbridge stood for his cross-examination.

"You heard about Kormik taking one of the priests' rifles," he said. "Were you aware that the priests loaded another gun and went to Kormik's tent and demanded the first rifle?"

"I saw them put cartridges in the gun outside," Koeha said.

"Who did you see putting cartridges in the gun outside—Ilogoak?"

"Ilogoak."

"Did you see him go towards the tent with the gun with the cartridges in it?"

"My wife and another man told them not to go into the tent."

"Ilogoak loaded a gun, and he was going to go to Kormik's tent, but your wife and another man held him back and wouldn't let him go, is that right?"

"Yes."

"Did they think he was going to shoot Kormik?"

"Yes."

Koeha described meeting Stefansson and R. M. Anderson, Joe Bernard, and John Hornby before he met Rouvière and LeRoux.

"Did you know the first time you saw Ilogoak that he was a priest, a missionary?" he asked. "Do you know what a priest is?"

Koeha said he did not.

"Did you know Kuleavik was a priest?"

"I didn't know."

"Did you think they were trappers or traders?"

"I think they come down for caribou, think they were hunters and traders."[7]

Asked if he had any more witnesses, McCaul said no. He would not call Sinnisiak. He would rest his case as it stood.

BEGINNING HIS defense, James Wallbridge called Sinnisiak to the witness stand. Wallbridge turned to Patsy Klengenberg.

"Tell him, first, I want him to speak to the big chief, and I want him not to be afraid, and to say everything. You tell him that. Tell him not to be afraid because all these people are here, to just talk to me as if he was talking to me alone."

Sinnisiak agreed, and kissed the Bible. Told he was not compelled to speak, Sinnisiak replied directly:

"I want to speak."

Sinnisiak testified that before the priests arrived, he had seen three white men: Stefansson and two prospectors. Though he didn't mention his name, or the circumstances surrounding their confrontation, one of the men was almost certainly John Hornby, with whom Sinnisiak had fought over the fishing line. Going step by step, Sinnisiak repeated the details of the killing exactly as he had told them to Denny LaNauze.

Wallbridge argued that despite LaNauze's obvious empathy for the prisoners, Sinnisiak's testimony had been given under extreme duress. How could it not have been, considering his custody in the hands of strange and well-armed men? Wallbridge asked Sinnisiak to go over the days and hours leading up to the murder. He asked him to reiterate how he and Uluksuk had been forced, under threats, to drag the priests's sleds, and how Father LeRoux had threatened to kill them each time they stopped pulling, or pulled slowly, or got stuck in the snow.

Sinnisiak repeated how he had started to cry and had gotten very cold. He told the jury again how he'd feared that he would be killed, or forced to live in a strange country, and that he would never again see his people.

"When we started off—every time we tried to get out of the harness the priest had his gun and was going to shoot me," Sinnisiak said. He then described the killing. He described chopping off one of the priests' feet.

"Why did you eat a piece of the dead man's liver?" Wallbridge asked.

"Because I heard from my grandfather," Sinnisiak said. "I heard about it from my grandfather."

"Did you know what it was going to do for you to eat the liver?" Wallbridge asked.

"The man might get up again if I didn't eat his liver."

"Do you like to talk about spirits?"

"I don't know."

"You don't know what? Do you like to talk about spirits?"

"I don't know how to speak about spirits."

"Do you know about spirits? Do you know anything about spirits?"

"I know about spirits."

"Has the eating of the liver anything to do with spirits?"

"I think maybe the spirits make the man alive."[8]

Wallbridge rested his case.[9]

The story's impact on the jury was hard to decipher. The reporters in the room, however, ate it up. "Crowded Court Hears Gruesome Confession of the Eskimos' Crime," the Edmonton *Morning Bulletin* told its readers in a marathon three-deck headline. "Story of Sinnisiak to Inspector LaNauze Describes in Plain Language, Direct and Matter of Fact in Its Simplicity, the Tragedy in the Far Northland—Gist of It Is That Eskimo Concluded Fr. LeRoux, Who Was Angry, Was Going to Kill Him, and He Resolved to Kill Both Missionaries." The accompanying article reproduced the entirety of Sinnisiak's description of the murder.

At least one man seemed to feel that its energy may have provided all the power he needed. When Sinnisiak completed his testimony, C. C. McCaul said he would not cross-examine. The witness's testimony was the same as the statement he had given at Bernard Harbor, McCaul observed, and that was good enough for him. McCaul said he would "go to the jury on the evidence in the shape in which it is."

JAMES WALLBRIDGE's closing comments lasted more than an hour. Given the degree to which his client had wilted under the Edmonton heat, he wondered aloud if Sinnisiak might have been more honorably treated if he had been killed at the moment of his arrest.

"Sinnisiak sits in his box," Wallbridge said.

> He sees with his eyes what is taking place, but he does not comprehend. He cannot understand what we are doing. It is a great question whether a man of a stone-age tribe, a man who hunts for his daily food, can in common justice have his deeds judged by the standards of modern civilization.
>
> These Eskimos are men absolutely unlettered, knowing nothing of civilization except such as they have gathered from the half dozen men they have seen in their lifetime up to the time of the tragedy. This must be to them a most strange proceeding, but probably not more strange than the other sights they have seen. Build-

ings like our Court House must be real mountains. Horses look like big caribou, and trains like ships that run on land.

The great charter of English liberties which we call the Magna Carta was passed many years ago, and provided that every man should be judged not by his superiors, but by his peers. Now we cannot judge this man by his peers. We have none of his peers here, if "peers" means "equal in his own land," but we can try in our minds to approach something of the same by trying to understand his point of view; and when you judge whether the conduct of these men was reasonable or unreasonable try, if possible, to put yourselves in the position of these untutored savages and say where *in their minds* they were justified or not."

Every killing was not murder, he reminded the jury. Given Sinnisiak's fear that he would be killed by the priests, his actions should be considered justifiable homicide. Sinnisiak clearly considered his own actions justified. It was the priests who were carrying loaded guns, not the Eskimos, and in any case Sinnisiak had no idea that the men were priests. He only knew they were white men with guns. Sinnisiak acted out of fear, not premeditation. If the Eskimos had wanted to kill the priests, they would have done so the night before, when the priests were asleep in their snowhouse.

"Any man, whether he is white or black, civilized or uncivilized, is justified in killing another in his own defense," Wallbridge said.

If he does kill in self-defense, that killing is what we call justifiable or excusable homicide. It is not an uncommon thing and it is not the first time the defense of justifiable homicide has been raised in our courts; and it is not necessary that the man who kills another in his own defense should be in immediate fear of death. As long as he reasonably believes that he is in danger of bodily harm or violence, then he is justified in defending himself up to the point of taking the life of another. And I ask you to find that what these men did was nothing more than any of you would have done if the cause in your minds had been the same. Now, I do not pretend to say that you would, under the circumstances, have believed that the priests were going to kill you. I will not suggest that you would have come to the same conclusion, knowing your fellow beings as you know them, that the priests were going to kill you. But with these Eskimos, these primitive men, savage men of the stone age, were they not justified in the conclusion which they came to; were they not justified in believing that these men were going to kill them? Was it not reasonable, considering the extent of their mind, the little knowledge they had of the white race, the two greatest fears they had—fear of the spirits and fear of the white man, the stranger—were they not justified in believing that their lives were in danger?

Wallbridge's remarks ended with a burst of hyperbole that several reporters featured in their stories the next day. He declared that "it would be the greatest crime in the world's history to condemn Sinnisiak to death for doing something he thought absolutely necessary, and which he had made no effort to conceal. The only evidence against him was his own statement of the crime."

IN HIS CLOSING statement, C. C. McCaul argued that Sinnisiak was entitled to the "advantage" of British justice, and not the "slaughter" that "the fool prospector" John Hornby had promised would result from the murder of a white man.

"My friend stated my opening address was inflammatory because I was unable to refer to the shocking death of these men without showing a little feeling," McCaul said. "I don't think a man could make the bare recital of those facts at all, unless he is so cold-blooded as to have the heart of a stone, could consider the awful position of these men and the awful death they suffered without at least feeling a little bit of emotion in regard to it."

McCaul dismissed Wallbridge's claims that the Eskimos should be treated as "stone-age, ignorant men, childlike men in many ways," and that their crimes should be judged somehow differently from crimes committed by an "ordinary white man." The jury must remember that the law that they were charged with considering was British, not native. "We cannot try these men according to the principles of Eskimo justice," he said. If we did, "they should have been properly murdered, an eye for an eye, a tooth for a tooth, a life for a life. Murder does not justify murder, but it does justify what we hope to be a fair and impartial trial."[10]

McCaul argued that Sinnisiak's actions had been premeditated. He had, after all, talked his plans over with Uluksuk. Not only that, he had confessed. But even without the confession, McCaul said he would not have been afraid to ask the jury to convict on the circumstantial evidence of the case. Koeha's testimony alone was enough to secure a conviction. McCaul said he was "shocked" to hear Wallbridge's suggestion that the prisoners should not be blamed for the murders. "I am not merely surprised, I am absolutely shocked to hear that come from a civilized human being who has heard the evidence and heard the circumstances of this trial," he said. "Premeditation, which is necessary to distinguish this case from manslaugher, was proved. You need not search for the motive, whether revenge or the object of stealing the rifle; we have the evidence of premeditation given clearly and squarely in the fact that these men discussed how they were to obtain their opportunity of killing the priests. That is premeditation."

Simple fear was not enough to justify a killing, McCaul argued. Killing a person required "the actual fear of immediate death, not merely injury."

"What are the facts?" McCaul continued.

These two savages, these two cannibals—this man says that he ate a portion of the liver, and adds a most extraordinary statement which opens up an enormous field for enquiry afterwards—information apparently he got from his grandfather. He says, because they used to kill white men they used to eat parts of them, a custom, a custom to kill white men by these Eskimo, and a custom to eat them. My friend asked you to admire their courage and bravery, the courage of a man who sneaked up behind the priest and drove his knife into his back when he wasn't watching, the courage of two men who threw the priest down, trampled him to death, stabbed him, took his rifle away from him, the courage and bravery my friend asked you to admire, the courage and bravery, my friend's idea of the man who fires at the poor fleeing priest, running over the snow, and kills him, and the two men come up, and he is stabbed and haggled with an axe. Brave men, Mr. Wallbridge said. Oh! Mr Wallbridge says, what bravery, what courage![11]

Once McCaul had finished, Judge Harvey charged the jury. His language would become one of the trial's most controversial legacies. "Gentlemen of the jury," he began. "The crime of which the prisoner is accused is the most serious that is known to our law, and naturally that will impress upon you the solemnity of your duty, because it is on you, and you only, that the duty is cast of determining whether or not he is guilty or not guilty of the charge."

The heart of the case, he said, was based almost entirely on Sinnisiak's confession, in which he admitted to the killing. It was up to the jury to determine whether the act was murder or justifiable homicide. There was no evidence, the judge said, that Father Rouvière had ever threatened the Eskimos. This made a plea of self-defense out of the question. Furthermore, Harvey asserted, the jury should feel no compunction about returning a guilty verdict. He would personally recommend that a death sentence not be carried out, and he felt quite confident his recommendation would be accepted by Canada's governor-general. Most likely, the two prisoners would be sent back north, and would show through their experience that, as one reporter put it, "the lives of white man were not to be trifled with."

To Wallbridge's astonishment, Harvey made no bones about his own feelings. "The fact that he is a poor, ignorant, benighted pagan," the judge remarked,

who comes from beyond the borders of our civilization, does not stand in the way of his receiving all the protection that our law can give any person charged with the same offense. As you have seen he has been furnished with counsel, not some junior counsel who might be desirous of getting the experience of defending an important case, but he has been provided as counsel with one of the leaders of the bar, who has left no stone unturned during the course of this trial to see that no unfair advantage was taken of the accused, and to see that everything that might be brought out in his favor should be brought out. Owing to the circumstances of this case, the particular circumstances, I instructed the sheriff, when empanelling the jury, to see that no person was put on the panel of jurors except men of the highest standing in the community. I thought it only fair that the prisoner should have the best that our country can afford in answer to a charge such as this.

Much has been suggested in the present case about the prisoner's lack of knowledge of our law and our customs, and his own custom. Of course, that applies to a greater or less extent to many of the foreigners who have come to our country; the Indians, although they have to become gradually more and more accustomed to our laws, but that cannot be dealt with by the court such as this in considering the liability for the crime. In law a person must be considered liable. In fact, there is a very great difference. That is a matter to be dealt with in the matter of punishment.

Harvey argued against the claim of self-defense, saying,

The question then would seem largely to be one between culpable homicide and excusable or justifiable homicide. Now, homicide is justifiable if it is done in self-defense, but self-defense does not mean prevention. We have, of course, in the last two or three years had pressed upon us very frequently the question of self-defense in a way that is more or less applicable to this. Germany has declared that she is making this war as a war of self-defense. Assuming that she is honest, all of us consider it is not self-defense as we look upon self-defense. It may be for the purpose of preventing what she fears, but it is not defending herself against an attack because she attacked first. That perhaps is her view of self-defense, and that is a view of self-defense that has been advanced as an excuse for killing within our own memory. We have accounts of it in the early unsettled portions of the country where the law is not strictly enforced of people taking the law in their own hands. Where they feared, and had good reasons to fear, men might kill them, they kill the person to prevent it. That is not self-defense. That is an attempt to prevent, but it is not under our law permissible. Now, the self-defense, as it is known to our law, that is, the excuse for the killing, is the defense against attack, a defense against an assault of some sort.

When I say that, I do not want you to misunderstand me. A man might point a gun which is loaded at you and which he has the ability to discharge and kill you. You would be justified, in self-defense, in shooting him first if you could prevent that, if circumstances were such as to satisfy you that he was likely to shoot you. But that is because he is assaulting you. That is an assault, the pointing of a gun under those circumstances. But if the man said, "I am going to shoot you, the next time I see you," that would not justify you in finding the first opportunity of shooting him. That would not be self-defense. The prisoner says that he was afraid he was going to be killed and that he could not get back home. There was no immediate danger. He does not support that there was. He showed a certain amount of cunning, a reasonable amount of cunning and reason by making a subterfuge to get out of the harness and get back to the sled where he could get control of the gun. The killing was done deliberately and intentionally and would, therefore, seem to be murder. There would have been no excuse, no justification, in the way of self-defense for that killing.

Harvey told the jury to deal with the case "calmly and deliberately and not to be affected by your sympathies, but allow your judgment full sway." He then went on to all but instruct the jury members to harden their hearts and pronounce the defendant guilty.

You are human, however, and you have your sympathies as you cannot help having them, and they, no doubt, will have some effect upon you; and I want to say to you, therefore, that while it is your duty to find a verdict of murder, if you view the case largely as I have suggested it to you and on that verdict, if you find it, it will be my duty to pass the sentence of death; that would be the only sentence I could pass. Yet I have no hesitation in saying to you that I would consider it a crime that this man should be executed for the act with which he has been, and for which he is being charged here. It is there that his condition, his absence of knowledge of our customs should have effect, and I would be bound, in the exercise of my duty, to recommend that the sentence of death should not be carried out, and I have no doubt whatever that the authorities would recommend to His Excellency, the Governor General, that he should not be executed, but that some other form of punishment would be imposed which would meet the requirements of the case, and which would take home to him and to the member of his tribe the knowledge of our laws and our measure of justice. I have no doubt that some such punishment as that would be given to him, and not that the extreme penalty of the law would be exercised. I tell you that so that you may feel freer perhaps to do what the law demands of you, but which might be abhorrent to your sentiments of humanity if you felt that the strict letter of the law would have to be carried out.

The moment Judge Harvey finished speaking, Wallbridge leaped to his feet to object to the judge's rhetoric. It was outrageous, he said, for the judge to imply his support for a guilty verdict. "I think your lordship should not have stated as you did in regard to the probability of the prisoner not being punished according to the law," Wallbridge said. "A man ought to be convicted or not convicted of murder according to his guilt or innocence. You should not have told them that the evidence of the prisoner does not suggest there was any immediate fear. I think the purpose of the evidence of the prisoner was fear, a continuous fear, and he thought that his fears would be realized. You should have directed the jury that a reasonable apprehension of violence—if it is justifiable and it is an apprehension—is sufficient to justify the act."

Harvey overruled the objection. "I think my declaration of the law to the jury on that point is correct," he said.[12]

The jurors began their deliberations at 12:03 P.M. They returned to the courtroom just an hour later. The throngs of onlookers, shocked that the debate had ended so quickly, rushed back to the courtroom and squeezed into their seats again. Given the forceful words of the judge, the spectators assumed that the jury could only have reached one conclusion. They were in for a surprise.

At 1:10 P.M., James Mould, the jury foreman, read the verdict. The court clerk, doubting he had heard correctly, asked him to read it again.

"Not guilty."

Patsy Klengenberg leaned over to Sinnisiak and translated the decision. Sinnisiak began trembling visibly. An odd look drew over his face.

"It is not true," he said. "I did kill him."[13]

Sinnisiak was led from the courtroom to a carriage outside the courthouse, and ushered off to the mounted police barracks, where he was told he would remain until the conclusion of Uluksuk's trial. Ilavinik and Patsy couldn't understand what had transpired. "I suppose it means this, that our two years' work is all for nothing," Ilavinik said to LaNauze. "I understand now, I am always finding out something new about the white man."[14]

—

CHAPTER TWELVE

A man knew so little that he had to be very careful in life. He had to observe the rules of life not only for himself but for others, since his failings could affect the hunting and welfare of the community as a whole. And as careful as he himself might be, others could behave in such a way as to bring disaster upon him.

—ANGAKOQ, AN ESKIMO SHAMAN

T HE EDMONTON VERDICT, C. C. MCCAUL WOULD LATER WRITE, shocked everyone in the courtroom. How could an all-white jury possibly have come to this conclusion? McCaul felt his case was rock solid. Were the jurors blind to the symbolic importance of the case? Had their judgment become clouded by all the strange anthropology that had swirled through the testimony? Had they become unconsciously sympathetic to the Eskimos, seen them as somehow victims rather than the murderers that they had confessed to being? McCaul quickly blamed the newspaper coverage of the trial. Reporters and headline writers, especially at the Edmonton *Morning Bulletin*, had created stories "calculated to bias and prej-

udice the public mind against the prosecution and in favor of the acquit-
tal of the prisoners."

He also blamed the jury, which, he believed, had been influenced in
dramatic and peculiar ways. A prominent local businessman and "Indian
agent" named H. A. Conroy "has had access to the prisoners and Eskimo
interpreters at the barracks ever since the prisoners were brought there,"
McCaul wrote. "From the information that I can gather I believe that he
has been active in spreading in this community prejudice against the
Crown and stirring up sympathy and sentiment in favor of the Eskimo
prisoners."

Some of this sympathy had reached the ears of the jury, McCaul said.
One juror, with whom McCaul admitted to having had "very pleasant and
satisfactory business relations, and who happens to be more or less a friend
of mine," described some of the jury's deliberations. The juror had come
to believe that the priests had caused some "trouble" among the Eskimos
before they left the mouth of the Coppermine. Some thought the priests
were "monkeying with the Eskimo women," he told McCaul. "Even a
white man would kill for this."

McCaul was outraged. "Not only was there not a tittle of evidence remotely suggesting this, but LaNauze had found that this story had been
spread by a disreputable half-breed trader who had a grudge against the
priests."

Another juror harbored resentment against Catholic missionaries,
McCaul believed. Alfred Fugl, who had been the manager of a northern
Hudson Bay outpost, blamed Gabriel Breynat for his own failed cam-
paign to join the legislature.

A third juror, H. Milton Martin, a professed Roman Catholic, told
McCaul that the Eskimos ought not to be convicted or punished because
"our missionaries have often been killed by the savages in much the same
way." When McCaul had said that even he, "a heretic," had felt sympathy
for the priests, Martin replied that his archbishop felt the Eskimos should
not be punished. "Just exactly what . . . H. Milton Martin meant by this
statement, I do not understand," McCaul wrote.

McCaul confessed to being bewildered about what to do next. Thankfully, given his initial decision to charge only Sinnisiak with the murder of Rouvière, he had plenty of options available. He promptly filed an affidavit asking for a change of venue. "On account of widespread prejudice among the community of Edmonton against the prosecution, and the alleged or rumored conduct of the priests with whose murder the prisoners were charged; and on account of the widespread sympathy and sentiment that has been developed in the said community by (as I verily believe from information received by me) interested persons; in my opinion a fair trial of the said prisoners of either of them on the charge of murder cannot be obtained in, or in the neighborhood of Edmonton."

McCaul also decided to file charges against both prisoners jointly for the murder of LeRoux. "You can easily imagine that I congratulated myself that I had only charged Sinnisiak with the murder of Father Rouvière, so that I had the new crime of the murder of Father LeRoux with which to charge him jointly with his fellow prisoner," he would write.

Edwin Keedy, the American lawyer who watched the proceedings in Edmonton and who had befriended McCaul, told the prosecutor that it was "quite unheard of for the prosecution to apply for a change of venue." Such a move would be "very prejudicial" to McCaul's case, Keedy said. McCaul dismissed Keedy's opinion as "an American notion."

Indeed, McCaul believed he had reason for optimism. Chief Justice Harvey, McCaul noted, "had been very much annoyed" at the verdict, coming as it did "dead in the teeth of his charge."

James Wallbridge, for his part, argued against moving the second trial, citing a case in which a change of venue was refused even though the judge in the first trial had been "hooted and nearly mobbed." The citizens of Edmonton were just as competent to sit on the LeRoux case as any jury that could be empaneled in Calgary, Wallbridge argued. The charge of prejudice was nonsense; McCaul would use the word to define any opinion contrary to his own. Wallbridge then asked Judge Harvey to recuse himself from the second case.

"In view of the fact that you have already expressed your opinion as to the guilt of the prisoners, would it not be possible to secure another judge to preside?" Wallbridge asked.

Impossible, Judge Harvey replied. The other judges were on vacation. The proceedings would move to Calgary, and the trial would begin in six days. Harvey, once again, would preside.

WHAT HAD INITIALLY been a few days' curiosity was suddenly turning into something of an epic. The trial of the Eskimos had already become "one of the most costly ever undertaken by the Dominion government," the Edmonton *Morning Bulletin* reported. Before the second trial even began, those in the city's legal circles estimated that the investigation and trials would cost more than $100,000.[1]

After they were moved to Calgary, Sinnisiak and Uluksuk were housed in a second-story room of the city's police barracks, along with Patsy, Ilavinik, and Koeha. The door to the room was not locked, though a guard was posted nearby. The two prisoners were given a ride around the city in a motorcar.

The Calgary newspapers were no less astonished than the Edmonton papers had been by the appearance of the accused. Alongside their photographs, the *News-Telegram* said the accused "might easily be taken for Russians of the Mongolian type. They are far from being unintelligent in appearance, having high foreheads and good large eyes."[2]

"The trial is unique in the history of Alberta," reported the Calgary *Daily Herald*. The "accused pagans" were "so steeped in ignorance that it is impossible to convey to them the meaning of an oath." The trial was especially vexing given that the prisoners had a "standard of morals necessarily approximate to those of the stone age, and the difficulty of conveying to them, through an interpreter himself only recently reclaimed from a state of savagery, the true meaning of the trial."[3]

"Eskimos Falling Easily into Ways of White People," another headline read. "They Eat Ordinary Food with Knives and Forks—Sleep on Beds." Admiring the adapabilty of these men who "are actually on the plane of our ancestors in the Stone Age," the paper reported that Sinnisiak and Uluksuk "use a knife and fork with more grace than many 'bohunks,' and have shown an appreciation of the white man's food, which, considering their previous upbringing, is certainly remarkable." Prison guards told the reporter that the inmates were "having the time of their lives." They had discarded all their native clothing and seemed to be getting used to the hot weather. One night, outside the police barracks, a journalist reported seeing Ilavinik "shiver and go inside the building." Another reporter wrote an entire story about Ilavinik realizing "the wish of his life" when a member of the police gave him a Waltham wristwatch.

"Ever since he had first seen one of the wonderful things that marked the time of the sun and kept some semblance of order in the police lives he had hungered for one, and at last he was appeased," the reporter wrote. Winding the watch for Ilavinik before he went to bed one night, a police officer told him the sun would rise when the hands reached a certain time. Sure enough, the next morning Ilavinik rose before everyone else and went outside to see if the watch would bring the sun. It did. The second night, however, he did not wind the watch, and when he arose the next morning, Ilavinik "was so worked up he forgot all about his powers as an interpreter, and nothing could be got out of him except pure Eskimo, in which the word 'taboo' shot out now and then. He kept pointing to his watch and then outside, and on examination of the watch it was found to have stopped at half-past two. Ilavinik was on the verge of tears."

Police officers rushed off to find Patsy. "He say something no good," Patsy told the officers. "Yesterday morning sun come when this hand here and that hand there. Now this hand and that hand not reached place yet and sun come. He want to know what matter with sun."

"It took a long time to explain that the sun was all right," the reporter wrote. "Ilavinik had always had the impression that the watches fixed the sun's getting up, and that was why he wanted one. His faith in the white man's time piece was considerably shaken when he was informed that the watches were governed by the sun, and not the other way around."[4]

None of the newspapers covering the case saw fit to offer an editorial opinion about it. They had other things to worry about. Writing about the "national egomania" under which the Germans were conducting the war in Europe, the editors of the *News-Telegram* opined that "an unwholesome mental diet is more of a menace to the welfare of the world than impure material food. Until they get this poison out of their minds, there can be no real peace, since in their present abnormal state they seem incapable of grasping the fact that other peoples have, like the Germans, inalienable rights. With this example before them, other civilized people must beware henceforth of that form of so-called patriotism which is mere megalomania, teaching that all the world beyond their own frontiers is a Naboth's vineyard."[5]

In addition to continuing coverage of the war ("19,000 Enemy Prisoners Taken"), local papers were also reporting other human-interest stories, such as the discovery of the body of a well-known Ontario doctor, found surrounded by three drunk (and unconscious) businessmen near the grounds of an oil company. The story appeared under the headline "Was Murder Committed in Liquor Orgy?"[6]

The second trial, *Rex v. Sinnisiak and Uluksuk*, opened at Calgary's Seventh Avenue courthouse at ten A.M. on Wednesday, August 22. An initial pool of twenty-five jurors was summoned to the courthouse and eventually winnowed to six. Once again, their names appeared in the local papers before the trial began: Hugh Melvin, William Ireland, J. K. Cummins, J. M. Baker, C. B. Clarke, and M. Allan. All had been residents of Calgary for at least ten years.

This time, though, Judge Harvey sequestered the jury. They would be put up by the court, and would not be allowed to communicate with anyone outside their own group without going through the sheriff's office. They were not to see any newspapers until the trial had been completed. This unusual step would prevent "too much sympathy being expressed on account of the actions of the priests," according to the Edmonton *Morning Bulletin*, which had been criticized by the judge for its coverage of the first trial.

Rather than the native skins in which they appeared at the first trial, Sinnisiak and Uluksuk were dressed in open-collared dress shirts. "White man's clothing," the *Daily Herald* called it. The prisoners "appeared to be in very low spirits, and sat much of the time during the morning with their sharp brown eyes downcast, and an expression of deep melancholy upon their faces," the *News-Telegram* reported.

Opening his case, McCaul spoke to the jury for fifteen minutes, a far cry from his epic two-hour opening statement at the first trial. He began slowly. "May it please your Lordship, and Gentlemen of the Jury: This trial has been perhaps appropriately ushered in by a little taste of arctic weather which we got yesterday afternoon and last night as the trial will be redolent of the atmosphere of the artic regions." He explained the law that allowed the state to try a case far from the scene of the crime if it occurs in an "unorganized terrirory." He said prosecuting the case was especially critical in such areas "to establish a feeling of good faith on the part of the Indians and to trust in the white man's justice, to establish in their minds the fact that an Indian or an Eskimo will be treated in exactly the same way and on exactly the same plane as any white man in the country." He showed the jury maps, and gave an overview of the investigation. He praised the Royal North West Mounted Police, who represented not "a punitive expedition, not an armed military force, as might have happened in some other countries, sent against the tribe to punish the tribe for the murders."

McCaul took a photograph of one of the prisoners to show the jury. This is Uluksuk, he said, and motioned for Uluksuk to stand up. Peering at the image, the jury quickly realized they were actually looking at a photograph of Sinnisiak. When Sinnisiak was told of the mistake, he broke into a wide grin. Recounting the mistake, one reporter noted that the moment proved "that the Eskimo is a human being and has a sense of humor."[7]

McCaul continued. White men are beginning to go into the Far North country, he said.

It is a matter of common knowledge that there are copper deposits which will, no doubt, be prospected on the Coppermine River. You can appreciate the extreme importance of these remote people being taught respect for the law which prevails throughout the entire Dominion of Canada, and that whatever their customs may have been, whether their justice was retributory justice, the law of an eye for an eye, a tooth for a tooth, a leg for a leg, that that has got to be replaced, not by retributory justice. Our justice is not administered in any feeling of revenge.

You are not asked here, no matter what you hear about the death of these priests, to avenge their death. You will be asked to give a verdict which will result in the punishment of these men, punishment so that it will act as a deterrent upon which British criminal justice, or criminal justice practically of all civilized nations, works.

As he had in Edmonton, McCaul warned that Eskimos were not a small band of people, but "a very large race" inhabiting most of northern Canada. "There are many thousands of them," he pointed out. He reminded the jury of the massacre Samuel Hearne had seen at Bloody Falls in 1771. "And it was just within a few miles of this spot that these unhappy and unfortunate priests were done unto death." McCaul did not dwell on the fact that Eskimos had been the victims, not the assailants, in the original Bloody Falls massacre.[8]

He sat down.

Wallbridge, too, opened as he had in Edmonton. The killings had been in self-defense, he said. Since the Eskimos could not possibly be judged by their peers, the jury must try to look beyond notions of civilized justice and understand the Eskimo point of view. Was it not reasonable, given their fear of strangers, especially strangers aiming rifles at them, that Sinnisiak and Uluksuk had been justified in believing that their lives were in danger?

—

THE FIRST WITNESS for the prosecution, once again, was Father Duchaussois, who had known Father Rouvière since their days as students in Belgium. As he had done at the first trial, Duchaussois described Rouvière as a gentle man of excellent judgment who rarely lost his temper. Looking over a pile of correspondence handed to him from the evidence table, he identified Rouvière's handwriting in one letter, which described the respect the priests were shown by their Eskimo hosts. Even after giving a tent over to the priests, Eskimos would always ask permission to enter. " 'They are always trying to do more for us,' " Duchaussois read. " 'How different to the Indians, who often content themselves looking at you as if you are in a bad case.' "

Taking a somewhat darker turn, the letter then described how the priests' mission was in part to reverse "the sowing of bad seed" by a Father Fry, a missionary with the Church of England. Reaching the Eskimos on the Arctic coast, Rouvière wrote, had been a race between the Anglican and the Catholic Churches.

Duchaussois identified the cassock, rosaries, breviaries, a blood-stained altar cloth, and, finally, the remains of Rouvière's diary. As at the first trial, the last words in the diary were open to interpretation. McCaul and Wallbridge spent considerable time arguing over the meaning of the word "disillusioned." Did it imply frustration with missionary work or Rouvière's fear that the priests' lives were in danger?

Corporal Bruce took the stand and identified the robe and the other articles he had gathered during the investigation. He offered his impressions of Eskimo culture. He boiled his remarks down to a few digestible sentences; the reporters covering the case tried to do the same. "There was no established authority among the Eskimos or courts by which a man could right a wrong if he wanted to do so," the Calgary *Daily Herald* quoted Bruce as saying. "They were a communistic people. They had no sense of religion compared to that of a white man, although they appeared to have some idea of a hereafter. There were many superstitions, such as a tradition that considered it unlucky for a woman to sew when the sun was high."

Corporal Wight spoke about the items he had discovered at the murder site, including the teeth and jawbone that had been scattered over an area of forty square feet.

During his turn on the stand, Ilavinik said it was common in the Far North to kill certain people, especially "the insane and incurable." He said that lying and stealing were far more serious offenses than the taking of human life and that rarely was there an instance of an Eskimo violating Eskimo traditions by telling a lie or thieving from another Eskimo. He described Sinnisiak as "a hunter by land and sea; a furrier; a fisherman; a guide; a carver; a metal sheather; a navigator of kayaks; and a driver of dogs, as he had followed the various occupations in turn and is equally adept at either."

Ilavinik described the moment when Sinnisiak was arrested:

" 'What you want?' Sinnisiak said.

" 'The police want you,' I say.

" 'What for?'

" 'You kill two priests.' "

Sinnisiak had said he didn't want to go, Ilavinik related. Ilavinik had translated this for LaNauze. LaNauze had said Sinnisiak had no choice. Ilavinik continued the story:

"You going to kill me?" Sinnisiak had asked.

"No, nobody going to kill you," LaNauze had said. "You got to come along."

"If you kill me, the boat will sink," Sinnisiak threatened.

"Did Sinnisiak say he was a medicine man?" McCaul asked.

Objection, Wallbridge said. Overruled, pronounced Judge Harvey.

"I did not know Sinnisiak to be a man that made storms," Ilavinik said.[9]

TAKING THE STAND, and using Patsy Klengenberg as his interpreter, Koeha spoke for over an hour. Koeha "is the most beautiful of the four full-blooded northerners who have been decorating the courtroom for the last two days," the Calgary *News-Telegram* reported. Koeha seemed far more relaxed than the two prisoners, often slouching in his seat and resting his chin on his forearm. "His rim of scraggy whiskers showed a more advanced state of vegetation than did those of the other representatives of the tribe, and his hair was longer and stiffer. When asked how old he was, he grinned until there were no eyes left visible in his copper-colored shiny face, and said he didn't know. When pressed to divulge his age, he said it was more than he could count on his fingers."

Koeha described hearing Sinnisiak's story, then spoke of finding the snow-covered bodies of the priests. He told of the Eskimo tradition of licking the blood off a killing knife to ward off evil spirits.

DENNY LANAUZE told the jury that Uluksuk had a "particularly happy" disposition and had probably been urged to the killing by Sinnisiak. When Rouvière raised his rifle "to an alarming position," LaNauze told the court, Sinnisiak said, " 'We ought to kill them, or they will kill us.' " " 'They can kill me if they want to,' " he quoted Uluksuk as responding. " 'I don't want to kill any people.' "

Asked by McCaul to compare the intelligence of the Eskimos to that of the Blackfoot Indians, LaNauze refused. He did say that when an Eskimo hunter returned with a kill, the people "shared the spoils in proportion to their families. It was a case of share and share alike."

Cross-examined by Wallbridge, LaNauze told the jury how cooperative the prisoners had been since their arrest. When Wallbridge asked LaNauze whether the Eskimos had any superstitions, LaNauze offered an enigmatic answer: "Well, it is not long since they burned the last witch in England."

McCaul let the witness stand down.

WALLBRIDGE BEGAN his defense by calling Sinnisiak, who repeated much of what he had said in Edmonton. Rather than let Sinnisiak's testimony stand, as he had in the first trial, McCaul decided to cross-examine him at length. "When Kuleavik [Rouvière] was running away, when you shot him, Kuleavik hadn't a rifle at all?" he asked.

"No, he had no rifle."

"He was unarmed? No arms?"

"He had nothing."

"Ilogoak, the other priest, was dead at the time you shot Kuleavik?"

"Yes."

"What were you afraid of Kuleavik for when he was running away and hadn't a rifle? Why were you afraid? Were you afraid of the spirits again, or what were you afraid of when Kuleavik was running away?"

"I don't know what I think. I shoot him."

McCaul asked Sinnisiak how far away Rouvière had been when he shot him. Sinnisiak pointed to a red house about seventy-five yards from the courthouse. McCaul had Sinnisiak identify photographs of Rouvière and LeRoux, and of John Hornby. He had Sinnisiak draw schematic diagrams of the sled, of the positions of the dogs in their harness, and of the priests. He had him draw himself and Uluksuk. He had him describe the struggle with Kormik over the rifle. He had him describe pulling the sleds.

"Quite a common thing for an Eskimo man to get into the harness and pull the sled, is it? The Eskimo men often put the harness on themselves and help the dogs pull the sled?"

"Yes. They always help pull."

"When the priests came up and you said the priests threw some stuff into the river. What did the priests throw into the river?"

"Axes, and some ammunition and some other stuff, I don't know."

"And did they throw the ammunition into the river?"

"Yes."

"They threw the ammunition into the river, and the axes they threw into the river?"

"Yes."

"The river was running?"

"Yes."

"Were the priests frightened of you and Uluksuk when they threw the ammunition into the river? Were the priests scared?"

"I don't know."

"Why did they throw the ammunition into the river then?"

"Because they were mad."

"They threw their own ammunition into the river because they were mad. Didn't they throw it into the river so you couldn't get it, and that fellow Uluksuk couldn't get it?"

"Maybe."

"When you tried to stop pulling the priest shoved you and told you to pull?"

"Shoved and pointed the rifle at the same time."

"Shoved you and told you to pull?"

"Yes."

"That made you angry, mad, hot inside?"

"I was scared."

"Were you mad, angry?"

"We weren't so very mad. We were very scared."

McCaul sat down.[10]

Wallbridge then called Uluksuk, who had not testified at the trial in Edmonton. As he took the stand, Uluksuk smiled broadly.

"Do not be afraid of these people," Wallbridge said. "Tell us whatever we ask you about. Speak out and do not be afraid."

"Yes."

"How old are you?"

Uluksuk, who appeared to be thirty years old, held up fingers on both hands. "Maybe I am eight years old." A ripple of laughter rolled across the audience.

"Are you married?"

"Yes."

"Babies?"

"No babies."

Uluksuk detailed the moments leading up to the murder.

"What did the priests say to you? Which priest was it, first?" Wallbridge asked.

"One took the rifle, the other took the knife."

"You said the priest came over from the sled to the pile of stuff. Which one came over, or both of them?"

"Both of them."

"What did they ask you to do?"

"I thought I was going to get shot."

Which priest had the gun? Wallbridge asked.

"Ilogoak [LeRoux] had the gun."

"Did the other priest have any arms at all?"

"He had nothing when he threw this stuff out. He had no knife."

The priests made them pull for a long time, Uluksuk said. "The priest pointed a gun every time I wanted to stop. I was afraid I get shot."

"Did you know how far the priests were going to take you away?"

"We think maybe take us a long way."

"Did you expect to see your people again?"

"I think we wouldn't see them again."

"Then Sinnisiak suggested you had better kill the priests?"

"Yes."

"And what happened then? What did you do after Sinnisiak said you had better kill the priests?"

"I don't want to. I scared of white man. I didn't want to tackle the white man."

Sinnisiak said he would kill the white men anyway, Uluksuk related. When LeRoux hit Uluksuk with a stick, Uluksuk reluctantly agreed to Sinnisiak's plan. Once the priests were dead, Sinnisiak hacked into Rouvière's leg with the axe. Uluksuk cut the priests open. They removed the livers, and ate small pieces. Then they went home and told their people what they had done.

"Did you know that Ilogoak and Kuleavik were priests, teachers of religion?" Wallbridge asked.

"I think they were just white men."

"What did you think they were doing?"

"I don't know what they were doing."

DURING HIS cross-examination, McCaul held up a sketch of a knife and asked if it was about the size of the one Sinnisiak had used to stab the priests. Yes, Uluksuk said.

"How long had you known Kuleavik before you killed him?" McCaul asked.

"Three summers I saw him. I knew him."

"Kuleavik good fellow?" McCaul asked.

"Yes."

"How long had you known Ilogoak before you killed him?"

"Two summers I know him."

"Ilogoak pretty good fellow too?"

"No."[11]

WITH THE TESTIMONY complete, Wallbridge offered a closing statement that closely resembled his argument in Edmonton. He began by outlining a bit of historical context, noting that the Eskimos had treated most of the priests' white predecessors, including the pioneer Stefansson, very well. Perhaps there was a reason for this, he suggested:

> Stefansson, when he went among them, was apparently endowed with that necessary amount of tact and good sense to make friends, and nothing happened to him because he treated the natives in the way they ought to be treated. Nothing has happened to Hornby. He also has good sense and good judgment, and if anything happened to the other men it must have been because they transgressed some law, wittingly or unwittingly, and ran contrary to what these people imagined a man should be. In the words of the witnesses, he "makes them afraid." They fear strangers, Stefansson

says. We do not know why. We only know it is a fact, and because they fear strangers, it is all the more reason why the strangers should be very, very careful not to do anything which would cause that fear."

There were two reasons why the jury should acquit the Eskimos, Wallbridge said.

First, they should be treated as young children or imbeciles, and I say that a young child or imbecile is incapable of committing a crime, and these men are incapable of appreciating the crime which they have committed. For hundreds of years, many hundreds, these Eskimos have been governing themselves by custom. The are like children turned loose on the prairie, if you can call the Arctic ice a prairie. They are turned loose without any semblance of government or order, just allowed to shift for themselves. When they have a dispute, they settle it among themselves. They cannot be treated like the civilized men of the city, cities that Stefansson says are ten thousand years ahead of the civilization of the Eskimos.

When strangers come from an unknown foreign land to an unknown people, savage people, people of the stone age, is it not a fact that they take their chance, that they believe by a certain course of conduct they can walk safely among them and come and go? Do they not take the chance of offending those people and paying the penalty of that offense?

The Magna Carta mandated that people be judged by their peers, Wallbridge noted, which in this case was a practical impossibility. But if members of the jury could put themselves in the place of the accused, up there near Bloody Falls, with the winter coming and strange white men holding them at gunpoint, they would surely conclude that the killings had been justified.

"When these men say that they were forced at the point of a gun to get into the harness and pull this sled, you cannot help but believe it," Wall-bridge said.

> There is no evidence to the contrary. If it were not for the state-ments of these men there would be no trial, because there was not a tittle of evidence to connect them. And I say that you must be-lieve them when they say that they were frightened, when they say that they were forced to get into the harness again to drag that sled against their will for we do not know how far in miles. And I say that when they say to you that they were afraid, that they believed their lives were in danger, that you must believe them. I say those fears, to them, whether they were real or otherwise, if you were judging them by their own standards, were very real when you have to look at it through their eyes, through their minds.
>
> Considering that these men were in the harness in front and the two priests behind, one of them armed with a rifle, I say it took a degree of courage on the part of these Eskimos to do what they did. These Eskimos, in their minds, thought they were doing a jus-tifiable act; they thought it was a case of necessity. The odds were against them, and they had to rely upon their wits as well as their strength. No matter how much we personally may want to blame these men for killing the missionaries, we cannot help but think that in their minds what they did was reasonable under the circum-stances; looking through their eyes and through their minds, that it was done from necessity.

Sinnisiak and Uluksuk did not murder simply to steal the rifles, the de-fense lawyer argued. If this had been their intention, they would have killed Stefansson, or Hornby, or the other whites they had encountered over the last few years. "There is no evidence of murder in their hearts, that they were doing anything other than what they said they were doing, killing these priests in self-defense."

Wallbridge reminded the jury that if they had the slightest doubt about the Eskimos' guilt, they should acquit them. More important, given the thrust of McCaul's rhetoric, the jury must resist the temptation to use their verdict as a chance to make the prisoners an example to the rest of their people. It was not possible to reach a guilty conviction to enact a kind of "policy."

"That, gentlemen, is not in accordance with our ideas of justice and fair play," he said. "If these men are guilty of murder, they should be found guilty of murder and should pay the extreme penalty. If these men are not guilty, then they should be sent to their homes, free. Either they are guilty or they are not guilty. There is no half-way measure."

Anticipating a reiteration of the exhortation Judge Harvey had issued from the bench in Edmonton, Wallbridge asked the jury to be circumspect about any guarantees that the prisoners would not be put to death. These men had already been under surveillance for eighteen months. If the jury compared the photographs of the rugged men Denny LaNauze had taken into custody in May of the previous year with the men before them now, they would see just how much they had already suffered. They had learned their lesson. Imprisoning them for even six more months would be "like condemning them to a slow death that is worse than hanging. There are natives who can be treated with the whip, natives of Africa I understand, thrashed into the way of the white man, made to do his bidding. But that is not the way with the Eskimo. He is a free, independent man. You cannot coerce him. His motto is the one made famous by Patrick Henry: 'Give me liberty of give me death.' "

Wallbridge then tried to take his preemptive tactic one step further, by reminding the jury of why the case was before them in the first place. "I think I should tell you why these men were brought from Edmonton to Calgary for trial," he said.

By now, Judge Harvey had had enough. "I think you had better confine yourself to the evidence," he interrupted.

"I just want to explain, your lordship," Wallbridge said.

"It is not at all necessary for you to do that," Harvey shot back. "It is quite improper."

Wallbridge asked again.

"It is quite improper for you to refer to that at all," Harvey said. "It does not come out in the evidence."

James Wallbridge sat down.[12]

AS HE HAD in Edmonton, McCaul, in closing, reminded the jury that British law does not say that a man may kill simply because he is afraid of being killed. At the moment of assault, he may kill only if he is unable to overpower his assailant. Picture the circumstances when the priests arrived at the mouth of the Coppermine, McCaul said. They were in a hostile village, far from any familiar faces or customs, and they were desperately hungry. Winter was coming on hard, and the village was already getting low on food. No longer were they being welcomed into the Eskimos' tents. The fear of being stabbed in the back for the rifles could not have been far from their minds.

McCaul advised the jury not to act out of caprice. They must carefully weigh the evidence and apply the law as it was written. And the circumstantial evidence, he said, was sufficient to convict the prisoners even without their confessions. Indeed, contrary to what Wallbridge argued, the confessions were the only evidence the defense had to maintain that the killings had been justifiable homicide. How could the jury be sure that Sinnisiak and Uluksuk had actually been going south to meet their people? Wasn't it possible that they had set out precisely in order to kill the priests and steal their rifles?

Once they'd killed LeRoux, why had they had to kill Rouvière? "Why didn't they let the poor fellow run?" McCaul asked. "Why didn't they let him go off and starve to death in the wilds? Why didn't they let him have a sporting chance of getting back to the village and getting assistance? Why didn't they let him have a sporting chance of meeting some of the people who were expected to come down from Imaerinik? No. My friend Mr. Wallbridge tells you they had to kill him in self-defense. In self-defense they had to kill this poor unfortunate priest who, when he was brought down with the second shot, was apparently too wounded to rise again."

McCaul then shifted his rhetoric. Beyond the cause of justice in this particular case, the jury had the opportunity to send a signal to all native people. It was an opportunity that should not be fumbled. "If these men are acquitted," McCaul continued, "it means that the jury find that they were quite right and justified in killing these missionaries under the circumstances that have been detailed. It means that these men go forth from this Court room without a shadow of a stain on their character, that they can return to their tribes and be able to say to their village community and to all the tribes that the white men, the big chief and his counselors, told us we were perfectly justified in killing the white men under the circumstances that we killed these men."

McCaul agreed that sentencing the Eskimos to death would be a "terrible thing," but that was not for the jury to worry about. "That is a matter that can be dealt with, and will, in the natural course of things, necessarily have to be dealt with." If McCaul had his way, Sinnisiak and Uluksuk would be convicted and have their sentence commuted to a short prison term. After this, they might be "an object lesson" to other Eskimos.[13]

WHEN THE LAWYERS had finished, Judge Harvey instructed the jury. His rhetoric closely resembled the language he had used in Edmonton. It might seem cruel to punish men for acts they did not consider to be wrong, he said, but as strange as they might seem to the jury, the Eskimos were still Canadian citizens, and subject to its laws.

"Nothing in the way of prejudice, nothing in the way of suspicion or of what might have been or of rumors, nothing in the way of sympathy, should enter into the decision of the case. Your judgment, and your judgment only, should be your guide," he said. The prisoners had confessed their role in the deaths of the priests. All that remained for the jury to decide was whether the murder was culpable or not culpable.

Harvey reviewed the facts of the case. There was nothing to indicate that the Eskimos had ever feared retribution for the killings. No one in their tribe would punish them, he said. These men were "quite intelligent enough to know what they were doing," Harvey maintained. They say they feared for their lives, that they killed the priests "to prevent the priests from taking them away where they would not get back to their own people and perhaps from killing them. That is their story."

Although the Eskimos might have felt the killings were justified, in British law they were not, the judge stated. "We find in this case that both the prisoners admit that they had decided and determined, before any attack was made at all, to kill the priests, so that there is no doubt that they intended to kill them and that it is murder unless there is something which reduces it to manslaughter." A charge of murder could be reduced to manslaughter only if the Eskimos had been provoked by fear. "It might possibly be that fear might cause a person to lose his self-control as much as anger would, so that he could not deal with the case as he would under normal circumstances, but I do not know of any case," Harvey said. "I have never known of an instance, where such has been the case. It appears to me that on the evidence there should be a verdict of murder rather than of manslaughter, but I don't feel like directing you any more definitely on that because I think there are such circumstances as make it incumbent upon me to leave it to you to say finally whether that is the case or not."

Judge Harvey recognized the difficulty of the jury's role. "You are human beings, and you cannot help feeling sympathy, and it is very difficult for one to guide one's conduct apart altogether from his feelings of that sort. You probably all feel as most of us must, that the penalty of death is not a proper penalty to impose in the case of these ignorant pagans for the act which they committed."

Harvey then told the jury of his intentions should they return a guilty verdict, as he hoped they would. If the verdict was one of guilty, and he could see no other verdict possible, he was certain that the usual penalty would not be consummated. "I feel that the prisoners should not have the death penalty imposed," he said. Harvey would consider it his duty to ask the governor-general for a lighter sentence.

"You may now retire to consider your verdict," he ordered. It was 5:20 P.M.

AS SOON AS the jury left the room Wallbridge once again objected to the way the judge had instructed the jury. Not only had Harvey made plain his own feelings about the verdict but he had not offered an alternative line of reasoning—that a reasonable fear of being killed makes homicide justifiable. Wallbridge also objected to Harvey's presumptuous declaration that he could somehow ensure that the death penalty would not be enforced. How could such a statement not prejuduce the jury in favor of a guilty verdict?

Harvey overruled each of Wallbridge's objections.

The jurors returned at 6:06 P.M. They had deliberated for forty-six minutes, even less than the Edmonton jury. The standing-room-only crowd fell silent as the foreman read the verdict:

"We find the prisoners guilty of murder, with the strongest possible recommendation to mercy that the jury can give."

Visibly pleased, Judge Harvey turned to the men in the jury box. "Gentlemen of the jury," he said. "You have performed a very unpleasant duty and, I think, have come to exactly the correct conclusion in all respects. I think the verdict is the only honest verdict that could be rendered on the evidence and the recommendation is most proper. It will be submitted by me with my own recommendation to the same effect at once." Harvey said he had "not any doubt in my mind" that the sentence would be greatly reduced.

He then addressed Patsy Klengenberg. "Patsy, tell them that the jury has found that they were guilty of killing the priests without right to do it; that under our law when people kill others that way they have to give their lives, but the great white chief further away than the distance they have come may interfere and show them mercy, be kind to them."[14]

Rather than turn to the defendants, Patsy hesitated. As one awkward moment gave way to another, a white observer said he must have been "lost somewhere in the mists that separate a taboo from a code of ethics." Perhaps he felt uncomfortable about delivering the news. Perhaps he was bewildered by how this second jury could have reached such a radically different conclusion from the first one. Patsy did not say. He did not speak at all.

Harvey asked LaNauze to press his interpreter, and this time Patsy repeated the words, as directed. Listening to his translation, the prisoners were silent, their faces reflecting the dramatic fluctuations in the judge's words. Their eyes widened. Hearing that they would have to sacrifice their own lives, they began visibly trembling. When Patsy said the Great White Chief would be merciful, they seemed to relax, "nodding their heads in a complete return of confidence in the goodness of the white man," one reporter wrote. They faced LaNauze and assented: "It is true, we will do anything you tell us to do."[15]

Harvey told the jury he would telegraph their verdict and his recommendation that very night. If the death sentence was in fact overturned, Harvey said, he would recommend that the convicts be transferred to a prison "more suitable to their constitutions."[16]

Harvey remanded the defendants to police custody to be taken back to the Supreme Court in Edmonton, and said he would telegraph the minister of justice in Ottawa. LaNauze, Bruce, and Wight escorted their prisoners back to Edmonton on August 24 to await their sentence. Patsy, Ilavinik, and Koeha went with them.[17]

With the possibility of a death sentence still hanging over the Eskimos' heads, the Calgary *News-Telegram* finally offered an editorial opinion on the case. "Were the death penalty to be imposed on Sinnisiak and Uluksuk, the two Eskimos convicted of murdering Father LeRoux in the far north, the cause of justice would not be served so well nor so fairly as it would be served were the two aborigines of the Arctic to be imprisoned for a time and then restored to their tribe," the paper opined. Their trial and sentence could serve as "object lessons which are intended to impress upon the primitive mind the fact that civilization does not allow murder to go unpunished. Had the authorities balked at the task of capturing these

Eskimos, their tribe would hold the lives of white persons very lightly, and the results would be unfortunate and most probably fatal. With the murderers instructed concerning the white man's unfailing law, the word will go forth through the north, and the lives of those who follow the unfortunate priests' steps will be safe."[18]

FOUR DAYS AFTER the end of the second trial, back in the Edmonton courtroom, Judge Harvey passed his sentence. In some ways, this was Harvey's moment. He could be tough and forgiving at the same time. He could dangle the power of British justice over the Eskimos' heads, then let them go. Most important, he could send them back to their people with a vivid impression of both the white man's severity and his wisdom.

"Patsy, tell the prisoners to stand up," Harvey said.

Tell them what I have to say. You told them in Calgary the other day that I would ask the Big Chief far away not to be too hard on them, and I have asked him by the way we have here, a long way, by telegraph, and he says because they did not know our ways, that they did not know what our laws are, he will not have them put to death for the killing of these men at this time. They must understand though that for the future they know now what our law is and if they kill any person again then they have to suffer the penalty.

I am going to pass sentence. I do not think it is necessary to explain the particulars of it now, but in the usual course action will be taken so that it will not be carried out. I impose the sentence of death in the usual form, and I will fix the date of the 15th of October as the date of execution. That is, of course, under the circumstances, something more or less a matter of form, but it is a form the Minister desires to have the proceedings take so that the commutation of the sentence may be in the usual way. He authorizes me to state the sentence will be commuted. You may tell them just what will be done I cannot say, but they will know in a few days.

They will probably be punished in some way, but I do not know just in what form it will be.

Patsy, you might tell them when they get back home, if they do, they must let their people know that if any of them kill any person they will have to suffer death. They know now what our law is.

Hearing Patsy's translation, Sinnisiak said nothing. Always the more voluble of the two, Uluksuk offered this: "Now I understand the ways of the white man. He speaks not with two tongues, and he thinks for us. If the police ever let me return to my people, and if I find that another man has taken my wife when I get there, I will turn around and travel the other way, because if I stayed there might be more trouble."[19]

At first, Sinnisiak and Uluksuk were to be jailed at the Royal North West Mounted Police's Herschel Island post, but a day later, court officials decided instead to send them to a jailhouse at Fort Resolution, on the southeastern shore of Great Slave Lake.[20]

A week later, Denny LaNauze took Sinnisiak and Uluksak to the railway station to see them off on their journey back north. The two convicts "whined and cried and seized us with both hands and clung to us," LaNauze wrote. "Patsy Klengenberg was cool and self-possessed as usual. Ilavinik was crying quietly. We shook hands, I swallowed hard and turned away to hide my feelings, for the Great Bear Lake patrol was ended." The patrol had taken two years and covered five thousand miles. It ended just in time, LaNauze wrote, to give its members the chance to serve in the Great War.[21]

EPILOGUE

—

The commercial world of the white man had caught the
Eskimos in its mesh, destroying their self-sufficiency
and independence, and made them economically its
slaves. Only in one respect did it benefit them:
it lessened the danger of those unpredictable
famines which had overtaken them every ten or
fifteen years, bringing suffering and death
to young and old without distinction.

—DIAMOND JENNESS, *The People of the Twilight*

AFTER TWO YEARS OF MINIMUM-SECURITY IMPRISONMENT
at Fort Resolution and some time spent working as guides for the Royal
North West Mounted Police, Sinnisiak and Uluksuk were released on
May 15, 1919, and eventually returned to their home territory. They were
told, in formal legal language, that "the proceedings in the present case
have served to inform them of their responsibilities, and that they are
solemnly charged with their duty to serve God and honour the King and
carefull to observe his laws."[1]

Despite the warnings, both Sinnisiak and Uluksuk apparently became
shiftless. In 1924, Uluksuk reportedly traded one of his sons to Sinnisiak
for a .22-caliber rifle, then took the boy back and disappeared. Sinnisiak

appealed to white police officers to intervene in the dispute. Before a patrol could find him, Uluksuk got into a quarrel with a man named Ikayena, who had shot one of Uluksuk's dogs. One night, Uluksuk sat outside Ikayena's tent while a card game went on inside. When Ikayena emerged, Uluksuk threatened him with a gun, and Ikayena shot him dead. Mounted police officers traveled 135 miles to make the arrest, and journalists used the occasion to comment on the intractibility of Eskimos. "The murder of Uluksuk brings to attention the possibility that the Eskimos' powers of perception are not developed sufficiently to understand the gentle paternalism of the white men in the matter of punishment," one newspaper reported.

Of Sinnisiak, less is known. He may have died of tuberculosis. People still say that he and Uluksuk brought white men's diseases like influenza back to their communities. In the eyes of some white men, Sinnisiak and Uluksuk continued to stand as models of the degenerate Eskimo. In July 1921, a police officer named Doak was sent out to investigate another Eskimo murder. At Fort Norman, the white explorer D'Arcy Arden told Doak to be careful. "Those Huskies are getting too cocky altogether for my liking and you would be taking a good chance of having your liver eaten," Arden said. "Look at what they did to the two priests, LeRoux and Rouvière, a few years ago. They are treacherous. Another stunt like that last jury pulled off and it won't be safe for a white man to enter Coronation Gulf."

Doak took a thousand-mile boat trip from Herschel Island east to Tree River, where he met and shared a meal with Sinnisiak. On the Kent Peninsula, Doak arrested two men, Aligoomiak and Tatamagana. Soon afterward, while under loose detention, Aligoomiak angered Doak by improperly softening his boots, then by spilling a pail of water. Doak shouted at him. Aligoomiak intended to shoot Doak in the leg to punish him for his sharp words. When the shot went high and Doak died, Aligoomiak decided to kill Doak's companion, a white trader named Otto Binder, as well. Once again, the Mounties were called in, and once again they found their men. This time, the trial was held in the north country: judge, prosecutor, defense attorney, and court clerk were all shipped two thousand miles north to a makeshift courtroom at Herschel Island. So was a hangman. The court scoured the countryside to find white jurors who did not know the deceased. In the end, both Aligoomiak and Tatamagana were convicted and sentenced to death. On February 1, 1924, they were hanged. Some in the Catholic Church felt that the severity of the punishment, compared to what had happened to Sinnisiak and Uluksuk, showed a two-tiered system of justice. The legal system did one thing for people convicted of killing Protestants and something else for those who killed Catholics. Some months later, Aligoomiak's elderly father left his community for a remote igloo. He strung a line between a harpoon and his igloo, and hanged himself.[2]

By 1930, Sinnisiak too was dead, though how he died is not known.

SOON AFTER the trials in Edmonton and Calgary, C. C. McCaul offered some ideas for fixing the north country—ideas that did not include missionaries. "I think that the Government ought to send a small expedition of education (not religion) to these people, accompanied, I would suggest, by no missionaries of any denomination whatever," he wrote. What was needed most of all was a full web of police barracks and courts to handle the inevitable increase in Eskimo crime. The Royal North West Mounted Police should set up a post with twenty officers at Fort Resolution, on Great Slave Lake, with another outpost at Fort Confidence, on Great Bear Lake, he proposed. The justice ministry should set up a central magistrate at Fort Resolution, with all the powers of a Supreme Court judge and the same salary ($10,000, plus a liberal travel budget) that was paid to judges in the Yukon. They should be promised a generous pension, since "no educated gentleman could be expected to ostracise himself from civilization and endure the hardships necessarily incident to the life and travel in this country for a longer period."

This increase in peace officers "would be able, probably, to keep the peace between the Great Bear Lake Indians and the Eskimos, between whom there is an ancestral feud," McCaul wrote. "They would also, of course, add greatly to, if not absolutely secure, the safety of all white men going to the Coppermine country. The magistrate would make it his duty to inculcate the general principles of both criminal and civil law among the natives, including the Eskimos, and could, I think, have an annual 'pow-wow' with them for this purpose. Some summer it would be a good plan, and an exceedingly interesting and not too rigorous or uncomfortable trip, for the Governor General and suite to visit these people, with an impressive escort of Royal North West Mounted Police."[3]

Sure enough, the reconfigured Royal Canadian Mounted Police saw its workload jump dramatically in the 1920s. Its feats of investigation became such a part of Canada's folklore that tales of wilderness crimes became standard yarns around the national campfire. Some were true, some were not, but all seemed to reflect something about the country's sense of itself. A story about wolves attacking a trapper in northern Ontario was uncovered as a fabrication when officers discovered photographs of animals that had been killed and arranged into fierce poses. Equally titillating, and equally untrue, was a rumor that a family of starving Eskimos living north of Saskatchewan had killed and eaten a group of Indians.[4]

Other legends were true. Three years after the Doak case, the police were called to investigate yet another missing white man: John Hornby. In June 1927, after a difficult winter spent northeast of Great Slave Lake, Hornby and two companions had starved to death. When Mounties arrived at the cabin some months later, they discovered two corpses lying outside and a third inside. The cabin's floorboards and bunks had been ripped up for firewood. A small tin trunk full of photographic equipment was flooded with water. The police officers found diaries and farewell notes. "We have suffered terrible and awful hardships," Hornby had written his cousin Margaret. In a rotten leather case, police also found a draft of a book Hornby had been writing. He had titled it "In the Land of Feast or Famine."[5]

—

DESPITE THEIR EARLY difficulties in reaching Eskimo communities, and disregarding McCaul's advice, missionaries did in fact continue to push northward. In 1916, not long after the Canadian Arctic Expedition and Denny LaNauze's patrol left Bernard Harbor, the Hudson's Bay Company established a trading post on the abandoned site. The Anglican Reverend Herbert Girling set up an outpost right next to it. The anthropologist Diamond Jenness considered Girling "a man of considerable culture and attainments, with large views and larger sympathies." Girling's "strong winning personality gained him a great influence over all the natives among whom he worked." There was one strange and terrifying moment early on in Girling's tenure. As he was helping unload a supply boat, a fuel tank exploded and ignited a fire that burned the boat to the hull. Though no one was killed, virtually all the supplies were lost. Girling would spend four years among the Copper Eskimos before dying of pneumonia in February 1920, at the age of thirty.[6]

That same year, Father Frapsauce, the Catholic priest who replaced Fathers Rouvière and LeRoux in the Far North, asked Bishop Gabriel Breynat to authorize resumption of the Eskimo mission. Since the verdict in the Calgary trial, Frapsauce said, he had had the chance to mix with the Eskimos, and found them "a naturally cheerful people; you never find one gloomy." The trouble was, Frapsauce said, "their morals are atrocious. They abandon all children born in the summer. They steal and lie and are utterly dissolute. There is a certain amount of good material there, and a few individuals whose habitual conduct is good; that of most of them, however, is simply deplorable. They are all addicted to witchcraft." A year later, Father Frapsauce fell through the ice on Great Bear Lake and drowned. His body was not recovered for months.[7]

Anglicans initially built St. Andrews Church in Bernard Harbor in 1915, but they moved it to the town of Coppermine, where the river dumps into Coronation Gulf, in 1929, soon after the Hudson's Bay Company built its outpost there. Catholics built their own church, Our Lady of the Light, right down the road. The Royal Canadian Mounted Police set up a post three years later.

In the spring of 1929, Breynat reported that he could fly the five hundred miles from Fort McMurray, north of Edmonton, all the way to Fort Simpson, on the Mackenzie River, in just ninety minutes. The trip used to take five days by dogsled. That same year, he traveled to the mouth of the Coppermine. There, in a "wretched little hut," Breynat and Father Pierre Fallaize, who'd replaced Father Frapsauce, gave the first mass ever celebrated on the Arctic coast. Their congregation consisted of a single Eskimo family. A week later Breynat performed his first Eskimo marriage. A month after this, Breynat lost another priest, Father Lecuyer, who drowned on the Arctic Red River. "It was a trial that gave me food for serious reflection," Breynat wrote. "We had reached the limit of our available strength. It was impossible to develop, or even hold our own, with a personnel so reduced as ours."

Breynat set off for Rome in 1930, to plead the case for more personnel with Pope Pius XI himself. The pope told Breynat that the first book he had ever read as a youth had been an account of the search for the Northwest Passage. He gave Breynat his full support and threw in $10,000 to help pay for a new mission boat. In August 1931, Breynat once again traveled to the coast, hoping to see the two crosses Corporals Wight and Withers had erected as a memorial to Fathers Rouvière and LeRoux. He took a canoe to Bloody Falls with Father Duchaussois and Patsy Klengenberg. Duchaussois kept pressing Patsy for details, pointing out "how improbable it was that desire to get hold of the carbine should have been the only motive for the double murder, when the victims had won the esteem and affection of so many of the Eskimos."

Finally, Patsy responded. "You should know, Father, that among the Eskimos nothing so important ever happens *without the medicine men having something to do with it.*"

Precisely what Patsy meant by this, Breynat did not fully tease out. Indeed, exactly what happened during those terrible moments near Bloody Falls remained a source of mystery for all who knew the Eskimos and the priests. That the priests had become unpredictable was beyond dispute, and unpredictability in the Arctic always created fear. In addition to being dangerously close to starvation, Fathers Rouvière and LeRoux had been physically weakened by injury and illness. Their backs to the Arctic coast, they had faced retreating over hundreds of miles of a bewildering landscape that for a century had swallowed explorers who possessed far more wilderness skills than they. Winter, the season of darkness and death, was on its way. The priests had no food, no shelter, and no real talent in securing either. In every way, their circumstances, even before Sinnisiak and Uluksuk had appeared, had become catastrophic. To the Eskimos, these facts alone suggested that the priests were perilously close to the edge. Would the priests have survived their journey back to their cabin on their own? It is hard to know. It does not seem likely.

Father Rouvière had always seemed a gentle man, but Uluksuk claimed that it had been Rouvière who had handed LeRoux the rifle. Then, just as impulsively, Rouvière had apparently changed his mind, and begun throwing the priests' cartridges in the river. This, to Sinnisiak and Uluksuk, must have been the clearest evidence of all that the priests had become unhinged. Rifle cartridges, even for skilled hunters, were precious beyond description. For the priests, they represented a last flicker of hope. With the cartridges washed downriver, the priests would have had no way of securing food for a journey that, given their inexperience and poor navigational skills, would have taken them many, many days.

The fact that Sinnisiak had to shoot Father Rouvière in the back seems clear evidence that Rouvière, in the end, refused violence. Father LeRoux, for his part, had always seemed petulant, even aggressive; that LeRoux, especially in such a state of desperation, would push a moment to its violent conclusion, would have surprised no one who had crossed his path in the Barren Lands.

Bishop Breynat, of course, reached his own conclusions. Patsy's comments about the medicine men only served "to strengthen our conviction that our missionaries were killed out of hatred of our holy religion, whose teaching threatened to destroy the domination, hitherto undisputed, exercised by these men of darkness, the sorcerers. If only we could discover soon the formal proof, which would allow the Church to bestow the palm and halo of martyrs on our beloved dead!"[8]

In August 1934, Father Pierre Fallaize made his own pilgrimage to find the memorial, now nearly two decades old. It was difficult to locate, partially because information about its emplacement was inexact. But Father Pierre Fallaize was determined. The site had become a symbol of the church's will to establish itself in the north country. Another priest hoped that one day, "all the Eskimos will pray there, remembering with gratitude those who laid down their lives for them."[9]

After making his way to the Arctic Ocean and traveling three hundred miles by boat from the Catholic mission base at Letty Harbor, Father Fallaize and three other priests, along with "a little Eskimo" named Peter Natit, took a motorboat twelve miles up the Coppermine to Bloody Falls, where they exited the boat and, in sealskin boots, climbed a steep bank. They then hiked over muddy, patchy ground, made slippery by the frozen subsoil that lay beneath. They stumbled over "women's heads," creeping plants, lichen, moss, and the tundra that extended over virtually the whole region. Since no one knew exactly where the memorial was, the small group took a number of wrong turns, scattering about as they made their way upstream. Finally, arriving at a ravine sometime in the afternoon, one of the priests called out. There, on the ground before him, lay a muddy, weather-beaten cross, about five feet in length, with a brief inscription: "In memory of the RR Fathers ROUVIÈRE and LEROUX, OMI. Killed by the Eskimos Nov. 1913. On a trip of Exploration for the Extension of the Gospel. R.I.P."

Behind, near the left arm of the cross, the priests noticed "the visible rents made by the claws of a powerful polar bear, no doubt the same animal which had leant against the cross and knocked it down." The priests stood the cross upright and secured it with a pile of rocks. They then knelt down to recite the De Profundis, along with a decade of the rosary, for their brothers "who had fallen victims to their apostolic zeal."[10]

—

PREDICTABLY, ALL OF this missionary activity had a dramatic impact on traditional customs. Suddenly, Eskimos were leaving sealing grounds two months earlier than previously, devoting themselves instead to fox trapping. In the winter of 1919, an entire population from southeast Victoria Island migrated to the Kent Peninsula, where a white trader had accumulated a large store of blubber for fuel. Hardly a hunting bow remained in the country, Diamond Jenness wrote. Nearly every man had a rifle. The destruction of the caribou was proceeding so rapidly that within ten years, scarcely one would be left in the vicinity of Coronation Gulf. The old copper culture had given way to iron; old dress was giving way to Western dress. Tuberculosis was beginning to take a toll that would ravage the Arctic for decades. By the mid-1930s, gold mines were being discovered near Great Bear Lake, and outfitters' businesses in the town of Yellowknife, on Great Slave Lake, began booming. American oil and mining companies began pouring into the Barren Lands, building roads and airfields.

The changes, of course, only broadened what had been going on in the north country for decades. In the hundred years between 1769 and 1868, London auctions had sold phenomenal quantities of furs and skins for the Hudson's Bay Company: 891,091 fox, 1,052,051 lynx, 68,694 wolverine, 288,016 bear, 467,549 wolf, 1,507,240 mink, 94,326 swan, 275,032 badger, 4,708,702 beaver, and 1,240,511 marten. Two contemporary companies, the North West Company and the Canada Company, also traded furs in comparable numbers. There are no figures for the number of native people in the region who perished because of diphtheria, smallpox, tuberculosis, poliomyelitis, and other diseases, but historians say that the figure may be as high as 90 percent. Smallpox carried off two thousand of the Greenland Eskimos in 1734 and 1735, and destroyed many of the Labrador natives as well.[11]

To Diamond Jenness, a similar fate awaited the central Arctic. In the late nineteenth century, it was estimated that the Eskimo population of the Mackenzie River delta numbered two thousand; by 1913 it was reduced to barely five hundred, the majority of the natives having died of measles. The influenza pandemic of 1918 took a terrible toll among the Eskimos of northern Alaska, nearly wiping out entire settlements. Among the Copper Eskimos, there had been a sharp rise in deaths from an influenza epidemic in 1912–13, immediately after the first encounter with Stefansson and the priests. The Oblate priest Father Fallaize, working Rouvière and LeRoux's territory in the Far North, reported that tuberculosis, meningitis, and other white men's diseases had begun to tear through the Eskimo population. A group of seventy-five people that Fallaize visited in 1924 was reduced by thirty-four in just six years. By the 1950s, the settlement at the mouth of the Coppermine had only seven families in permanent residence, but the ebb and flow of more migrant groups enabled it to support both an Anglican and a Catholic church. Both missions maintained health clinics, but it is hard to miss a certain irony in this. Throughout the 1950s and '60s, these clinics handled terrible outbreaks of measles, German measles, and Asian flu, all brought in by white visitors.

"The journey of the two French missionaries to the mouth of the Coppermine river in 1913 must have opened the eyes of the Eskimos to difficulties under which the majority of white men labor when they try to cope with Arctic conditions of life and travel," Jenness wrote. "For many different reasons, therefore, the natives conceived a certain amount of contempt for white men, contempt that was qualified only by a desire to gain some of their most valued possessions, their knives and axes and particularly their rifles and ammunition."[12]

"Even while we said our farewells," Jenness wrote,

the traders were all heading eastward to the new land where beautiful fox skins were valueless and a fortune could be gained in a night. White men have invaded it from every quarter, and the twilight of ignorance and superstition is yielding to the dawn of great knowledge. Bows and arrows have passed with other weapons into the

darkness of the past, and a new mechanical age has brought magazine rifles, shotguns, steel traps, and even gasoline engines. The
caribou are passing with the bows and arrows; of all the herds that
once crossed the narrow strait to Victoria Island hardly one now
reaches the Arctic shore. "Furs, furs, more furs," is the white man's
cry. "Without furs there is no salvation, no ammunition to shoot the
scattered game and satify your hungry children." The tribal bands
where each man toiled for all and shared his food in common are
resolving into their constituent families, and every family vies with
the rest in the race for wealth and worldly prosperity.

Whither will it all lead? Fifty years ago the cyclone swept over
the Eskimos of the Mackenzie River delta, and of its two thousand
inhabitants a scant two hundred survive. Fifty years earlier it struck
Baffin Island with similar result. Will history, fifty years hence,
record the same fate for this twilight land where two years ago we
carried on our mission? Were we the harbingers of a brighter dawn,
or only messengers of ill-omen, portending disaster?"[13]

EIGHTY-NINE YEARS after the murder of Fathers Rouvière and
LeRoux, I flew in to the tiny outpost of Kugluktuk, the village that had for
several generations been known as Coppermine, now renamed with an
Inuit word that means "Where the Waters Fall." Even as our First Air jet
passed over the borderless country that lies between Great Slave Lake and
the Arctic Ocean, I was aware that my own journey was just another in a
long series of expeditions taken by inhabitants of more southern climes
who can never quite shake a fascination with the Far North. My interest in
the murder and its aftermath had little to do with the grim details of the
crime or the dramatic peculiarities of the trial that followed, though in
time both events would come to intrigue me for their own reasons. What
had drawn me north was a line of inquiry I find preoccupying like few others: the relationships that human beings develop with the land on which
they choose to live. Landscapes, particularly harsh landscapes, operate on

human history like the hand of a novelist, pressuring people to act and react in ways that illuminate their character.

To my mind, the lives and deaths of the two priests was a story full of moral ambiguity. Their deaths, according to white missionaries, police officers, and lawyers, were the result of criminal Eskimo behavior. But their deaths were also intricately tied up in the distinctly nonmoral facts of Arctic life: cold, hunger, and fear. Their deaths reflected the sharp and uncompromising differences between European and native notions of wisdom. One was based on Western principles of sanctity and sin, on following codes of conduct that had first arisen in a place whose most striking physical attributes were heat and sand and organized agriculture. The other was based on the physical experience of living in a place that demanded absolute discernment simply to survive from one day to the next. The Eskimos did not believe they had come to the Arctic across the Bering Straits. They had arisen straight from their land. Among the Eskimos, there were no leaders. There were experts. Hunters. Fishermen. Bootmakers. Shamans. Eskimos had a relationship with their landscape that over centuries had evolved to great subtlety. Hunters could come to a place they had last visited forty years before and remember it exactly. The landscape required understanding, not controlling. Christian missionaries asked their constituents to spend their time preparing for the world to come. The Eskimos could afford no such luxury. Bishop Breynat had once described the Canadian natives to whom he ministered as "disinherited souls." Disinherited from what exactly? The Eskimos had been living season to season in the Arctic for five thousand years. Could it be that the priests were the real nomads, wandering in the wilderness?[14]

The troubling links between proselytizing religion, commerce, and justice that have become such an emblem of the last two hundred years seemed perfectly captured in this little story of life and death in a very remote place. To many of the first whites in the Arctic, the Eskimos were just another in a long line of native people to be poked, prodded, and, in some cases, brought back for museum display. One young girl, apparently kidnapped by whalers hoping to sell her as a slave in the Caribbean, ended up in France and was given the name Mademoiselle le Blanc. She amazed the French with her running speed; reportedly, she ran slightly sideways, like a wolf. A small party of Eskimos brought back to the United States by Admiral Robert Peary in 1897 quickly sickened and died from bacterial infections for which they had no immune defense. Their flesh was stripped from their bodies, and their skeletons, articulated with wire, were displayed in the American Museum of Natural History.[15]

Exploring a moment in history in which two remarkably different cultures violently intersected also seemed an opportunity for me to understand some basic cultural impulses. The looking glass that colonial powers hold up to native people always turns out to be more mirror than lens. For Europeans, Francis Spufford writes, "studying the Inuit was like rereading the very first pages of a long, long novel—whose plot the Victorians thought they knew, because they thought that they themselves lived its last pages. Everything that they may become, that they will become, waits to be revealed. In the Inuit the Victorians glimpsed the primitive, the lumpishly original forms of human making and doing."[16]

For Catholic missionaries, of course, the stunning challenge of converting Eskimos seemed heroic, and if a priest died in the act, well, he fell into a long and honorable line. "The blood of martyrs is the seed of Christians," one missionary wrote, quoting Tertullian from a time "when the newborn Church was bled every day in the arenas of the pagan Roman emporers."[17]

WHAT I DISCOVERED in Kugluktuk in the summer of 2002 was both irrelevant to and utterly bound up with the story you have just read. The town celebrated the Nunavut Land Claims Agreement Act and the Nunavut Act in 1993, marking the handover of vast amounts of Arctic territory to its original inhabitants. Yet to my eyes there was also a peculiar and unmistakable misery. Suicide continues to be a curse, particularly among the young. When I asked a local what a prefab house was doing rotting down by the beach—not fifty yards from my campsite—he said the townspeople had dragged it there after the home owner, in a fit of jealous rage, had killed his wife, all but one of his children, and himself inside it. A young woman I met, the wife of the newly arrived Pentecostal minister, seemed overwhelmed by her new home. "There has been so much death here," she said.

The twin demons of North American native people, alcoholism and diabetes, were also in full bloom and seemed, like all the town's troubles, somehow more despairing for the unimaginable remoteness of the place itself. Though the town was officially "dry," liquor fetched $300 a bottle on the black market, and was widely consumed. The current Anglican minister, Malcolm Palmer, had had to stop storing altar wine in his home because people kept breaking in to steal it. One of his predecessors, Bishop John Sperry, considers Kugluktuk to be suffering from "urbanization," an astonishing—but accurate—way to think about a tiny town whose nearest neighbor is hundreds of miles away. Kugluktuk now has all the problems of big cities: a high rate of unemployment; AIDS; cancer; domestic violence; drug abuse; pollution (mostly the result of nuclear fallout and the aerial disposal of PCBs, which are now showing up in the fat cells of caribou and seals); and global warming, which is already causing changes in both seasonal ice melts and caribou migration patterns. "These days, the clergy may not have to pull teeth or deliver babies," Sperry writes, "but almost daily, their ministry involves counselling people suffering from marriage breakdowns, spousal, elder, or child abuse, or chronic depression. They may need to attend court sessions, talk to parents about delinquent children, or deal with suicide attempts."[18]

It's not that Kugluktuk is hard to get to; in this era of regular, safe air travel, quite the opposite is true. Getting to Kugluktuk today requires a ninety-minute plane ride from Yellowknife, the capital of the Northwest Territories, which is itself a ninety-minute trip north from Edmonton. Yet the place feels profoundly separate from the rest of the world. A giant container ship arrives once a year, as it has for decades, to disgorge everything from fuel oil to prefabricated housing materials to snowmobiles and children's bicycles. In a local supermarket, you can buy a wolf pelt for $750, or a pineapple for $14. People live in prefab houses that rent for $35 Canadian a month. Trucks deliver fresh water to every house in town every two days. Teenagers drive around on four-wheel ATVs. Most elders in the town are Christian. Malcolm Palmer conducts every part of his Anglican church services in the local dialect, except for the sermon, which he reads in English. During the service I attended, people sang "Onward, Christian Soliders" in Inuinnaqtun. It seemed an oddly appropriate song, given the battles Catholics and Protestants had been waging to establish themselves in the region. In Kugluktuk, the Catholic church has been closed for years, but a new Pentecostal church was just getting started. If they chose different religions, people from the same families had to be buried in separate cemeteries.

But traditional life is not that long gone. Sitting around a plywood table in the Kugluktuk Chamber of Commerce, I spoke with a number of older people who had lived in igloos and caribou-skin tents until 1965. People still go "out on the land" during the warmer weather, disappearing to remote hunting and fishing cabins for months at a time. They don't need maps or compasses to find their way. Aimee Ahegona, an elderly man whose grandparents had once taken Diamond Jenness into their tent, told me how he had killed a polar bear when he was just fifteen years old. Peter Kamingoak, who had served as a guide for Anglican bishop John Sperry, said snowmobiles were useful, but usually burned out after a year of hard use. Dog teams were still considered far more durable.

When I visited, everyone I spoke to had watched the Twin Towers burning on CNN, and had feelings of deep sympathy for Americans. Yet when I tried to explain where New York City was, even pointing to it on a map in one family's house, the distance from Kugluktuk to Manhattan seemed interplanetary. Imagining life and death at Ground Zero seemed no more possible from the shores of Coronation Gulf than imagining life in Kugluktuk had been from the banks of the Hudson River. I thought of the last hundred years, and the degree to which Western culture had, and had not, managed to envelop the people of Coronation Gulf. And I thought of what Denny LaNauze had written, soon after the epic journey he had taken to bring Sinnisiak and Uluksuk to justice in Edmonton.

"White trappers and traders are expected also to enter Coronation Gulf this summer, and as the natives are only too anxious to learn white man's ways and habits, the advent of civililzation amongst them will not tend to their betterment," LaNauze had noted. "Game will in course of time grow scarcer with the advent of a large supply of arms and ammunition, and the people will begin to wear white man's clothes in preference to their own sensible deer skin clothing, which cannot be excelled. Should any epidemic ever strike these people, no doubt many deaths would result, for the people usually live in large communities. Indeed, to us who have had the good fortune to see these people live their strenuous, healthy existence on the Arctic coast, we cannot wish them better fortune than to hope that civilization may ever be kept at arms' length from them."[19]

ACKNOWLEDGMENTS

—

As someone who has traveled to remote places with all kinds of different people, I know a good team when I have one, and my trip to Kugluktuk and Bloody Falls in the summer of 2002 was a real pleasure thanks in large part to the companionship of my brother, Brian Jenkins, and my dear friend Chris Sheldrick.

In Kugluktuk, I was fortunate indeed to come to know Malcolm Palmer, the current Anglican minister, and his wonderful wife, Ruth, who managed the town's visitors' center. The Palmers were unfailingly generous and hospitable. Also in Kugluktuk, thanks to Alex Buchan, Alistair and Dan Harvey, Aimee Ahegona, Larry Whitaker, Tommy and Elva Piglalak, and Peter Kamingoak.

The transcripts for the Edmonton and Calgary trials can be found in the Royal Canadian Mounted Police files at the National Archives of Canada. The Royal North West Mounted Police report detailing the search for Sinnisiak and Uluksuk can be found in the Alberta Provincial Archives, as can the Commissioners Report detailing other RNWMP activities. I received invaluable assistance from a number of researchers and staff librarians, including Kay Forsyth and Jonathan Davidson at the Alberta Provinicial Archives; Chantal Nadeau at the Archives Deschatelets in Ottawa; and Diane Lamoreaux at the archive of the Oblates of Mary Immaculate. Thanks to Kirsten Olson at the Legal Archives Society of Alberta and Margit Nance and Curt Griffiths at Simon Fraser University's Northern Justice Society. Photographs of the people and places described here can be found in a number of places, and for this reason I am indebted to several people who work in archives in the United States and Canada: at Dartmouth College's Rauner Collection, Sarah Hartwell; at the Northwest Territories Office of Education, Culture and Development in Yellowknife, Amanda Halldorson; at Canada's National Archives, Doug Whyte, Richie Allen, and Rowanne Mokhtar.

Once again, the staff at the University of Delaware's interlibrary loan office deserve special mention, especially Ann Pfaelzer Ortiz. Eric Wilson helped out early on as an undergraduate research assistant, and Leigh Snyder and Trish Jenkins contributed valuable insights as independent study students.

Although this book comes with a complete bibliography, I thought it proper to mention some particularly important influences. Barry Lopez, Hugh Brody, and Francis Spufford are among the most eloquent and textured writers I have read on the Far North; the region's literature is vastly richer for their contributions. R. G. Moyles set the stage for this book when he first dug up some of the story's most important documents for his book *British Law and Arctic Men*. George Whalley's research into the case and his biography of John Hornby were extremely helpful, as was George Douglas's account of his trip to the Arctic coast.

Thanks to my dear friends and exquisitely intelligent readers Chris Sheldrick, Tim Dilworth, and Wes Davis, whose intellectual capacities and enthusiasms continue to astound me. I must also tip my hat to the Village Idiots, Tom Thompson, Matt Thompson, James Guyton, Gerry Hanlon, Andrew Holt, and Kevin O'Malley, with whom I played bluegrass every Thursday night during the course of this writing. Mike Sproge and Linda Brunson at Baltimore's spirited Evergreen Café supplied the coffee that made this book possible.

I am fortunate to have had Lee Boudreaux as editor on this project. Though she inherited it from Courtney Hodell, with whom I had worked on a previous book, Lee proved an exceptionally enthusiastic and curious guide, and a razor-sharp line editor as well. Her assistant, Laura Ford, was unfailingly professional and generous with her time, and Bonnie Thompson's copyediting was brilliant. And, as always, I am indebted to my wonderful agent, Neil Olson.

Finally, I am grateful to my wife, Katherine, who has always been a subtle and painstaking editor; to my son, Steedman, who charms my every day; and to my baby daughter, Annalisa Swan, who waited so patiently in utero while I finished this manuscript. She began her entrance into this world exactly thirty minutes after I printed out my first draft.

NOTES

—

PROLOGUE

1. John R. Sperry, *Igloo Dwellers Were My Church* (Calgary: Bayeaux Arts, Inc., 2001), p. 120.
2. Roger P. Bulliard, *Inuk* (New York: Farrar, Straus and Young, 1951), pp. 76–77.
3. Edmonton *Morning Bulletin*, August 14, 1917.
4. "Address of C. C. McCaul, K. C., in Opening the Case for the Prosecution of Sinnisiak, an Eskimo Charged with Murder, Before the Hon. Chief Justice Harvey and a Jury, at Edmonton, Alberta," August 14th, 1917, Alberta Provincial Archives, pp. 4–6; Edmonton court transcript.
5. *Ibid.*

CHAPTER ONE

1. George Whalley, *The Legend of John Hornby* (Toronto: Macmillan, 1962), pp. 5–22, 27, 54–55; George Douglas, *Lands Forlorn: A Story of an Expedition to Hearne's Coppermine River* (New York: G. P. Putnam's Sons, 1914), pp. 50–51; Gabriel Breynat, *The Flying Bishop: Fifty Years in the Canadian Far North* (London: Burns and Oates, 1955), pp. 20, 155; George Whalley, "Coppermine Martyrdom," *Queens Quarterly* 66 (winter 1959–60), pp. 591, 593–95, 610. Hornby had gone to Harrow, spoke in a soft scholarly voice, and knew bits of French, German, and Italian. He had first come to Canada from England in 1904, a wandering twenty-three-year-old son of a cotton-spinning family. His father, "Monkey" Hornby, had been an all-England cricketeer. John Hornby was not the first of his tribe to travel far afield; one brother had died in Africa in 1905; another was a veteran of the Boer War. John trained for

the diplomatic service in Germany; he learned to ski there, a story went, and just three weeks later reached the finals of the world ski-running championships.

2. Breynat, pp. 226–27.

3. Breynat, pp. 61, 107, 155; Whalley, "Martyrdom," p. 593.

4. Breynat, 20–21, 154. Mazenod would become beatified by Pope Paul VI in 1975 and canonized by Pope John Paul II in 1995. As he lay dying on May 21, 1861, Mazenod was said to have offered his final wish to his followers: "Practice amongst yourselves charity, charity, charity . . . and zeal for the salvation of souls."

5. Breynat, p. 154. By the end of the nineteenth century, missions to the Canadian Arctic were being bled by the limitless spiritual needs of gold prospectors in the Yukon. Yet the church still maintained ten missions to serve northern Indians, mostly along the Mackenzie River corridor and the shores of the region's big lakes, Athabasca and Great Slave. Of these missions, only four had churches: Fort Resolution and Fort Providence on Great Slave Lake, and Fort Norman and Fort Good Hope on the Mackenzie. Others conducted services in small house chapels. Manning these missions were a dozen priests, a dozen lay brothers, and ten nuns from the Sisters of Charity or the Grey Sisters of Montreal. In 1895, the church had purchased a sixty-foot steamer, the *Saint-Alphonse,* for "revictualling" the missions; the money came from societies of the Propagation of the Faith and the Holy Childhood. A new steamer, the *Sainte Marie,* would arrive in 1906.

6. J. F. Rymer, "The Dream of the North; or, Catholic Work Amongst the Indians," *Catholic Registry,* January 11, 1912.

7. Breynat, pp. 44–45. One old man, known as "Man's Shadow," despite being sick, set off from his camp Easter morning and crossed the lake to receive Holy Communion. The following morning, still feverish, he left the mission for a two-hour hike to inspect his fishing nets. As soon as he arrived, he learned that his son Henry had killed a bear and three elk out on the land. Over the protests of his wife, who was herself prostrate with the flu, Man's Shadow set off to find his son and a recuperative meal. A few days later, in a dismantled encampment, some Indians discovered the man's body, half burned and partly devoured by his own dogs, who were still in harness.

8. Breynat, pp. 110, 154–55; R. G. Moyles, *British Law and Arctic Men: The Celebrated 1917 Murder Trials of Sinnisiak and Uluksuk, First Inuit Tried Under White Man's Law* (Saskatoon, Saskatchewan: Western Producer Prairie Books, 1979), p. 7; Whalley, *Hornby*, p. 27; Calgary *Daily Herald*, August 22, 1917.

9. Breynat, pp. 20, 27, 41. Breynat's first midnight mass among his new congregation was one he would never forget. Inside the little hall chapel, men packed into one side, women into the other, all of them kneeling or squatting on their heels. The altar was adorned with candles fashioned from caribou grease. The faithful burst forth with the Kyrie, Gloria, and Credo, then sang hymns in the Indian language Montagnais. During communion, the preparation prayers were recited in chorus; then men, women, and children dutifully filed toward the Holy Table, still singing "Behold the Gentle Lamb." Most of the Indians living near the mission stuck around only until New Year's Day, when the Hudson's Bay Company factor presented a giant feast. The Indians, who to the settlers' incredulity had been living almost exclusively on caribou for six months, received, among other things, a couple of cakes of tobacco, half a pound of tea, a pound or two of flour, and a few lumps of sugar. They then "set off happily for the respective camping grounds, undaunted by the prospect of five or six days afoot and nights in the open," Breynat wrote. "Blessed Caribou-Eaters, God bless them!"

10. Breynat, p. 41.

11. Breynat, pp. 54–57.

12. Vilhjalmur Stefansson, *My Life with the Eskimos* (New York: Macmillan, 1913, 1927), pp. xiv, 1, 3, 10, 12, 14, 149, 176–79, 180–81, 208–09; Francis Spufford, *I May Be Some Time: Ice and the English Imagination* (New York: Picador, 1997), p. 191. Stefansson was a Manitoban born to Icelandic parents who by 1911 had already made archaeological trips to Iceland in 1904 and 1905, and to the north coast of Alaska and the mouth of the Mackenzie River in 1906–07. But it was to the east, the very place Father Rouvière would come several years later, that Stefansson wanted to explore. After interviewing Eskimos near the Mackenzie, Stefansson became certain that no natives east of Cape Parry, along the Dolphin and Union Strait, had ever seen a white man. This, he felt sure, was the only such group left on the North American continent. "Finding

them," he wrote, "would be the unbelievable adventure of stepping thousands of years into the past, back into the unknown history of the Stone Age." Given his years of experience, Stefansson was supremely confident in his ability to survive. "Carrying food to the Arctic," he observed, "was carrying coals to Newcastle." In 1908 Stefansson had launched an expedition with the Canadian zoologist Rudolph Martin Anderson to find and live among the Eskimos near Coronation Gulf. In essence, he set out on an anthropologist's headiest adventure: to discover one of the last of the world's people to have remained outside the ken of the European world. Stefansson and Anderson decided to travel light, carrying only cameras and film, rudimentary gear, and rifles and shotguns for themselves and to trade to the Eskimos. Years later, Stefansson would write *The Lost Franklin Expedition*, a polemic critical of the stubborn European habit of ignoring native navigation and survival techniques. Stefansson's own reaction to the Copper Eskimos bordered on ecstatic.

"These were not such men as Caesar found in Gaul or in Britain," he wrote.

> They were more nearly like the still earlier hunting tribes of Britain and Gaul living contemporaneous to, but oblivious of, the building of the first pyramid in Egypt. Their existence on the same continent with our populous cities was an anachronism of ten thousand years in material development. They gathered their food with the weapons of the Stone Age, they thought their simple, primitive thoughts, and lived their insecure and tense lives — lives that were to me the mirrors of the lives of our far ancestors, whose bones and crude handiwork we now and then discover in river gravels or in prehistoric caves. I had nothing to imagine; I had merely to look and listen; for here were not remains of the Stone Age, but the Stone Age itself, with its men and women, very human, entirely friendly, who welcomed us to their homes and talked with us.

13. Stefansson, *My Life*, pp. 75–76, 81–82. When he had begun his expedition in 1908, Stefansson had immediately noticed a pair of dramatic changes among the Mackenzie River Eskimos from his previous visit just

two years before. First, they were altering their seasonal hunting habits in order to secure molasses, sugar, and tea from the dozen or more whaling ships that wintered at Herschel Island. As they had become more and more dependent on trade and throw-offs from the whaling ships, the Eskimos had begun to lose their autonomy. Some had became dissolute as a result, causing a number of explorers to consider the degradation of the people to be as much a legacy of European contact as trade. "The net result was that between 1889 and 1906 there had been greater change wrought than the Hudson's Bay Company has been reponsible for among any of the northern Indians in a hundred years," Stefansson wrote. "The condition was now serious, for the whaling industry was beginning to show the signs of a gradual breakdown, which has since terminated in a collapse."

CHAPTER TWO

1. Samuel Hearne, *A Journey from Prince of Wales Fort in Hudson's Bay to the Northern Ocean, 1769, 1770, 1771, 1772*, ed. Richard Glover (Toronto: Macmillan, 1958), pp. 98–100.

2. George M. Douglas, *Lands Forlorn: A Story of an Expedition to Hearne's Coppermine River* (New York: G. P. Putnam's Sons, 1914), pp. iii, 6–7; George Whalley, *The Legend of John Hornby* (Toronto: Macmillan, 1962), p. 51.

3. Douglas, pp. 44–47.

4. Barry Lopez, *Arctic Dreams: Imagination and Desire in a Northern Landscape* (New York: Bantam Books, 1987), p. 243.

5. Whalley, *Hornby*, p. 1.

6. Francis Spufford, *I May Be Some Time: Ice and the English Imagination* (New York: Picador, 1997), p. 189. Some contemporary linguistists argue that "Eskimo" may actually have evolved from a word describing a technique for tying snowshoes.

7. Hugh Brody, *The Other Side of Eden: Hunters, Farmers, and the Shaping of the World* (New York: North Point Press, 2000), p. 111.

8. Spufford, p. 212; John R. Sperry, *Igloo Dwellers Were My Church* (Calgary: Bayeaux Arts, Inc., 2001), p. 14.

9. Gabriel Breynat, *The Flying Bishop: Fifty Years in the Canadian Far North*

(London: Burns and Oates, 1955), pp. 155–56; George Whalley, "Copper-mine Martyrdom," *Queens Quarterly* 66 (winter 1959–60), pp. 595–96.

10. Douglas, pp. 52–54.
11. Whally, *Hornby*, pp. 56–57; Whalley, "Martyrdom," pp. 596–97.
12. Douglas, pp. 66–71.
13. Whalley, "Martyrdom," pp. 596–97; Douglas, p. 86.
14. Douglas, pp. 90, 136–37; Whalley, *Hornby*, pp. 57–58; Whalley, "Mar-tyrdom," p. 597.

CHAPTER THREE

Epigraph: John R. Sperry, *Igloo Dwellers Were My Church* (Calgary: Bayeaux Arts, Inc., 2001), p. 72.

1. George M. Douglas, *Lands Forlorn: A Story of an Expedition to Hearne's Coppermine River* (New York: G. P. Putnam's Sons, 1914), pp. 93–104.
2. Douglas, pp. 107–10.
3. Douglas, pp. 139–40; George Walley, *The Legend of John Hornby* (Toronto: Macmillan, 1962), p. 60.
4. Gabriel Breynat, *The Flying Bishop: Fifty Years in the Canadian Far North* (London: Burns and Oates, 1955), pp. 156–58; George Whalley, "Coppermine Martyrdom," *Queens Quarterly* 66 (winter 1959–60), pp. 598–99.

CHAPTER FOUR

Epigraph: Daniel Merkur, *Powers Which We Do Not Know: The Gods and Spirits of the Inuit* (Moscow: University of Idaho Press, 1991), p. x.

1. Vilhjalmur Stefansson, *My Life with the Eskimos* (New York: Macmil-lan, 1913, 1927), p. 37.
2. Stefansson, *My Life*, p. 127. Stefansson began his trip east to Coronation Gulf on April 21, 1910. Within a few short weeks, he would make one of his signature, and most controversial, discoveries: a group of people who came to be known as "Blond" Eskimos. Upon encountering people he felt resembled sunburned Europeans (though none were actually blond; Stefansson blamed the term on overly exuberant newspapermen), Stefansson

developed a theory that they may have descended from early Nordic explorers, perhaps from companions of the marauder Erik the Red. Banished from Iceland in the tenth century, Erik had sailed for a frozen place he subsequently named Greenland in hopes of attracting settlers. Erik's son Leif Eriksson sailed in 1000 to visit his father, but went too far south and hit North America. When he finally did make it to Greenland, he brought along a group of missionaries to set up a Christian colony. Just two hundred years later, there was already a bishopric, a monastery, a nunnery, and sixteen churches. Eventually, Stefansson postulated, some of these people either intermarried with Eskimos or gradually migrated west.

3. Stefansson, *My Life*, pp. 180–81, 187, 194–96. At one point, Stefansson met an Indian named Jimmy Soldat who offered to take him to John Hornby in exchange for an introduction to Stefansson's Eskimo companions. Stefansson felt ambivalent about introducing Soldat or anyone else from the south to his new friends. "I did not desire to bring my unspoiled Coronation Gulf people into contact with civilization, with the ravages of which among the Eskimos of Alaska and the Mackenzie I am too familiar," Stefansson wrote. "But it seemed that this could not be staved off for more than a year or two, in any case, for our having lived with the Eskimos was bound to become well known, and both the traders and missionaries who operate through Fort Norman would be sure to make use of the information." Stefansson finally agreed to lead Soldat to within a mile of the Eskimo encampment, then went off to ask their permission to bring him into their camp. At first they refused; they had had little contact with Indians, and their ancestors had had little good to say about them. In the end, Stefansson persuaded them to meet Soldat, provided that he leave all weapons behind. Soldat initially rejected this plan, assuming that the Eskimos meant to kill him. When at last the meeting took place, Soldat lost little time handing out colorful religious prints. He asked Stefansson to tell the Eskimos that he was "an ambassador of a bishop of the Roman Catholic Church, and that the bishop said that if they were good men and never killed any more Indians and abjured their heathenish practices, he would come and build a mission among them and would convert them to the true faith." Stefansson declined. "This speech," he later wrote, "which meant so much to the Indian, would, of

course, have meant nothing to the Eskimos, for they had never heard of the good bishop or of the faith he preaches. I, therefore, did not bother to translate anything, but merely took the pictures, which were the ordinary religious chromos, and gave them to the Eskimos."

4. John R. Sperry, *Igloo Dwellers Were My Church* (Calgary: Bayeaux Arts, Inc., 2001), p. 39; Diamond Jenness, *The Life of the Copper Eskimos: A Report of the Canadian Arctic Expedition, 1913–1918* (New York: Johnson Reprint Corporation, 1970), p. 235. In addition to his remarkable ethnographies of the Copper Eskimos, Jenness is credited with discovering the ancient Dorset culture of Baffin Island.

5. Barry Lopez, *Arctic Dreams: Imagination and Desire in a Northern Landscape* (New York: Bantam Books, 1987), p. 201.

6. Jenness, *Life of the Copper Eskimos*, pp. 172–81.

7. Stefansson, *My Life*, p. 185.

8. Stefansson, *My Life*, p. 36.

9. Hugh Brody, *The Other Side of Eden: Hunters, Farmers, and the Shaping of the World* (New York: North Point Press, 2000), pp. 233–35.

10. Jenness, *Life of the Copper Eskimos*, pp. 185–88.

11. Jenness, *Life of the Copper Eskimos*, pp. 194–95, 200, 211; Richard Condon, with Julia Ogina and the Holman Elders, *The Northern Copper Inuit: A History* (Norman: University of Oklahoma Press, 1996), p. 36.

12. Jenness, *Life of the Copper Eskimos*, p. 217.

13. Brody, *Eden*, pp. 230–31.

14. Roger P. Bulliard, *Inuk* (New York: Farrar, Straus and Young, 1951), pp. 266, 268.

CHAPTER FIVE

1. George M. Douglas, *Lands Forlorn: A Story of an Expedition to Hearne's Coppermine River* (New York: G. P. Putnam's Sons, 1914), pp. 136–40; George Whalley, "Coppermine Martyrdom," *Queens Quarterly* 66 (winter 1959–60), p. 599; Diamond Jenness, *The Life of the Copper Eskimos: A Report of the Canadian Arctic Expedition, 1913–1918* (New York: Johnson Reprint Corporation, 1970), pp. 97, 101.

2. Jenness, *Life of the Copper Eskimos*, pp. 104–05.

3. Jenness, *Life of the Copper Eskimos*, pp. 113–14.
4. Jenness, *Life of the Copper Eskimos*, pp. 107–08.
5. Douglas, pp. 158–59, 162.
6. Whalley, "Martyrdom," p. 600; George Whalley, *The Legend of John Hornby* (Toronto: Macmillan, 1962), p. 64.
7. Douglas, pp. 131–33, 152–53. Lionel had not stopped with house construction. He had also made a strong table, around which he had placed four wooden folding chairs the team had appropriated from the *Mackenzie River* steamer. Along the wall near the fireplace, he built a makeshift kitchen—a row of shelves bursting with pots and pans and tins and biscuit boxes filled with flour, sugar, rolled oats, beans, and dried apples. Sleeping quarters were arranged with cots for George and Sandburg and a hammock for Lionel.

    Meals were simple affairs. Breakfast, served at nine-thirty, typically consisted of oatmeal porridge, sometimes served with bacon and beans, but more often with a caribou or ptarmigan hash, dried potatoes, bannock (a flat, unleavened bread made from oatmeal), and tea. Lunch, served at three-thirty, was typically soup, caribou steaks, stews, or roasted ptarmigan, along with more dried potatoes and bannock and stewed apples. Dinner, at eight, was usually the day's light meal, just bannock and chocolate. For a weekly treat, Sunday breakfasts were served with coffee instead of tea, and hominy instead of oatmeal.

    Labor among the three was laid out as neatly and efficiently as the cabin's interior. Chores rotated each week between the cook, the woodchopper, and the hunter. As the chef took stock of supplies and prepared meals, the woodchopper would locate and fell dead spruce trees, drag them to a wood pile, and saw and split firewood. The hunter would go out on daily expeditions in search of game. Between the two wandering members of the party, the land surrounding the little cabin had snowshoe tracks strung over a radius of ten miles. The local wildlife became very familiar neighbors, Douglas wrote, though mostly through the tracks they left in the snow. Occasionally they would catch sight of a wolf or an arctic fox, but these were rare; wolverines were never spotted in the flesh. Herds of caribou were exceedingly scarce during the winter months, but ptarmigan, their next favorite source of meat protein, were abundant.

During October and November, the hunter, carrying a .22 rifle, routinely brought home five ptarmigan a day, and by the end of November they had accumulated a stock of fifty frozen birds, all plucked, cleaned, and ready for the pot.

8. Douglas, pp. 140–43.
9. Douglas, pp. 146–47; Whalley, "Martyrdom," p. 599.
10. Douglas, pp. 160–64, 169; Whalley, "Martyrdom," pp. 600–01.
11. Douglas, pp. 179–231; Roger P. Bulliard, *Inuk* (New York: Farrar, Straus and Young, 1951), p. 227.
12. Whalley, "Martyrdom," p. 602; Whalley, *Hornby*, pp. 81–83; Douglas, pp. 179–231, 284. The Douglases and Hornby had left for the coast back on April 30, taking two toboggans, each pulled by three dogs. They had passed Bloody Falls, where, 141 years before, Samuel Hearne had watched his Indian guides slaughter a community of Eskimos. Sure enough, they had met Eskimos there, but had been treated well. They had been offered musk-ox skins. They had continued to the coast, becoming one of the earliest white expeditions to reach the Arctic Ocean by an overland route from the south. They greeted a family living in a tent by the shore. Douglas snapped a picture of the parents with their four children, all of them dressed in full caribou skins.

On their way south, they stopped for a visit with a cheerful Eskimo family of five: parents with girls aged thirteen and seven, and a ten-year-old boy. Later, they were joined by another woman and her husband, who had been out hunting ptarmigan. George Douglas shot a photograph of a man, his bow stretched tight, standing over a small shrub. Though the family had no news of Stefansson, they did possess several tin cooking pots, which must have come from one of the Arctic expeditions. George Douglas trotted out the French-Eskimo dictionary compiled by Father Petitot, the priest who, driven nearly mad by the darkness forty-four years before, had fled the Arctic in a panic. Douglas tried out a few words. At first the Eskimos were confused, but when Douglas spoke a word they understood, they cheered and crowded around the book "as though they expected to *hear* something from it."

The Douglases visited with another group of Eskimos farther south. This group carried a skinless kayak, which made for easy portaging on windy days, and a number of things they wanted to trade to the Indians, including sealskin shoes and parchment made of young sealskin. Though the Douglases declined to take anything, they left the Eskimos with some forks and spoons. One woman was so eager to have a fork that she offered an entire wolfskin in exchange. It wasn't an eating utensil she fancied; it was a comb. She also desperately wanted Hornby's fur capote, even putting on a kind of dance to plead for it. George Douglas was be-mused, but remained typically circumspect. The Eskimo woman was not "one whit more extravagant in her folly than some 'civilized' women I have since seen, whose sense of the fitness of things has been completely obsessed in their infautation over a fashionable craze," he wrote.

13. Douglas, p. 252.
14. "Report of the North West Mounted Police," *Sessional Papers*, 1916, no. 28.
15. Stefansson, *My Life with the Eskimos* (New York: Macmillan, 1913, 1927), p. 371; Hugh Brody, *The Other Side of Eden: Hunters, Farmers, and the Shaping of the World* (New York: North Point Press, 2000), pp. 40, 190, 282.
16. Whalley, "Martyrdom," p. 604; Whalley, *Hornby*, pp. 87–88; "Report of the North West Mounted Police," p. 210.
17. Whalley, "Martyrdom," pp. 604–05. Hornby had never had any trouble getting along with Rouvière. They had spent the entire previous winter sharing a cabin, and this new separation caused him a loneliness he had never before felt in the North. Rouvière, of course, had no choice but to side with his fellow priest, the man with whom he would soon be sharing very close quarters in very trying circumstances. Whether Rouvière ru-minated on the fate of the murder-suicide the Douglases had described, he did not say. But the rift between LeRoux and Hornby could not have but deeply soured their relationship. Hornby kept to his own cabin at the head of the Dease River and stopped visiting with the priests, who were now fully moved into the Douglas cabin six miles away. If the situation was irritating to Hornby, in practical terms it meant only fewer chess games and more dinners alone. For the priests, isolation from Hornby was plainly dangerous. Suddenly, Rouvière was the most experienced wilderness traveler at hand, and by far the most temperamentally adapted

to the ceaseless challenges of living far from home. If Rouvière had learned anything so far, it was that survival in the Barren Lands meant interdependence and cooperation. Destroying a relationship as useful as the one they had established with Hornby would have been a bad idea in summertime. Destroying it just as the two priests were preparing for the first winter together, and just before setting their sights on mission work on the Arctic coast, was self-destructive. In mid-January, Rouvière decided to accompany Hornby on a trip back to Fort Norman to check in with Father Ducot. Whether Hornby would ever return to his cabin, Rouvière could not tell. Hornby, who had never relished sharing the Barren Lands with other whites, seemed altogether sick of sharing space with Father LeRoux. For the first time since he had arrived in the region in 1908, Hornby was considering walking away from the Barren Lands, at least as long as the priests remained.

18. Whalley, "Martyrdom," pp. 606–07.
19. Edmonton trial transcripts, pp. 32–34; R. G. Moyles, *British Law and Arctic Men: The Celebrated 1917 Murder Trials of Sinnisiak and Uluksuk, First Inuit Tried Under White Man's Law* (Saskatoon, Saskatchewan: Western Producer Prairie Books, 1979), p. 7; Whalley, "Martyrdom," p. 607; Whalley, *Hornby*, pp. 92–93.
20. "Report of the North West Mounted Police," p. 205.
21. Whalley, *Hornby*, p. 97.

CHAPTER SIX

1. Diamond Jenness, *The Life of the Copper Eskimos: A Report of the Canadian Arctic Expedition, 1913–1918* (New York: Johnson Reprint Corporation, 1970), pp. 110–11.
2. "Report of the North West Mounted Police," pp. 205, 210, 214.
3. George Whalley, *The Legend of John Hornby* (Toronto: Macmillan, 1962), p. 96.
4. Gabriel Breynat, *The Flying Bishop: Fifty Years in the Canadian Far North* (London: Burns and Oates, 1955), pp. 171–74.
5. "Report of the North West Mounted Police," *Sessional Papers*, 1916, no. 28, p. 206.
6. George Whalley, "Coppermine Martyrdom," *Queens Quarterly* 66 (winter 1959–60), pp. 609–10.

CHAPTER SEVEN

1. "Report of the North West Mounted Police," *Sessional Papers*, 1916, no. 28, pp. 244, 246–48.

2. R. G. Moyles, *British Law and Arctic Men: The Celebrated 1917 Murder Trials of Sinnisiak and Uluksuk, First Inuit Tried Under White Man's Law* (Saskatoon, Saskatchewan: Western Producer Prairie Books, 1979), p. 15.

3. George Whalley, "Coppermine Martyrdom," *Queens Quarterly* 66 (winter 1959–60), p. 610; Gabriel Breynat, *The Flying Bishop: Fifty Years in the Canadian Far North* (London: Burns and Oates, 1955), p. 168.

4. Breynat, p. 168; "Report of the Commissioner of the Royal North West Mounted Police," November 1916, pp. 7, 9, 16–24.

5. Edmund Kemper Broadus, *Saturday and Sunday* (Freeport, N.Y.: Books for Libraries Press, Inc., 1967), pp. 65–66.

6. Broadus, p. 76; Moyles, p. 10.

7. Charles D. LaNauze, "Murder in the Arctic," a four-part series of articles published in *The Annals of the Propagation of the Faith* (June-July 1937, August-September 1937, December 1937–January 1938, February-March 1938), Part I, p. 51; Edmonton *Morning Bulletin*, August 10, 1917; August 17, 1917.

8. Moyles, pp. 11–12.

9. LaNauze, Part I, p. 5; "Report of the North West Mounted Police," pp. 190–91.

10. LaNauze, Part I, pp. 52–53; "Report of the North West Mounted Police," pp. 191–93. On August 12, the patrol set out for the treacherous journey across Great Bear Lake to the northeastern shore, where Rouvière, Hornby, and the Douglases had spent their winters. Given the violently unstable weather that routinely moved across the lake, LaNauze could tell the trip across would be one of the most dangerous legs of the entire expedition. The shoreline had never been properly surveyed, and the weather was wild. Within a few days of their departure a howling northwesterly gale blew across the lake, forcing D'Arcy Arden, an expert sailor, to reef the York boat's sail and limp into a makeshift anchorage. As Rouvière and the Douglases had learned, the wide-open York boat was inadequate for crossing what amounted to an inland sea. Great Bear Lake, at its

widest, is nearly 250 miles across. "A thoroughly sea-going craft, such as a 50-foot schooner well decked in and with proper anchors is the only safe way of taking supplies across the lake," LaNauze wrote. Even a short wave, coming in broadside, can flip a canoe or a York boat in a blink; Great Bear Lake routinely had waves reaching eight or ten feet, with storm surges reaching twice that.

Although the patrol managed to avoid weathering so much as a single violent breaker, just holding the tiller against the Arctic wind gradually damaged the structural integrity of the boat, until, with a crack, the rudder broke. There was little to do now but limp to shore and wait out the gale. At night, a watchman had to remain vigilant to be sure the winds didn't rip the boat from its mooring. At last, in early September, with the York boat creaking and groaning and taking on water, they came across the Douglases' boat the *Jupiter*. In the best tradition of the Far North, they scavenged the *Jupiter*'s rudder and fixed it to their own boat. They arrived at the forested northeastern shore of the lake at the end of the first week of September.

11. "Report of the North West Mounted Police," p. 194.
12. "Report of the North West Mounted Police," pp. 194, 227.
13. LaNauze, Part I, p 53; "Report of the North West Mounted Police," pp. 194–95; 227.
14. LaNauze, Part I, p. 53; "Report of the North West Mounted Police," pp. 196–97.
15. LaNauze, Part II, p. 70. During one particularly nasty stretch of cold weather, a woman went into labor. She lay in her tent, some distance from the patrol's camp, screaming through the night. Finally, a group of Indians came to LaNauze for help. They were able to follow the woman's moans all the way to her camp. He arrived at a torn and drafty tepee pitched near the shore of lake. The inside was lit and warmed only by a small fire in the middle. A group of women huddled around the shrieking mother, supporting her on their knees. They had been relieving each other for three days and nights. The woman was delirious, constantly calling out the name of her husband; he, alone in a corner, sat quietly sobbing. LaNauze seemed at a loss. He gave the woman a shot of whiskey and some bovril, with little effect. Her pulse was strong, and her temperature seemed normal. He decided to give her fifteen drops of chlorodyne

over six hours, and—because of the medication or not he could not say—
she finally gave birth to a healthy girl. Just two weeks later, the father,
mother, and baby left the camp for distant hunting grounds.

CHAPTER EIGHT

1. "Report of the North West Mounted Police," *Sessional Papers*, 1916, no. 28, pp. 248, 279.
2. "Report of the North West Mounted Police," pp. 244, 247–48, 266.
3. "Report of the North West Mounted Police," p. 245.
4. "Report of the North West Mounted Police," p. 247.
5. "Report of the North West Mounted Police," p. 270.
6. "Report of the North West Mounted Police," p. 277.
7. Charles D. LaNauze, "Murder in the Arctic," a four-part series of articles published in *The Annals of the Propagation of the Faith* (June-July 1937, August-September 1937, December 1937–January 1938, February-March 1938), Part I, pp. 52–53; "Report of the North West Mounted Police," pp. 228–29.
8. "Report of the North West Mounted Police," p. 229.
9. LaNauze, Part II, pp. 72–73; "Report of the North West Mounted Police," p. 230.
10. "Report of the North West Mounted Police," p. 230.
11. "Report of the North West Mounted Police," p. 232.
12. LaNauze, Part II, pp. 72–73.
13. "Report of the North West Mounted Police," p. 198.
14. "Report of the North West Mounted Police," pp. 205–06.
15. LaNauze, Part III, pp. 110–12; "Report of the North West Mounted Police," pp. 198–99, 234–35.
16. "Report of the North West Mounted Police," pp. 208–09, 214.
17. "Report of the North West Mounted Police," pp. 209, 215.
18. "Report of the North West Mounted Police," pp. 204–08.
19. Diamond Jenness, *The Life of the Copper Eskimos: A Report of the Canadian Arctic Expedition, 1913–1918* (New York: Johnson Reprint Corporation, 1970), pp. 94–96.
20. LaNauze, Part III, p. 113; "Report of the North West Mounted Police," p. 282.

CHAPTER NINE

1. "Report of the North West Mounted Police," *Sessional Papers*, 1916, no. 28, pp. 198–99, 233; Charles D. LaNauze, "Murder in the Arctic," a four-part series of articles published in *The Annals of the Propagation of the Faith* (June-July 1937, August-September 1937, December 1937–January 1938, February-March 1938), Part III, pp. 110–12.

2. "Report of the North West Mounted Police," pp. 206, 235; LaNauze, Part III, pp. 113, 118.

3. "Report of the North West Mounted Police," p. 207.

4. "Report of the North West Mounted Police," pp. 235, 239; LaNauze, Part III, pp. 113, 118.

5. LaNauze, Part III, pp. 113, 118; "Report of the North West Mounted Police," p. 200.

6. "Report of the North West Mounted Police," pp. 204, 215, 235–36; LaNauze, Part III, p. 118.

7. "Report of the North West Mounted Police," pp. 204, 215–16.

8. Diamond Jenness, *The Life of the Copper Eskimos: A Report of the Canadian Arctic Expedition, 1913–1918* (New York: Johnson Reprint Corporation, 1970), p. 11.

9. "Report of the North West Mounted Police," pp. 213, 218

10. "Report of the North West Mounted Police," pp. 220–26; LaNauze, Part IV, pp. 11–12.

11. "Report of the North West Mounted Police," pp. 202, 220–26, 238–39; LaNauze, Part IV, pp. 11–12.

12. "Report of the North West Mounted Police," pp. 211–12.

13. "Report of the North West Mounted Police," pp. 203–05, 223–26.

14. "Report of the North West Mounted Police," p. 197.

15. "Report of the North West Mounted Police," p. 240. On June 6, a group led by Rudolph Anderson came in from Bathurst Inlet. They said they had met Constable Wight at the mouth of the Coppermine, on his way to investigate the murder site at Bloody Falls. Anderson's colleague K. C. Chipman had decided to accompany D'Arcy Arden back to Great Bear Lake in hopes of reaching Fort Norman for the first trip of the season aboard the steamer owned by the Hudson's Bay Company.

A week later, George Wilkins of the expedition's northern party arrived by sled from Victoria Island's Point Armstrong—across the Prince of Wales Strait, from Banks Island—where Stefansson's new ship, the *Polar Bear*, had spent the winter. Wilkins reported that Stefansson planned to use the *Polar Bear* to explore the northwest coast of the land north of Prince Patrick Island, then pass the summer in the northern islands.

16. "Report of the North West Mounted Police," p. 241. When the fog finally lifted, the *Alaska* turned around, and once again had to navigate a narrow strait full of enormous fields of ice. Captain Sweeney steered the ship toward shore to try to work through the looser ice, but this proved impossible. He dropped anchor, then had to change his position again and again to avoid being crushed. The crew spent the night watching the antics of innumerable bearded seals.

Finally, on July 22 substantial leads finally opened up in the ice, and Captain Sweeney was able to steer his ship back into open water. The ship pulled into Cape Parry on July 24, then sailed across Franklin Bay, where the crew had a good look at the "Smoking Mountains," a series of high shale cliffs that had been burning for years. LaNauze saw smoke billowing from fifteen distinct points in the rock. Later that day, the *Alaska* arrived at its first "civilized" port: Baillie Island, a Hudson's Bay Company outpost situated on a sand spit near Cape Bathurst, where the ship had wintered in 1914–15. LaNauze took his prisoners ashore here, "so as to break them gradually into western civilization."

Stepping off the boat, Sinnisiak and Uluksuk once again seemed nervous, and they were hardly reassured when a group of local Eskimo children ran away from them. When LaNauze and his men produced a meal of seal meat and fish, however, the locals seemed to warm to the newcomers. Its compass more reliable here, the *Alaska* left Baillie Island on the evening of July 26, pointed toward Herschel Island, and was soon out of sight of land. A pair of bowhead whales spouted a quarter mile from the ship. More astonishing still, the ship nearly ran over a polar bear swimming amid the loose ice.

17. "Report of the North West Mounted Police," pp. 202, 226–27, 242–43.
18. "Report of the North West Mounted Police," pp. 249–50.

19. LaNauze, Part IV, pp. 12–13; "Report of the North West Mounted Police," p. 216.

20. Edmonton *Morning Bulletin*, August 8, 1917; August 11, 1917; August 14, 1917.

21. Edmonton *Morning Bulletin*, August 8, 1917.

22. Edmonton *Morning Bulletin*, August 9, 1917; August 13, 1917; Calgary *Daily Herald*, August 14, 1917.

CHAPTER TEN

1. Calgary *Daily Herald*, August 14, 1917.

2. Edmonton *Morning Bulletin*, August 10, 1917; August 11, 1917.

3. Charles D. LaNauze, "Murder in the Arctic," a four-part series of articles published in *The Annals of the Propagation of the Faith* (June-July 1937, August-September 1937, December 1937–January 1938, February-March 1938), Part IV, pp. 12–13; Calgary *Daily Herald*, August 23, 1917.

4. Edmonton *Morning Bulletin*, August 14, 1917.

5. Edmonton *Morning Bulletin*, August 15, 1917; Edwin Keedy, "A Remarkable Murder Trial," *University of Pennsylvania Law Review*, vol. 100, no. 1 (October 1951), pp. 51–52.

6. Calgary *Daily Herald*, August 15, 1917; August 17, 1917; Edmonton *Journal*, August 14, 1917.

7. Edmund Kemper Broadus, *Saturday and Sunday* (Freeport, N.Y.: Books for Libraries Press, Inc., 1967), pp. 74–75.

8. LaNauze, Part IV, p. 13; Alan Ridge, "C. C. McCaul, Pioneer Lawyer," *Alberta Historical Review*, vol. 21, no. 1 (winter 1973).

9. McCaul, "Notes Written to E. L. Newcombe, K.C., Deputy Minister of Justice, Ottawa, Oct. 31, 1917," Alberta Provincial Archives; Calgary *Daily Herald*, August 21, 1917.

10. Edmonton *Morning Bulletin*, August 15, 1917.

11. "Address of C. C. McCaul, K. C., in Opening the Case for the Prosecution of Sinnisiak, an Eskimo Charged with Murder, Before the Hon. Chief Justice Harvey and a Jury, at Edmonton, Alberta, August 14th, 1917," Alberta Provincial Archives, p. 4.

12. McCaul, "Address," pp. 5–6.

13. McCaul, "Address," p. 7; Edmonton *Morning Bulletin*, August 15, 1917.

14. McCaul, "Address," pp. 8–9.

15. Edmonton *Morning Bulletin*, August 15, 1917.

16. McCaul, "Address," pp. 11–14; McCaul, "Notes."

17. Edmonton *Morning Bulletin*, August 15, 1917.

18. McCaul, "Address," p. 15.

19. Edmonton trial transcripts.

20. Edmonton trial transcripts, pp. 22, 38; Edmonton *Morning Bulletin*, August 15, 1917; McCaul, "Notes."

21. "Report of the North West Mounted Police," *Sessional Papers*, 1916, no. 28, pp. 272–76; Edmonton trial transcripts, pp. 42–55.

22. Edmonton trial transcripts, pp. 55–78; Keedy, pp. 52–53; Calgary *Daily Herald*, August 16, 1917; LaNauze, Part IV, pp. 12–14.

23. Edmonton *Journal*, August 18, 1917.

24. McCaul, "Notes."

CHAPTER ELEVEN

1. Edmonton *Morning Bulletin*, August 15, 1917; August 16, 1917; Edmonton *Journal*, August 15, 1917; August 16, 1917.

2. C. C. McCaul, "Notes Written to E. L. Newcombe, K.C., Deputy Minister of Justice, Ottawa, Oct. 31, 1917," Alberta Provincial Archives; R. G. Moyles, *British Law and Arctic Men: The Celebrated 1917 Murder Trials of Sinnisiak and Uluksuk, First Inuit Tried Under White Man's Law* (Saskatoon, Saskatchewan: Western Producer Prairie Books, 1979), pp. 43, 49.

3. Edmonton trial transcripts; Calgary *Daily Herald*, August 16, 1917.

4. Edwin Keedy, "A Remarkable Murder Trial," *University of Pennsylvania Law Review*, vol. 100, no. 1 (October 1951), footnote to pp. 54–55.

5. Diamond Jenness, *The Life of the Copper Eskimos: A Report of the Canadian Arctic Expedition, 1913–1918* (New York: Johnson Reprint Corporation, 1970), pp. 232–33; Hugh Brody, *The Other Side of Eden: Hunters, Farmers, and the Shaping of the World* (New York: North Point Press, 2000), pp. 197–98, 203.

6. Edmonton trial transcripts; Edmonton *Morning Bulletin*, August 16, 1917; August 17, 1917; Charles D. LaNauze, "Murder in the Arctic," a

four-part series of articles published in *The Annals of the Propagation of the Faith* (June-July 1937, August-September 1937, December 1937–January 1938, February-March 1938), Part IV, pp. 13–14; Keedy, p. 55.

7. Edmonton trial transcripts; Keedy, pp. 58–59; Edmonton *Morning Bulletin*, August 18, 1917; Edmonton *Journal*, August 17, 1917; Calgary *Daily Herald*, August 16, 1917.

8. Edmonton trial transcripts, pp. 190–218; Keedy, p. 61; LaNauze, Part IV, pp. 13–14; Edmonton *Morning Bulletin*, August 17, 1917.

9. In the audience, the American law professor Edwin Keedy wrote furiously. Was this kind of ritual cannibalism evidence of a primitive depravity? Back home, he would discover that a man's liver had in fact been considered the "seat of his soul" in literature written by Babylonians, Assyrians, Hebrews, Chinese, Etruscans, Greeks, and Romans. In the *Iliad*, Hecuba, the mother of Hector, vows that "she will not rest until she has devoured the liver of Achilles" (Keedy, p. 61).

10. Edmonton trial transcripts, pp. 222–24; Edmonton *Morning Bulletin*, August 18, 1917; Moyles, p. 53.

11. Edmonton trial transcripts. pp. 224–33; Keedy, pp. 61–62; Edmonton *Journal*, August 17, 1917.

12. Edmonton trial transcripts, pp. 234–44; Edmonton *Morning Bulletin*, August 18, 1917; Calgary *Daily Herald*, August 17, 1917; Edmonton *Journal*, August 17, 1917.

13. Keedy, pp. 63–64.

14. Edmonton *Morning Bulletin*, August 18, 1917; Calgary *Daily Herald*, August 17, 1917; LaNauze, Part IV, pp. 13–14.

CHAPTER TWELVE

Epigraph: Jean Blodgett, *The Coming and Going of the Shaman* (Winnipeg: Winnipeg Art Gallery, 1978), p. 27.

1. C. C. McCaul, "Notes Written to E. L. Newcombe, K.C., Deputy Minister of Justice, Ottawa, Oct. 31, 1917," Alberta Provincial Archives; Edmonton *Morning Bulletin*, August 21, 1917; Calgary *Daily Herald*, August 20, 1917.

2. Calgary *News-Telegram*, August 25, 1917.

3. Calgary *Daily Herald*, August 21, 1917.

4. Calgary *News-Telegram*, August 25, 1917.

5. Calgary *News-Telegram*, August 22, 1917.

6. Calgary *News-Telegram*, August 21, 1917; August 22, 1917.

7. Calgary trial transcripts; Edmonton *Morning Bulletin*, August 23, 1917; Calgary *Daily Herald*, August 22, 1917; August 23, 1917; Calgary *News-Telegram*, August 21, 1917.

8. Calgary *News-Telegram*, August 23, 1917.

9. Edmonton *Morning Bulletin*, August 24, 1917; Calgary *Daily Herald*, August 23, 1917; Calgary *News-Telegram*, August 23, 1917.

10. Calgary *Daily Herald*, August 23, 1917; August 24, 1917; Calgary trial transcripts; Edmonton *Morning Bulletin*, August 23, 1917; Calgary *Daily Herald*, August 22, 1917; Calgary *News-Telegram*, August 21, 1917; McCaul, "Notes," p. 7.

11. Calgary trial transcripts, pp. 50–63; Calgary *Daily Herald*, August 24, 1917. Here is the transcription of Uluksuk's statement: "I was at the mouth of the Coppermine river after the lakes froze over," Uluksuk began.

We were fishing there, Kormik and the two white men Ilogoak and Kuleavik had one camp between them.

Kormik wanted to kill the two white men because they were angry with him as he had put away their rifle, and his wife had put away some of the white man's food. After the white men left to go up the river, Sinnisiak and I followed their trail. We wanted to get to the people who were left behind. It was three days after the priests had left that we met them on the river.

The tall white man Ilogoak said to me "If you will help us I will give you traps. We want you to go with us as far as the trees."

On the first day the priests were not angry with us. We camped with them one night and we did not reach the trees, we made a small snow house for the priests. The next day the priests were angry and said "if you will take us to the woods we will give you traps." We started, I was behind pulling the sled. Sinnisiak was close to the sled and the two white men were behind.

I wanted to speak. Ilogoak put his hand over my mouth. I wanted to talk of my wife sewing clothes for Ilogoak in the fall.

Kuleavik [Rouvière] gave Ilogoak a rifle and a knife and Ilogoak pointed the gun at us. I was afraid and I was crying.

Every time I wanted to talk, Ilogoak came and put his hand over my mouth.

We went on and Sinnisiak said to me, "We ought to kill these white men before they kill us," and I said "They can kill me if they want to, I don't want to kill any people." Sinnisiak then said, "I will kill one of them anyway. You had better try and be strong too." Ilogoak turned round and Sinnisiak stabbed him from behind in the back. Ilogoak then hit me with a stick and I stabbed him twice with a knife and he dropped down.

I took the rifle from on top of the sled and threw it down in the snow. The other white man Kuleavik started to run away and Sinnisiak picked up the rifle and missed him the first shot. The second shot he wounded him and the priest sat down.

Sinnisiak dropped the rifle and took an axe and a knife. I had a knife and we ran after him. When we got up to Kuleavik, Sinnisiak told me to stab him again, I did not want to stab him first, then Sinnisiak told me to stab him and I stabbed him again in the side and the blood came out and he was not yet dead. I did not stab him again and Sinnisiak took the axe and chopped his neck and killed him. Sinnisiak said to me "You had better cut him open." I did not want to. He told me again and I cut open his belly and we eat a piece of the liver each. We then left Kuleavik on the top of the snow and went back to the other man Ilogoak and I cut him open when Sinnisiak told me to. We eat a small piece of his liver also.

I wanted to throw the rifles away and Sinnisiak said "Take one, and I will take one."

We took three boxes of cartridges each. We then went back to the mouth of the river where the other people were. We took nothing from the sled except the rifles and the cartridges. We got back to the camp when it was night time; Sinnisiak went to Kormik's tent, I went to my tent.

I told the people we had killed the two white men and that I did not want to, but Sinnisiak had killed them first.

> Kormik and his wife Hoaha and Angebrunna then went to get the priests' stuff. They came back the same night with the stuff.
>
> The people took the rifles and cartridges from me.
>
> I have no more to speak about.

12. Calgary trial transcipts.
13. Calgary trial transcripts.
14. Calgary trial transcripts; Edmonton *Morning Bulletin*, August 24, 1917; Calgary *Daily Herald*, August 25, 1917; Calgary *News-Telegram*, August 25, 1917; Charles D. LaNauze, "Murder in the Arctic," a four-part series of articles published in *The Annals of the Propagation of the Faith* (June-July 1937, August-September 1937, December 1937–January 1938, February-March 1938), Part IV, pp. 12–13; R. G. Moyles, *British Law and Arctic Men: The Celebrated 1917 Murder Trials of Sinnisiak and Uluksuk, First Inuit Tried Under White Man's Law* (Saskatoon, Saskatchewan: Western Producer Prairie Books, 1979), pp. 65–66.
15. Edmonton *Morning Bulletin*, August 24, 1917; Edmund Kemper Broadus, *Saturday and Sunday* (Freeport, N.Y.: Books for Libraries Press, Inc., 1967), p. 83.
16. Edmonton *Morning Bulletin*, August 24, 1917; Edmonton *Journal*, August 25, 1917; Edmonton *Morning Bulletin*, August 24, 1917; Calgary *Daily Herald*, August 25, 1917.
17. Calgary *Daily Herald*, August 25, 1917.
18. Calgary *News-Telegram*, August 29, 1917.
19. Calgary trial transcripts; LaNauze, Part IV, pp. 12–14.
20. Edmonton *Morning Bulletin*, August 29, 1917; August 30, 1917.
21. LaNauze, Part IV, pp. 12–14.

EPILOGUE

1. R. G. Moyles, *British Law and Arctic Men: The Celebrated 1917 Murder Trials of Sinnisiak and Uluksuk, First Inuit Tried Under White Man's Law* (Saskatoon, Saskatchewan: Western Producer Prairie Books, 1979), p. 85.
2. Philip H. Godsell, "Arctic Murder: The Crimson Epic of the R.C.M.P.," in *True Detective Mysteries*, vol. 18, no. 4 (July 1932), pp. 7–15, 71–73.

3. C. C. McCaul, "Notes Written to E. L. Newcombe, K.C., Deputy Minister of Justice, Ottawa, Oct. 31, 1917, Alberta Provincial Archives.

4. *Provincia*, April 17, 1926.

5. George Whalley, *The Legend of John Hornby* (Toronto: Macmillan, 1962), pp. 127, 183, 304, 310, 322.

6. Diamond Jenness, *The Life of the Copper Eskimos: A Report of the Canadian Arctic Expedition, 1913–1918* (New York: Johnson Reprint Corporation, 1970), p. 11; John R. Sperry, *Igloo Dwellers Were My Church* (Calgary: Bayeaux Arts, Inc., 2001), p. 49.

7. Gabriel Breynat, *The Flying Bishop: Fifty Years in the Canadian Far North* (London: Burns and Oates, 1955), p. 182.

8. Breynat, pp. 217–21.

9. Roger P. Bulliard, *Inuk* (New York: Farrar, Straus and Young, 1951), p. 28.

10. Breynat, pp. 236–37.

11. Barry Lopez, *Arctic Dreams: Imagination and Desire in a Northern Landscape* (New York: Bantam Books, 1987), pp. 10, 337.

12. Jenness, *Life of the Copper Eskimos*, pp. 241–42, 248–49.

13. Diamond Jenness, *The People of the Twilight* (Chicago: University of Chicago Press, 1928, 1959), pp. 246–47.

14. Hugh Brody, *The Other Side of Eden: Hunters, Farmers, and the Shaping of the World* (New York: North Point Press, 2000), pp. 70–74, 86, 237.

15. Francis Spufford, *I May Be Some Time: Ice and the English Imagination* (New York: Picador, 1997), pp. 226–27.

16. Spufford, p. 210.

17. Bulliard, p. 29.

18. Sperry, pp. 50, 128–30, 138, 159. Unlike most of his predecessors, Sperry was so proficient in Inuinaqtun that he managed to translate not only the New Testament and Book of Common Prayer, but two hundred Christian hymns as well. His memoir *Igloo Dwellers Were My Church* is a remarkably honest account of both the contributions and the complications of missionary work.

19. "Report of the North West Mounted Police," *Sessional Papers*, 1916, no. 28, pp. 204, 217, 238–39.

—

Blodgett, Jean. *The Coming and Going of the Shaman: Eskimo Shamanism and Art.* Winnipeg: Winnipeg Art Gallery, 1978. Exhibition catalog for show of same name, March 11–June 11, 1978.

Breynat, Gabriel. *The Flying Bishop: Fifty Years in the Canadian Far North.* London: Burns and Oates, 1955.

Broadus, Edmund Kemper. *Saturday and Sunday.* Freeport, N.Y.: Books for Libraries Press, Inc., 1967.

Brody, Hugh. *Living Arctic: Hunters of the Canadian North.* Vancouver: Douglas & McIntyre, 1987.

———. *The Other Side of Eden: Hunters, Farmers, and the Shaping of the World.* New York: North Point Press, 2000.

———. *The People's Land: Eskimos and Whites in the Eastern Arctic.* New York: Penguin Books, 1975.

Bulliard, Roger P. *Inuk.* New York: Farrar, Straus and Young, 1951.

Condon, Richard, with Julia Ogina and the Holman Elders. *The Northern Copper Inuit: A History.* Norman: University of Oklahoma Press, 1996.

Diubaldo, Richard J. *Stefansson and the Canadian Arctic.* Montreal: McGill–Queen's University Press, 1978.

Dorais, Louis-Jacques. *Language in Inuit Society.* Iqaluit: Nunavut Arctic College, 1996.

Douglas, George M. *Lands Forlorn: A Story of an Expedition to Hearne's Coppermine River.* New York: G. P. Putnam's Sons, 1914.

Eber, Dorothy Harley. *Images of Justice: A Legal History of the Northwest Territories as Traced Through the Yellowknife Courthouse Collection of Inuit Sculpture.* Toronto: McGill–Queen's University Press, 1997.

Franklin, John. *Narrative of a Journey to the Shores of the Polar Sea in the Years 1819–20–21–22.* London: J. Murray, 1823.

Godsell, Philip H. "Arctic Murder: The Crimson Epic of the R.C.M.P.," in *True Detective Mysteries*, vol. 18, no. 4 (July 1932), pp. 7–15, 71–73.

Hearne, Samuel. *A Journey from Prince of Wales Fort in Hudson's Bay to the Northern Ocean, 1769, 1770, 1771, 1772.* Edited by Richard Glover. Toronto: Macmillan, 1958.

Horrall, S. W. *The Pictorial History of the Royal Canadian Mounted Police.* Toronto: McGraw-Hill Ryerson Ltd., 1973.

Jenness, Diamond. *The Life of the Copper Eskimos: A Report of the Canadian Arctic Expedition, 1913–1918.* Ottawa: F. A. Ackland, 1922; New York: Johnson Reprint Corporation, 1970.

———. *The People of the Twilight.* Chicago: University of Chicago Press, 1928, 1959.

Keedy, Edwin. "A Remarkable Murder Trial." *University of Pennsylvania Law Review*, vol. 100, no. 1 (October 1951).

King, J. C. H., and Henrietta Lidchi, eds. *Imaging the Arctic.* Seattle: University of Washington Press, 1998.

LaNauze, Charles D. "Murder in the Arctic." A four-part series of articles published in *The Annals of the Propagation of the Faith,* June-July 1937; August-September 1937; December 1937–January 1938; February-March 1938.

"Les Cloches de Saint-Boniface." *Organe de L'Archivteche et de Toute la Province Ecclésiastique de Saint Boniface.* Vols. XV-XVII (January 1, 1916–December 15, 1918).

Lopez, Barry. *Arctic Dreams: Imagination and Desire in a Northern Landscape.* New York: Bantam Books, 1987.

MacDonald, John. *The Arctic Sky: Inuit Astronomy, Star Lore, and Legend.* Toronto: Royal Ontario Museum–Nunavut Research Institute, 1998.

Martyrs aux Glaces Polaires: La Meilleure Composition dans Chaque Genre du Concours Rouvière et LeRoux. Montreal: Editions Beauchemin, 1939.

McCaul, C. C. "Address of C. C. McCaul, K. C., in Opening the Case for the Prosecution of Sinnisiak, an Eskimo Charged with Murder, Before the Hon. Chief Justice Harvey and a Jury, at Edmonton, Alberta, August 14th, 1917." Alberta Provincial Archives.

———. "Notes Written to E. L. Newcombe, K.C., Deputy Minister of Justice, Ottawa, Oct. 31, 1917." Alberta Provincial Archives.

Merkur, Daniel. *Powers Which We Do Not Know: The Gods and Spirits of the Inuit.* Moscow: University of Idaho Press, 1991.

Mowatt, Farley. *Coppermine Journey: An Account of a Great Adventure— Selected from the Journals of Samuel Hearne.* Boston: Atlantic Monthly Press, 1958.

Moyles, R. G. *British Law and Arctic Men: The Celebrated 1917 Murder Trials of Sinnisiak and Uluksuk, First Inuit Tried Under White Man's Law.* Saskatoon, Saskatchewan: Western Producer Prairie Books, 1979.

Niven, Jennifer. *The Ice Master: The Doomed 1913 Voyage of the* Karluk. New York: Hyperion, 2000.

Norman, Howard. *Northern Tales: Traditional Stories of Eskimos and Indian Peoples.* New York: Pantheon Books, 1990.

Olson, Sigurd. *Reflections from the North Country.* New York: Alfred A. Knopf, 1976.

Oswalt, Wendell H. *Eskimos and Explorers.* Lincoln: University of Nebraska Press, 1979.

Pielou, E. C. *A Naturalist's Guide to the Arctic.* Chicago: University of Chicago Press, 1994.

Rasmussen, Knud. *The Netsilik Eskimos: Social Life and Spiritual Culture, Report of the Fifth Thule Expedition, 1921–1924.* Copenhagen: Gyldendal, 1931; reprint; New York: AMS Press, 1976.

"Report of the North West Mounted Police." *Sessional Papers,* no. 28. Printed by J. de L. Tache, Printer to the King's Most Excellent Majesty, Ottawa, 1916.

Ridge, Alan D. "C. C. McCaul, Pioneer Lawyer." *Alberta Historical Review,* vol. 21, no. 1 (winter 1973).

Rymer, J. F. "The Dream of the North; or, Catholic Work Amongst the Indians." *Catholic Register,* January 11, 1912. In Archives Provinciales, Edmonton.

Speake, Jennifer, ed. *Literature of Travel and Exploration: An Encyclopedia.* New York and London: Fitzroy Dearborn, 2003.

Sperry, John R. *Igloo Dwellers Were My Church.* Calgary: Bayeaux Arts, Inc., 2001.

Spufford, Francis. *I May Be Some Time: Ice and the English Imagination.* New York: Picador, 1997.

Stefansson, Vilhjalmur. *The Friendly Arctic: The Story of Five Years in Polar Regions.* New York: Macmillan, 1932.

———. *My Life with the Eskimos.* New York: Macmillan, 1913, 1927.

———. *The Northward Course of Empire.* New York: Macmillan, 1924.

Valentine, Victor F. *Eskimo of the Canadian Arctic.* Toronto: McClelland and Stewart, 1968.

Whalley, George. "Coppermine Martyrdom." *Queens Quarterly* 66 (winter 1959–60), pp. 591–610.

———. *The Legend of John Hornby.* Toronto: Macmillan, 1962.

Zaslow, Morris. *The Opening of the Canadian North, 1870–1914.* Toronto: McClelland and Stewart, 1971.

INDEX

―

ABOUT THE AUTHOR

MCKAY JENKINS is the author of *The Last
Ridge: The Epic Story of America's First
Mountain Soldiers and the Assault on Hitler's
Europe*; *The White Death: Tragedy and
Heroism in an Avalanche Zone*; and *The South
in Black and White: Race, Sex, and Literature
in the 1940s* and is the editor of *The Peter
Matthiessen Reader*. He holds degrees from
Amherst, Columbia's Graduate School of
Journalism, and Princeton, where he received
a Ph.D. in English. A former staff writer for
the *Atlanta Constitution*, he is currently
Tilghman Professor of English and a member
of the Program in Journalism at the University
of Delaware. Jenkins lives in Baltimore
with his family.